'Stefano Carta is a truly original and deep thinker, and with his personal and well-researched approach he conveys an inspiring and valuable contribution to the continuing contemporary discussion of Jung's thought. Stefano Carta deserves great credit for this impressive work that will undoubtedly stand as a milestone in Jungian literature for many years to come.'

Misser Berg, *Jungian Analyst, President of the International Association of Analytical Psychology*

'The extraordinary breadth and scope of Stefano Carta's two volume set *The Infinite Ladder* is a boon to scholars of Analytical Psychology. The careful synthesis of essential Jungian concepts spanning an enormous range from biological to cultural considerations within a psychological perspective, integrated into a contemporary multidisciplinary framework is a rare achievement as well as a gift to the field. Together these volumes will also serve as a very valuable hub in guiding researchers who explore the interconnectedness of Analytical Psychology with the most advanced contemporary thought in numerous related fields.'

Joseph Cambray, *PhD, IAAP, Past President and CEO, Pacifica Graduate Institute*

'Stefano Carta's two volumes are a courageous attempt to reassert the importance and validity of C.G. Jung's fundamental ideas on the central role of emotions, archetypes and the Self within an evolutionary framework. Employing the compelling metaphor of the infinite ladder, Carta demonstrates how psychology reveals its transformative function of the biological foundations of life into the cultural realm. His books, firmly rooted in cutting-edge research, are indeed a unique, fascinating and challenging contribution that will bring the reader to new heights of understanding.'

Carolyn M. Bates, *PhD, North American Co-editor in Chief for the* Journal of Analytical Psychology

'These two volumes are the fruit of a lifelong exploration of Jungian psychology in a contemporary scientific environment. Some of C. G Jung's important ideas are scrutinized in terms of their connectivity to today's scientific thinking. Questions that Jung was already pondering are placed in a new, contemporary context. "What has not been appreciated enough in the past in Jung's theories and yet could be connected to today's ideas?" To answer this question, the author takes the reader on a stimulating, thoughtful and thought-provoking intellectual journey.'

Verena Kast, *Jungian Psychoanalyst and Former Professor at the University of Zurich*

'This is an exciting book the likes of which I have been waiting for. It is far-reaching and comprehensive in its profound understanding of Jungian thought and connects these insights with findings of contemporary neuroscience. By using Jung's writings as a starting point, the author opens up a treasure trove of knowledge and understanding by covering topics such as affectivity, neurobiology, psychosomatics, spirituality and culture. In two volumes, the author succeeded in his declared aim to look for those of Jung's contributions that seem valuable for analytical psychology today.'

Arthur Neisser, *Co-editor in Chief for Europe,* Journal of Analytical Psychology, *London, UK, and Schwendi, Germany*

'Professor Stefano Carta has provided us with a veritable *magnum opus* in many respects. In these two volumes, not only does he systematically cover an astonishing range of themes and masterfully amalgamate insights from a staggering range of sources, disciplines and traditions, but he also dares to confront central assumptions of Jungian psychology and to re-examine its very foundations. Moreover, he carves out innovative pathways that enable us to re-view central tenets of Jungian thought and their presuppositions, whilst seamlessly addressing both theory and practice. It is for these reasons that this work will become an indispensable guide to anyone who wishes to seriously delve into the intricacies of Jungian ideas, with their multiple implications and applications.'

Renos K Papadopoulos, *PhD, FBPsS, Professor of Analytical Psychology, Department of Psychosocial and Psychoanalytic Studies, University of Essex; Editor of* C.G. Jung: Critical Assessments *(in four volumes) and of* The Handbook of Jungian Psychology

'Stefano Carta makes my head spin with his intelligence and scholarship. Among the many original contributions in these groundbreaking texts, Carta discovers deep inherent resonance and integrates Jung's foundational ideas with the scientific insights coming from contemporary evolutionary biology, neuroscience and cultural anthropology. Carta takes his place among the most creative and innovative thinkers in the history of analytical psychology with these two brilliant volumes.'

Thomas Singer, *Editor of Award-Winning* Cultural Complexes and the Soul of America (Routledge, 2020)

'In this impressive study, Stefano Carta proves himself to be a "faithful interpreter" who trusts his author. His criticism is constructive as he sets out to create a psychology fit for our time by using the materials left to us in C.G. Jung's precious legacy.'

Murray Stein, *PhD, ISAP-ZURICH*

'In *The Infinite Ladder*, Stefano Carta takes the reader on a remarkable journey, one that assesses the relationship between Jung's conceptual framework and the practice of analytical psychology in our contemporary world. Drawing from a wide variety of sources, such as neuroscience, infant development, philosophy, and affective research, Carta evaluates which of Jung's ideas retain utility as clinically relevant concepts. Few could offer the breadth of perspective and deep critical analysis that Carta offers in these two volumes. Essential reading for all contemporary Jungians.'

Mark Winborn, *PhD, Jungian Psychoanalyst and Clinical Psychologist. Author of* Interpretation in Jungian Analysis: Art and Technique *and* Jungian Psychoanalysis: A Contemporary Introduction

From Biology to Psychology in Jungian and Evolutionary Theory

This groundbreaking book repositions C.G. Jung's legacy, and the field of analytical psychology, within the panorama of contemporary knowledge in biology, psychology and anthropology, on the grounds of the role of affects and emotion as the foundation of all psychic activity.

Within this new volume, Stefano Carta aims to provide a new, up-to-date way of understanding Jung's work and to show the effect to which his central positions can be better understood in relation to topics such as the nature of the psyche, of the Self, of the collective unconscious and of archetypal theory. From an evolutionary and biological perspective, this book describes, with extensive substantiations and an original discussion, the transformation of the biological processes into psychological ones. Additionally, the book aims to identify current tendencies which view analytical psychology in increasingly reductionistic ways and reaffirm the dynamism of Jung's paradigm.

Spanning two volumes, which are also accessible as standalone books, and with international appeal and original and interdisciplinary in scope, they will be of great interest to Jungian scholars and analysts, as well as students and those on Jungian-oriented training courses.

Stefano Carta is a psychologist and a Jungian analyst graduate at the C.G. Jung Institute in Zurich. He is Professor of Dynamic and Clinical Psychology and Ethnopsychology at the University of Cagliari, Italy, and has been Honorary Professor at the Department of Psychoanalytic Studies at the University of Essex, UK. He is a member of the International Association of Analytical Psychology and former President of the Associazione Italiana di Psicologia Analitica (AIPA). Among his many publications, he has edited the three-volume entry on "Psychology" for the *Encyclopaedia of Life Support Systems* by UNESCO.

From Biology to Psychology in Jungian and Evolutionary Theory

The Infinite Ladder

Volume 1

Stefano Carta

Routledge
Taylor & Francis Group

LONDON AND NEW YORK

First published 2025
by Routledge
4 Park Square, Milton Park, Abingdon, Oxon OX14 4RN

and by Routledge
605 Third Avenue, New York, NY 10158

Routledge is an imprint of the Taylor & Francis Group, an informa business

British Library Cataloguing-in-Publication Data
A catalogue record for this book is available from the British Library

ISBN: 978-1-032-95730-2 (hbk)
ISBN: 978-1-032-95729-6 (pbk)
ISBN: 978-1-003-58625-8 (ebk)

DOI: 10.4324/9781003586258

Typeset in Times New Roman
by Apex CoVantage, LLC

Contents

Foreword

This book, together with its companion Volume 2, *A Jungian and Evolutionary Approach to Psychology and Culture*, were born from a conversation I had with Sonu Shamdasani in September 2023 at a dinner table – one of the best places at which to exchange thoughts, memories and projects. We were discussing the relationship of the Jungian community with regard to Jung's ideas, also under the light of some issues in which I had been involved – the role of affects, the Self and its relations to the Ego, together with the evolutionary framework needed to make sense of archetypal images. It was then that Sonu asked me, "Why don't you write a book?"

I thought that I would give it a try, in an attempt to reflect and summarize my ideas and what I know of the state of contemporary knowledge on these questions. I did not expect that I would produce two volumes, and that even so, I had to select only a part of the present state of research that seems convergent with some of Jung's most important hypotheses.

The overall project of this work was to try to trace a possible bottom-up evolutionary path through which, from the biological strata, images imbued with affect and meaning may emerge. It was always clear to me that the function of this bottom-up ladder is to – somehow teleologically – progressively form ontologically higher-level organizations which then regulate top-down those lower levels that expressed the constraints within which they emerged. This is the reason why the first volume begins with a biological discussion on "instincts" and the second volume ends with a brief amplification on the symbolic image of the Trinity. If the latter emerges bottom-up from the biological, ontologically "lower" level, its meaning is graspable only top-down, hence, eventually at the highest possible symbolic level – a level to which the Trinity belongs. This meaning shines its light on what such an image hints to and, at the same time, on the lower processes out of which this symbolic image emerged. An example may be the situation in which the areas of the brain that light up under an fMRI become meaningful through and by the correlation to the higher-level, psychological processes and not the other way around. To paraphrase Wittgenstein: The physiological is the symbol of the (psycho)logical.

Thus, this evolutionary infinite ladder describes a sort of a helix, a Moebius strip. The pivotal construct of this perspective – which is Jung's perspective – is the Self, for whose realization the Ego is instrumental. This perspective describes a psychology that cannot be reduced only to infancy and the developmental years, as most contemporary psychologies (if not all of them) maintain, but which is teleologically directed towards the future realization of the Self – what Jung called the "individuation process".

Throughout the writing of these two books, several friends and colleagues accompanied me. I wish to thank some of them.

I wish to thank Sonu Shamdasani for the impulse he gave me and for his support and encouragement. I am particularly grateful to Silvano Tagliagambe, whose knowledge and wisdom I would now like to acknowledge. Our discussions and his ideas have been an invaluable influence on me and have given me the necessary support to feel that my own theoretical basis was epistemologically cogent. His extensive final essay, at the end of the second volume, may provide a further contribution to my overall effort.

My most grateful recognition goes to Carolyn Bates, who read the very first draft of these volumes; her encouragement at that moment – when no one had yet read them – has been indeed important.

My gratitude also goes to Joe Cambray, Pina Galeazzi, Verena Kast, Angelo Malinconico, Arthur Niesser, Tom Singer, Murray Stein and Mark Winborn for their encouraging and supportive comments.

I am grateful to Renos Papadopoulos for his constant support and his everlasting friendship.

I would also like to thank Katie Randall and Berset Manon of Routledge for their steadfast, patient, wonderful assistance throughout the production of these two volumes.

In closing, I wish to thank my wife, Beth, for her enduring patience and encouragement, for her almost heroic effort in reading both volumes twice, for providing her insightful comments and, last but not least, for correcting my written English text.

The discussions we are having here could be represented pictorially by a helix; we keep on coming back to the same point, only on different levels of the helix.

Bion, W.R. (2014). Brazilian Lectures. Rio de Janeiro, 1974. In: *The Complete Works of W.R. Bion*. Vol VII, p. 82. London: Karnak

The spirit of our time spoke to me and said: "What dire urgency could be forcing you to speak all this?" This was an awful temptation. I wanted to ponder what inner or outer bind could force me into this, and because I found nothing that I could grasp, I was near to making one up. But with this the spirit of our time had almost brought it about, that instead of speaking, I was thinking again about reasons and explanations. But the spirit of the depths spoke to me and said: "To understand a thing is a bridge and possibility of returning to the path. But to explain a matter is arbitrary and sometimes even murder. Have you counted the murderous among the scholars?"

Jung, C.G. (2009). *The Red Book. Liber Primus*. San Francisco: W.W. Norton. Fol. i(v)/ii(r), p. 230

Chapter 1

Introductory Remarks

1.1 Approaching Jung's Text

This book, along with its companion Volume, *A Jungian and Evolutionary Approach to Psychology and Culture*, are not an attempt to summarize, reconstruct, criticize or analyze Jung's theory and thought. Although they deal with Jung's legacy and writings, their intent is to look for those contributions of his that seem to me valuable for analytical psychology today. In fact, I am not personally interested in being a historian of Jung's thought and one of his exegetes. There are quite a number of such books that have done and are doing a job much better than the one I could ever do.

What some of these authors do is to analyze Jung's theory from the answers he gave to the specific problems – mostly clinical but also psychological in general – with which he was dealing. What I wish to do is to start from Jung's problems, to see whether his theoretical, methodological and empirical answers not only seem to respond to them but also whether they are in line with contemporary science. I wish to embark upon this attempt because my position is not just a matter of competence, it is also a choice derived from my concern about remaining entangled in the discussion on Jung and, therefore, stuck with my gaze towards the past. My desire is to *use* those Jungian ideas and concepts that seem to me to be valid and vital for analytical psychology today, so as not to risk losing its core meanings without necessarily even realizing it.

In a few words, my desire is to speak of analytical psychology, which I think to be a unique form of psychology in the contemporary panorama, and to extrapolate those principles that may legitimately root it in today's world of research and science. Obviously, the only way to do this is to turn towards Jung and the part of his legacy (which may eventually be *all of it* – who knows? The debate is not closed) that may serve such a purpose.

I believe that an interpreter may take two main different positions vis à vis his text. I exclude the possibility that he looks and assesses its internal coherence without ever trying to understand its legitimacy or meaningfulness. Ricoeur (2008, p. 33) called the first attitude *hermeneutics of suspicion*, while Gadamer called the second *hermeneutics of faith* (1989).

DOI: 10.4324/9781003586258-1

The suspicious interpreter is interested in looking essentially for what the text conceals, or for what does not work. He is in the position of one who has a legitimate claim on the text that the text seems not to satisfy. In this situation, the only intentions and expectations that move the hermeneutic relationship between text and interpreter are those of suspicion, and he approaches the text as if it is a defendant in a courthouse. His attitude is, therefore, inquisitive, skeptical and always relentlessly critical.

For the second attitude, the interpreter tends to have faith and give credit to the text and tries to understand and infer what the text might wish to express – *the text's intentions*. In the mind of the faithful interpreter, there is the constant assumption that the text must mean something coherent and legitimate. He actively looks for this coherence not just because he wishes to redeem the text from its obscurities or shortcomings but also because he feels that in taking the faithful stand, he might end up thinking and understanding something, thanks to the interpreting activity that this probably imperfect text is implicitly asking him to do.

I do recognize the importance and fruitfulness of the suspicious attitude, which Ricoeur attributed to three giants such as Marx, Nietzsche and Freud. It helps to validate or discard the text to substitute it with another one,[1] yet it does not produce much new understanding in the interpreter's mind. It mostly regards the text itself.

In these books, I have chosen to take the faithful stand, as I am not interested in assessing Jung's text to decide whether it is guilty or innocent. What I wish to do is to give such a difficult, ambiguous text credit because I think that this choice might produce or confirm new legitimate and not-too-confusing ideas and new meanings for the interpreter, in this case not just for myself but especially for the analytical psychology that is part of my cultural, philosophical and scientific background. Perhaps it is not needless to say that Gadamer's faithful stand was the one Jung felt closest to. At least *this* is a first piece of coherence.

Hence, starting from the empirical and theoretical problems Jung was facing, throughout this book, if I have not selected all his quotes to analyze the coherence of his exposition, I have looked for a thread that may be useful for analytical psychology. In so doing, I might have selected some of his positions and excluded others, and if such a selection seems to the exegete's eyes to invalidate a fair description of Jung's ideas, I wish to remind him, or her, to consider those concepts and ideas that I am using in this book as part of Jung's attempt to give the best solution possible to the problems he was tackling.

Therefore, if, for instance, through my discussion one of the many critics of Jung that dismiss a certain number of his ideas because "Jung was confused" does not read in my pages that he was confused, it is because, if he ever really was so, *in this context*, I do not care. Once again, I would rather extrapolate what I think are (and, of course, I may be partially or totally wrong) the interesting and valid principles that Jung left us under the form of what we call analytical psychology.

Another important example could be the discussion on archetypes. I will extrapolate some of Jung's passages to show that they may be legitimate within the scope of contemporary science and research. If the legitimacy of the archetypal hypothesis is recognized as valid through just *some* passages, while other defini-tions are judged contradictory or plainly wrong, my task will be accomplished anyway, as, once again, I am not exegetically interested in Jung's coherence.

In a few words: I will be a cherry picker.

1.2   General Issues

Throughout my discussion, I will confront myself with those authors that think that those specific principles that I discuss (because I think they are valid and persua-sive) are ungrounded or that cannot be fruitfully connected and reinvigorated under the light of contemporary science and research. In fact, in the past years, there has been an interesting ongoing discussion on some of Jung's foundational concepts, especially archetypes, which he supposed to be collective pre-conscious complexes of biological, evolutionary origin.

Among the most important protagonists of this discussion on both sides, I am indebted to Knox (2001, 2003, 2004a, 2004b, 2009, 2010), Pietikäinen (1998a, 1998b), Roesler (2012, 2022), Goodwyn (2010a, 2010b, 2012), Haule (2011), Maloney (2003a, 2003b), Merritt (2012), Stevens (2002, 1998), Jones (2003), Hogenson (1998, 2003a, 2003b, 2004, 2010), McDowell (2001), Merchant (2006, 2010, 2012, 2015, 2016, 2019, 2020) and Saunders and Skar (2001).

From this list, I wish to underscore the particular importance of the contribu-tions by Stevens (2002), Merritt (2012), Haule (2011) and Goodwyn (2012). The two volumes by J.R. Haule – *Jung in the 21st Century* – should be considered a sort of complementary source to these two volumes of mine. While it has a differ-ent scope and architecture, this work of mine may be complemented by Haule's important contribution to analytical psychology.

Also Goodwyn's *The Neurobiology of the Gods* (2012) is for me something like a complementary contribution to these two volumes. In fact, in his opening page, Goodwyn, speaking of:

Gods, demons, angels. . . . Muses, spirits, ghosts . . . fairies, devils, imps, fauns, unicorns, dragons, poltergeist, ghouls, vampires, djinns, werewolves . . . saviors.

writes:

Many have tried to explain this phenomenon. . . . Theoretically, any set of arbi-trary ideas could be passed on easily, promote social cohesion or be intuitive and as would still have no idea what they represented. Thus, we must not only ask why these ideas are so persistent and ubiquitous, but also what they *are*, and why they are so emotionally starring.

(Goodwyn, 2012, p. 3)

While Goodwyn's book is an important attempt to discuss exactly this matter, my work focuses on the *legitimacy* of the hypothesis about the existence of archetypes and on the fundamental role that affects and emotions play throughout their emergence. The sign of the continuity of my effort with Goodwyn's is noticeable also by that fact that some of the literature to which I refer is the same to which he refers.

The discussion carried out by some of these authors (like Knox, 2001, 2003, 2004a, 2004b, 2009, 2010; Pietikäinen, 1998a, 1998b; Roesler, 2012, 2022; Maloney, 2003a, 2003b; Merchant 2006, 2009, 2010, 2012, 2015, 2016, 2019) has important implications not only because it involves the issue of the possible universality (i.e., biological nature of the fundaments of the human mind) but also – and perhaps especially – because it rests and refers to cognitive and infant research and findings in such a way that, in my, opinion, it risks departing from the core assumptions of the Jungian theory without realizing it, or just without saying it.

This work will essentially deal with two aspects of analytical psychology that make it unique and specific within the larger world of contemporary psychologies and psychotherapies: a) the dispositional primary role of affects and b) Jung's archetypal hypothesis. Both these tenets have been under scrutiny since Jung formulated them up until today. I wish to participate in this discussion to try to prove that, essentially, Jung's hypotheses were coherent and sound.

In the psychological literature, there is great terminological confusion between affects and emotions. It is, therefore, important to clarify how I will use these words. For "affects", I will refer to the organic, "ectopsychic"[2] precursors of feelings. When I will refer to Panksepp's theory of primary affective emotions, I will call them "affects".

The following is Jung's definition of affect:

> By the term affect I mean a state of feeling characterized by marked physical innervation on the one hand and peculiar disturbance of the ideational process on the other.
>
> (Jung, 1921, §681)

Here, Jung is referring to a state of feeling as a transformation of the affect-sensation (like a muscular tension, or a heavy breathing) into that *subjective* experience we call "feeling". Referring to contemporary affective neuroscience, I will refer to affects as *a-noetic* feelings, i.e., motivational factors still devoid of representations that organize the organism at a *non-reflectively conscious* level. Affects are functions of the Self – the so called "minimal self", or "nuclear self" (Gallagher & Zahavi, 2008) – while feelings are inextricably bound with subjectivity and representational non-reflective (noetic) or self-reflective (meta-noetic) consciousness.[3] As Jung writes, with the existence of a conscious Ego:

> I distinguish . . . *feeling* from affect, in spite of the fact that the dividing line is fluid, since every feeling, after attaining a certain strength, releases physical innervations, thus becoming an affect. For practical reasons, however, it is advisable to distinguish affect from feeling, since feeling can be a voluntary disposable function, whereas affect is usually not. Similarly, affect is clearly

distinguished from feeling by quite perceptible physical innervations, while feeling for the most part lacks them, or else their intensity is so slight that they can be demonstrated only by the most delicate instruments, as in the case of psychogalvanic phenomena.

. . .

I regard affect on the one hand as a psychic feeling state and on the other as a physiological innervation state, each of which has cumulative, reciprocal effect on the other. That is to say, a component of *sensation* allies itself with the intensified feeling, so that the affect is approximated more to sensation and essentially differentiated from the feeling state.

(Jung, 1921, §681–682)

Hence, we may follow the APA definition of "feeling" as follows:

a self-contained phenomenal experience. Feelings are subjective, evaluative, and independent of the sensations, thoughts, or images evoking them.

(APA, 2018)

This slides towards becoming an affect the more it is associated with physical sensations (meaning sensory activations, like heart pounding, stomachache, etc.).

Jung's reference to sensation is important, as it refers to the biological, organic level (not only the neuroanatomy, the embryology and the neuro-transmettitorial nature of the brain but also of the sympathetic, parasympathetic and autonomous systems) out of which affects and then emotional feelings emerge. Differently from Jung, I regard emotions as complex states that express feelings, sensations and cognitive and relational contents.

As we shall see (vol. I, § 4.2), feelings are primary, irreducible experiences that found and organize self-reflective consciousness (Edelman & Tononi, 2000).

Throughout the whole discussion that will develop, affects, primary, secondary and tertiary emotions will have a pivotal role. I consider emotional feelings the transformed product of the integration of primary affects with representational/cognitive structures *within a co-evolutionary field* or, said differently, *within a relational and social network*. Affects belong to the deepest strata of our biological endowment. Nevertheless, they must be interpreted as part of the organism's regulating functions within its specific environment. Throughout ontogenesis and socialization, such affects and their regulatory functions are transformed into and expressed by emotions within the intersubjective and social fields. Therefore, it should be clear from the start that affects, and even more so emotions, should not be treated as reified "things" but as dynamic relational processes occurring between the interiority of the individual and his social milieu. Emotions are, therefore, transformations of endogenous biological universal affective structures expressed in an indefinite number of culturally determined, specific, meaningful relational forms. Seen this way, emotions may be interpreted extrovertedly as forms of *symbolic actions* (Rosaldo, 1980) and introvertedly as functions connecting and interpreting the subject's experiences with her inner and outer world under the form of feelings.

My discussion on the relationship between the role of affects, emotions and feelings and (human) cognition will merge with Jung's theory of complexes. This implies a discussion not only on the affective side of the complex but also on their epistemic side and, therefore, on the nature of images and of their supposed universality – i.e., on Jung's archetypal hypothesis.

Throughout these books, images will be interpreted as *cognitive patterns and formats that, activated and guided by affects, reflectively re-present, give shape and, therefore, provide intelligibility to those affects*.

Therefore, after having listed what I think are some of the most critical issues Jung was dealing with, my point of departure will be the difference and the relationship between the role of the affects, feelings and cognition and the *dispositional* nature of the psyche. This dispositional nature implies a biological evolutionary endowment of some sort of constrained and specific forms of intelligences – cognitive science's "modules". Such a "modularization" would confer to the flow of the psyche's activity its "archetypal structure and organization" – Jung's "personal and cultural complexes".

On the contrary, a *situational* interpretation of the psyche, which implies the hypothesis of a *general*, non-specific form of intelligence, would justify the opinion for which there are no relevant fixed, inherited universal psychoid imaginal structures (Jung's "archetypes").

As I will try to argue, much of the contemporary Jungian literature on complex formation, of which perhaps the most influential has been Jean Knox's theory on archetypal complexes, has been mostly based on studies on the ontogenesis of cognition in an infant research perspective. In my opinion, this reference to infant research has produced several important misunderstandings, as most[4] of these elegant and unvaluable research efforts quoted by the Jungian critics are necessarily limited by their own scope and methods. In fact, they *are not interested in the whole child but only in the child as a cognitive problem-solver*. Therefore, to scientifically study this specific aspect of the mind and to proceed in a methodologically correct way, they devise a Galilean, quantitative experimental environment that must eliminate all the emotional variables – the extra-cognitive variables. Hence, if the findings of cognitive studies in infant research *are* obviously fundamental and *must* be taken into consideration, extending their vision of such a child – a product of a specific Galilean setting aimed at the study of cognition – to the whole child and to the whole human being produces a distortion that must be corrected. This is what I will try to do.

Along with Jung, my aim is, therefore, to claim the primacy of affects and to reposition the role of cognition as an evolutionary *means* to allow the dispositional affects to attain their role in furthering the goal Jung called "individuation" as an expression of the Self by the Self.[5]

Yet, as you will see, a very large part of these books will be dedicated to cognition, and this may seem a paradox, or a contradiction. This is so for two main reasons. The first is that cognition is the only way we formulate theories and explanations;

therefore, a theory on affects and their evolutionary nature as movers and fundamental organizers of all psycho-biological life ends up by being formulated through cognitive descriptions. The second reason being that, at present, among the many theories of affects, feelings and emotions, there is not yet any consensus on what an emotion is!

I hope that the vast reference to cognitive studies and issues will not mislead the reader and that she will always keep in mind that the great importance of cognitive processes and structures must be interpreted as evolutionary reflective representations stemming *from* and descriptive *of* affects. In fact, these books do not intend to prove that cognition is not as relevant as it seems. Instead, they will try to do the following:

a) Strongly reaffirm the dispositional nature of psychic life.
b) Reposition the discussion on cognition in such a way as to show how much Jung's ideas are relevant and coherent with today's state of the art science.
c) Put affects as the real origin and key organizers of cognition.
d) Underscore and properly place Jung's "cognitive" theory of the unconscious, for which unconscious processes are already organized as emotional/epistemic devices to cope with "reality". This issue deeply differentiating Jung from Freud; in fact, it is important to stress that Jung's complexes, including those that, due to their supposedly unconscious, collective and archaic features he called "archetypes", differently from Freud's drives, which have a purely bio-energetic component, are made up of two aspects – an affective/emotional aspect and a cognitive aspect.

In so doing, I will highlight the interpretation of the unconscious as a form of unconscious consciousness, as Jung wrote in his *On the Nature of the Psyche* (Jung, 1947/1954, §6), together with the role and meaning of images as direct non-arbitrary representational patterns of affects.

1.3 Looking at Problems, not Answers

When someone develops a theory, he does so because he sees a problem and, therefore, attempts to construct an explanation and a possible solution. In these books, I will attempt to formulate an answer to what for Jung were "problems" and to consider *how* he tackled them, i.e., what answers did he give to such problems. My goal is not to salvage or condemn Jung but to contribute to analytical psychology. Therefore, I wish to very schematically sketch out what the problems are that Jung was trying to address with his model. They belong to two different categories:

Category A)

1) What are the fundamental motivational forces that move human psychology?
2) Do psychological universals, almost-universals or conditional universals exist, and if so, at which level of complexity?

3) How, how much and at what level of complexity do humans learn?
4) May learning transform and modify those universals (if they exist)?
5) How do we define "learning"?

Category B)

1) Why are there phenomena like those that Jung called "synchronistic"?
2) Why does mathematics seem to work so well also when applied to non-directly experienced empirical reality? What Eugene Wigner described as the *unreasonable effectiveness of mathematics*?

If these problems exist, there is no psychological model – with the exclusion of analytical psychology – that is able to give a proper answer to all of them nor that is even *attempting to do so for those of category B*, as they represent typical "paradigmatic anomalies" within any theory of which I have knowledge.

All the theories we know, mostly from cognitive science, general psychology and infant research, work wonderfully, as they are able, through observations and ingenious experiments, to progressively redefine and respond to the problems at stake but at the cost of *eliminating* those problems – like synchronistic occurrences – which, for Jung, were crucial. Obviously, the elimination of any anomalies, the simplification of complexity not by a more encompassing view but by the denial of their existence, generates a feeling of safety and of cognitive control, but at the cost of blinding ourselves.

The formulation of these issues and the answers Jung gave to them is the core of his legacy, for which the Ego is not an intelligent entity who just adapts to the situational conditions, i.e., as a structure essentially carved *by* these conditions. Jung is the only psychologist that seriously shifted the role of the protagonist from the Ego to the Self, and this is the basis of Jung's real interest: psychotherapy. All the main forms of psychotherapy that I know of only deal with the formation of the Ego, as if the Ego is the beginning and the end of the whole story. Obviously, the Ego is the necessary condition for something, but in todays' main forms of psychotherapies, this "something" seems to be lost within a generic form of adaptation. I am referring to this issue because, as I will show, some important contributions from the Jungian perspective have shifted towards this incompatible perspective for which the Ego is the protagonist. Perhaps, only Bion, Winnicott and Erik Erikson, in very different ways, indicate that the Ego, whose maturation is often thought to end at the end of adolescence – a very long time before death – actually undergoes further transformations throughout its life. Nevertheless, also, these theories in different ways overlook the teleological nature of this process. And while all the contemporary studies on infant research, or on attachment, or, on a different level, all references to the organic neurobiological interpretation of reality must be taken into consideration, they should always be approached in the following way:

• From what I will call the domain of secondary *epistemological knowledge*, they should always be interpreted as causes-for-aims. In a few words: if there is a child in the adult, there is a potential adult in the child, and it is the future "adult" that will ultimately give meaning to the child.

- From what I will call the domain of primary *gnostic knowledge* – i.e., the empirical domain of the subjective psychological experience (the only experience we may have) – all domains of knowledge must be approached as a form of amplification of an underlying enigmatic reality (See: Polanyi, 1974. But also: Feyerabend, 2010).

Therefore, to look for the most useful and acceptable answers that Jung proposed for these problems, this book will try to highlight the following:

- The nature of representations and that of affects, which must be carefully distinguished.
- Their ontogenetic development, which, once again, must be differentiated.
- The relationship between affects, feelings and representations within the structure of the complex.
- And the nature of the organization between these two components. The questions being, in a few words, as follows:

  - How is the relationship between affects, feelings and representations organized throughout experience – i.e., as *personal* complexes?
  - Is their relationship organized *also* through nonpersonal constants, as in what we now call *cultural complexes*?
  - Is their relationship organized also like Jung's *archetypes*? And if so:

- How could we describe (if it is possible) the development from minimal bio-psychological constraints to those complex formations that a person might experience as "archetypal images"? This is a crucial issue because it implies the possibility of a progressive emergence of something universal and very complex without the need for any pre-written genetic program. The last part of this book is devoted to studying such a possibility.

To pursue this, I will refer to the following:

- the concept of co-evolutionary fields both within phylogenesis and ontogenesis; and
- a more differentiated categorization of universals.

Notes

1 But will they be skeptical also with regard to this latent text now made manifest, or will they defend it from now on as a scientific religion? (I apologize for the oxymoron). I think the answer, at least for part of Marx's and Freud's followers, is already well-documented.
2 I will discuss this concept in the next pages.
3 To be precise, we should distinguish between noetic *presentations* and meta-noetic *representations*.
4 Not all of them. A vast number of studies are carried out within something like a "clinical" perspective, and while they remain mostly cognitive, they keep a larger scope within

which such processes are interpreted. I am thinking about authors like Louis Sander, Edward Tronick, Colin Trevarthen or Daniel Stern.

5 I use this cautious wording because the term "Self" has many different meanings and references, from neurobiology to analytical psychology to social psychology, etc.

References

American Psychological Association [APA]. (2018). *APA Dictionary of Psychology*. https://dictionary.apa.org/feeling.

Didi-Huberman, G. (2017). *The Surviving Image: Phantoms of Time and Time of Phantoms: Aby Warburg's History of Art* (trans. Mendelsohn Harvey). University Park: Pennsylvania State University Press.

Edelman, G., Tononi, G. (2000). *A Universe of Consciousness: How Matter Becomes Imagination*. New York: Basic Books.

Feyerabend, P. (2010). *Against Method*. London, New York: Verso.

Gadamer, H.-G. (1989). *Truth and Method*. New York: Continuum.

Gallagher, S., Zahavi, D. (2008). *The Phenomenological Mind*. New York, NY: Routledge.

Goodwyn, E. (2010a). Approaching Archetypes: Reconsidering Innateness. *Journal of Analytical Psychology*, 55, 4, 502–521.

Goodwyn, E. (2010b). The Author Replies. *Journal of Analytical Psychology*, 55, 4, 550–555.

Goodwyn, E. (2012). *The Neurobiology of the Gods. How Brain Physiology Shapes the Recurrent Imagery of Myths and Dreams*. London, New York: Routledge.

Haule, J.R. (2011). *Jung in the 21st Century*. 2 Vols. London, New York: Routledge.

Hogenson, G.B. (1998). Response to Pietikäinen and Stevens. *Journal of Analytical*, 43, 3, 357–372.

Hogenson, G.B. (2003a). Reply to Maloney. *Journal of Analytical Psychology*, 48, 2, 265–266.

Hogenson, G.B. (2003b). Reply to Raya Jones. *Journal of Analytical Psychology*, 48, 5, 714–718.

Hogenson, G.B. (2004). What Are Symbols Of? Situated Action, Mythological Bootstrapping and the Emergence of the Self. *Journal of Analytical Psychology*, 49, 1, 67–81.

Hogenson, G.B. (2010). Response to Erik Goodwyn's "Approaching Archetypes: Reconsidering Innateness". *Journal of Analytical Psychology*, 55, 4, 543–549.

Jones, R.A. (2003). On Innatism: A Response to Hogenson. *Journal of Analytical Psychology*, 48, 5, 705–714.

Jung, C.G. (1921). Psychological Types. In: *The Collected Works of C.G. Jung*. Vol. 6. London: Routledge.

Jung, C.G. (1947/1954). On the Nature of the Psyche. In: *The Collected Works of C.G. Jung*. Vol. 8. London: Routledge.

Knox, J.M. (2001). Memories, Fantasies, Archetypes: An Exploration of Some Connections Between Cognitive Science and Analytical Psychology. *Journal of Analytical Psychology*, 46, 613–635.

Knox, J.M. (2003). *Archetype, Attachment, Analysis: Jungian Psychology and the Emergent Mind*. London and New York: Routledge.

Knox, J.M. (2004a). From Archetypes to Reflective Function. *Journal of Analytical Psychology*, 49, 1, 1–19.

Knox, J.M. (2004b). Developmental Aspects of Analytical Psychology: New Perspectives from Cognitive Neuroscience and Attachment Theory. In: *Analytical Psychology: Contemporary Perspectives in Jungian Analysis*. J. Cambray, L.C. Hove (Eds.). New York: Brunner-Routledge.

Knox, J.M. (2009). The Analytic Relationship: Integrating Jungian, Attachment Theory and Developmental Perspectives. *British Journal of Psychotherapy*, 25, 1.

Knox, J.M. (2010). Response to Erik Goodwyn's "Approaching Archetypes: Reconsidering Innateness". *Journal of Analytical Psychology*, 55, 4, 522–533.

Maloney, A. (2003a). Archetype theory, Evolutionary Psychology and the Baldwin Effect. A Commentary on Hogenson's Paper. *Journal of Analytical Psychology*, 48, 1, 101–116.

Maloney, A. (2003b). Reply to Hogenson. *Journal of Analytical Psychology*, 48, 2, 263–265.

McDowell, M.J. (2001). Principle of Organization: A Dynamic-Systems View of the Archetype-as-Such. *Journal of Analytical Psychology*, 46, 4, 637–654.

Merchant, J. (2006). The Developmental/Emergent Model of Archetype, Its Implications and Its Application to Shamanism. *Journal of Analytical Psychology*, 51, 1, 127–146.

Merchant, J. (2009). A Reappraisal of Classical Archetype theory and Its Implications For theory and Practice. *Journal of Analytical Psychology*, 54, 3, 339–358.

Merchant, J. (2010). Response to Erik Goodwyn's "Approaching Archetypes: Reconsidering Innateness". *Journal of Analytical Psychology*, 55, 4, 534–542.

Merchant, J. (2012). *Shamans and Analysts: New Insights on the Wounded Healer*. London: Routledge.

Merchant, J. (2015). Foetal Trauma, Body Memory and Early Infant Communication: A Case Illustration. *Journal of Analytical Psychology*, 60, 3, 601–617.

Merchant, J. (2016). The Image Schema and Innate Archetypes: Theoretical and Clinical Implications. *Journal of Analytical Psychology*, 61, 1, 63–78.

Merchant, J. (2019). The Controversy Around the Concept of Archetypes and the Place for An Emergent/Developmental Model. *Journal of Analytical Psychology*, 64, 5, 701–719.

Merchant, J. (2020). Archetypes and the 'Impoverished Environment' Argument: A Response to Erik Goodwyn. *Journal of Analytical Psychology*, 66, I, 132–152.

Merritt, D.L. (2012). *The Dairy Farmers Guide to the Universe*. 4 Vols. London, New York: Routledge.

Pietikäinen, P. (1998a). Archetypes as Symbolic Forms. *Journal of Analytical Psychology*, 43, 3, 325–343.

Pietikäinen, P. (1998b). "Archetypes as Symbolic Forms": Response to Hester Mcfarland Solomon, George B. Hogenson and Anthony Stevens' Knox, J.M. (2003). In: *Archetype, Attachment, Analysis: Jungian Psychology and the Emergent Mind*. London, New York: Routledge.

Polanyi, M. (1974). *Personal Knowledge: Towards a Post-Critical Philosophy*. Chicago: University of Chicago Press.

Ricoeur, P. (2008). *Freud and Philosophy. An Essay on Interpretation*. D. Savage (Transl.). New Haven, CT: Yale University Press.

Roesler, C. (2012). Are Archetypes Transmitted More by Culture Than Biology? Questions Arising from Conceptualizations of the Archetype. *Journal of Analytical Psychology*, 57, 2, 223–246.

Roesler, C. (2022). *Development of a Reconceptualization of Archetype Theory. Report to the IAAP*. https://iaap.org/wp-content/uploads/2022/04/report-archetype-theory-roesler-1.pdf.

Rosaldo, E. (1980). *Knowledge and Passion: Ilangot Notions of Self and Social Life*. Cambridge: Cambridge University Press.

Saunders, P., Skar, P. (2001). Archetypes, Complexes and Self Organization. *Journal of Analytical Psychology*, 46, 2, 305–323.

Stevens, A. (1998). Response to P. Pietikäinen. *Journal of Analytical Psychology*, 43, 3.

Stevens, A. (2002). *Archetype Revisited: An Updated Natural History of the Self*. London: Routledge.

Chapter 2

Explanations and Experience

Buttate pure via
Ogni opera in versi o in prosa.
Nessuno è mai riuscito a dire
Cos'è, nella sua essenza, una rosa.

[Do throw away
Every work in verse or prose
No one could ever say
What, in essence, is a rose]
       Giorgio Caproni (2002)
  Elogio della rosa. Torino: Einaudi

As I will focus on the issues and problems that Jung was trying to answer by developing his own theory, I will implicitly differentiate two radically different epistemological aspects. The first, that deals with problems, is marked by an empirical experiential nature. In fact, a "problem" is something one *has an experience of*, one "has" a problem (may that be theoretical, practical, ethical, etc.). The second aspect, on the contrary, deals with the attempt to formulate an explanation; it has an analytical nature. Contrary to the nature of the problem, one does not (*and should not think to*) have an explanation; one *thinks or formulates* an explanation, and no explanation may exhaust or substitute the experience one had of the problem.

My point of view follows Karl Jaspers' distinction between *verstehen* and *erklären*:

> To avoid ambiguity and obscurity we will always employ the expression "understand" [verstehen] for the intuitive vision of the spirit, from within. We will never call com-prehending, but "explaining" [erklären] the knowing of objective causal connections that are always seen from the outside. . . . It is therefore possible to explain something without understanding it.
>
> (Jaspers, 2000, p. 30, my transl.)

DOI: 10.4324/9781003586258-2

And further:

> The rigorous exactness of the sciences is not the whole truth. Such exactness, in its universal validity, does not bind us in all respects as real men, but only as beings endowed with intellect.
>
> (2000, p. 26)

This concept of "constraint" is of great interest here: the scientific community identifies and compares protocols and shares research results, but what is called into question is only the system of the intellect, not the human being in its entirety. This is an important point that I will try to elucidate in the next pages.

This book is written by an analyst and has an analytical perspective. All I will say has to do with what happens during an analysis or, better yet, to all of us during our psychological existence. Yet I will also refer to what was used to be described as "natural sciences", especially biological principles and research.

Jung's position, in relation to "natural" and "human" sciences, is, as it often happens, peculiar:

> In respect of its natural object and method, modern empirical psychology belongs to the natural sciences, but in respect of its method of explanation it belongs to the human sciences as he thought that his object belonged to *natural* sciences, while his method belonged to the *human* sciences. Obviously, this complicates the issue further.
>
> (Jung, 1924, § 166. Transl. modified by Shamdasani, 2003)

Natural sciences deal with objectivity, whereas hermeneutics is rooted in the practical, empirical life of the subject. With Jung, the affair becomes more complicated. For him, objectivity and subjectivity are not always opposed (yet they may be and often are), but it is possible to find an objective "object" *within* the subject and her subjective, empirical life.

Under the sociological frame of reference – the one of Durkheim, or Weber – it is easy to find an "objective" knowledge in a subject that is fully identified with his social group (this may be the case of the Persona, but it also applies largely to the use of our natural language). On the contrary, there is a fierce debate, also among the Jungian community, about the existence of forms of objective "knowledge" (I mean emotional or pragmatic knowledge, not declarative knowledge) that belong not to the *social* group but to the human individual as such. As we will see, this debate is crucial, as it may bring us to paradoxical conclusions such as that of a Nazi person under Nazism: he would be considered healthy because he is "objectively" socially well-adapted (this is why Georges Devereux wisely distinguished between "normal societies" and "sado-masochistic" ones).

The notion that objective knowledge rests on "collective" social structures on the one hand and with universal archetypal structures on the other is a pivotal one since, as we will see, Jung's very idea of individuation, which is the very reason of all his endeavors, is centered on such a possibility – the possibility to attain a form of "universal,[1] objective", yet at the same time, subjective, personal experiential understanding. This understanding is a deeply emotionally charged meaning *felt* as universal and *referring to something universal* (or quasi-universal) – an understanding with which the Ego (the subjective subject) should *not* identify because it would inflate it and make it feel that its own objective-subjective knowledge must be valid for everyone else. This is how fundamentalisms work.

This relationship between subjectivity and objectivity is also the relationship between the Ego and the Self – the active emotional entity against which the Ego struggles and longs for at the same time and to which it is (partly or wholly) subjected.

My position with regard to these two approaches to reality is "interactionist". In fact, while the reality we gather from our emotional experience represents the core of human nature, it is also true that every human being constantly tries to *make sense* of his own experiential reality. To formulate coherent explanations, whenever we do not actively choose to employ a Galilean approach (i.e., when we are outside the "experimental laboratory"), we all unconsciously produce what are called "folk theories" (this means that this happens also to every scientist when he lets himself just "live"). This is clear at the beginning of an analysis: the patient comes to us with her theory about her symptoms, or condition; often, it is a folk theory that needs scrutiny. (I will come back to folk theories in vol. II, § 6.1.) My effort is aimed at discussing some theories that may shed some light on the complexity of human emotional experience.

The search for causes and reasons happens in analysis all the time. The question "Why did *this* happen?" cannot be ignored, yet no explanation of what an apple *is* may substitute or exhaust the experience of biting into an apple nor of *seeing* or smelling an apple. Yet I think that a purely felt (emotional) experience is not fully complete unless it is an object of reflection and is *open to being included in a causal and teleological explanatory context*. Our patients do look for explanations, yet this does not mean that to be full and legitimate, a psychological experience must necessarily be explained; it means that it should be *open* to and *available* for such an enquiry and that this enquiry is infinite. Therefore, we must ask: What is the role of any possible attempt at an *explanation* of such an *experience*, which, differently from its explanation, represents what is real? And what is the role of what we may say *about* this emotional-imaginal experience? And most of all: What may be the role of my own attempt to formulate some possible explanations on some important psychological issue vis à vis the experiences that these explanations are trying to understand?

I will try to respond in the following way: No explanation, no paradigm, theory or model has the right to mystify, substitute or minimize this experiential reality, as *this* is the only real one. In other words: no *scientia* can substitute its object – *experientia*.

We should also notice that that a theory, like an emotional image or a dream or a patient's narrative which for her is felt as (emotionally) meaningful, is also a product of the psyche. In fact, theories or models may also sometimes become emotionally charged and represent "narcissistic" aspects of the theorizer. When, for instance, a scientist defends his theory with arguments *ad hominem* or expels someone who disagrees from his community (*Alas!* This has been part of the regressive religious aspect of many psychoanalytical communities), they become *beliefs* that the proponent defends as an intimate part of his own narcissistic self.

Theories, like the ones I will discuss, are reflections *on* "reality" (i.e., on what affects us affectively) and, therefore, pertain to the human domain of the *intellect* and the thinking function. They are unavoidable and useful but should always serve empirical emotional experience. Later, I will draw a more precise distinction between primary knowledge through emotional experience (what I will call *gnostic* knowledge) and secondary knowledge *about* primary gnostic knowledge (which I *will call epistemic* knowledge).

2.1 Jung's "Empirical" Stance

What I just wrote is connected with Jung's idea of what is real. Perhaps the main theme of this book is the role of affects, emotions and feelings in human psychology and, therefore, also within the human cognition. Hence, I wish to start from the following propositions: for Jung, who in this case is fundamentally inspired by Charles S. Pierce's and William James' pragmatic approach:

- Affectivity corresponds to effectivity (Jung, 1933).
- Whatever affects us (therefore, whatever is affective) is real.

This point of departure defines Jung's ontology: there is an Unknowable (or better said: infinitely knowable, therefore, never completely knowable) underlying reality, which emerges via the empirical, subjective experience of whatever affects us. Such emotional affects are conveyed by "images".

Jung refers to this emotional quality as "numinous". It represents a fundamental aspect of analytical psychology, as it connects the human epistemic activity with a specific qualitative experience of reality, meaning and value, conveyed by the numinous feeling.

The foremost example of this phenomenological, empirical approach, for which what is real is what affects us affectively, is not expressed in clear terms in Jung's works, but it clearly shows itself in his *Red Book*. It is in this diary that Jung describes what is the reality to which he is referring, precisely his own direct qualitative experience of the numinous images emerging from his unconscious.

Therefore, we necessarily must remember that our real object of enquiry, and therefore, of any analysis, is the object of our direct empirical subjective experience of emotional images. Obviously, under this perspective, dreams and active imagination reveal their fundamental character as the very stuff we humans are made of.

The role of primary emotional experience, vs. secondary explanatory knowledge, is unfortunately foreshadowed by the publication of Jung's collected works *before* the publication of his *Red Book* and *Black Book*. As Sonu Shamdasani pointed out, it is from the *Red Book* and the *Black Book* that we may really understand Jung's empirical, pragmatic approach, as for Jung the images he was dealing with *were real*. On the contrary, Jung's more scholarly texts, published in his collected works, cannot but mix primary, immediate psychological descriptions with discussions based on secondary knowledge (I want to avoid the term "explanations", as Jung was always quite careful not to fall into the semiotic, reductive trap of substituting primary experience with its explanation).

Therefore, as this book is mostly on theories and secondary explanatory knowledge, all that I will write must be taken with the proper caution, as it will try to discuss what ultimately counts – subjective experiences of the numinous (emotional) images, which *can never* correspond to its own explanations since an explanation is always a cognitive transformation and a substitution (*"this* means *that"*) of a subjective experience.

In fact, Jung was quite clear on the dangers of explaining away the only reality that exists – the empirical, subjective experience of numinous images. Therefore, I would like to be as consequential and clear as possible and say that within this pragmatic definition of reality, *I consider any attempt at an explanation – may this be neurobiological, biological, developmental, social, anthropological, etc. – a specific form of amplification, insofar it has any meaning for who formulates it.*

As I am referring to the direct, empirical *subjective* experience of effective affects – a feeling – a short clarification on subjectivity is necessary.

Here, "subjective" does *not* at all mean only "private" or isolated from the world. In fact, the way perception and affectivity subjectively affect us involves and encompasses our "environment",[2] especially at a socio-cultural-historical level. In fact, culture and history symbolically organize the individual subjectivities in somehow coherent wholes – in social groups. In this sense, subjectivity not only does not exclude sociality but also implies it. This directly involves what we call *cultural complexes*, which I will discuss in volume 2.

An important consequence of what I have written so far has to do with the kind of language that is most effective in describing human psychological reality. In fact, it becomes clear that such a language will be the more "real" the more it will express and adhere to the original language of the psyche and to its primary experiential form of knowledge – a symbolic and imaginal language.

The need to use a language that does not betray the symbolic nature of the experience that it wishes to express springs from a paradoxical hermeneutic situation in which any clear-cut, cartesian form of understanding would mean the immediate collapse and death of the meaning that this language should serve (Jung, 1911–12/1956; Carta, 1985).

This situation reminds one of Heisenberg's uncertainty principle, for which the very attempt to know something destroys the possibility to know it. In the symbolic domain – which for Jung is the genuine domain of the psyche – the symbol acts upon us as a vector towards a horizon that can never be really reached, as the real goal is the *process* towards understanding. In fact, during a psychotherapy, espe-cially a long one, or when reflecting upon one's life, one may remember, for exam-ple, a certain dream or even a certain occurrence that carried a symbolic character, and realize that the dream, or the meaning of the occurrence, has been constantly active beneath the surface of one's life. The dream, or the occurrence, may have never been really interpreted because their real interpretation corresponds to the unfolding of the life process itself.

During his analysis, a 45-year-old patient experienced a transformational leap that he shared with me during a moving session.

He was a philosophy teacher and was used to his everyday teaching routine. He was a good teacher, respected by his students and colleagues. Everything always seemed just normal; his teaching was his job. He was a music lover, and one day, he decided to explain the Pythagorean theory of harmonics. At the beginning of the lesson, he thought he was going to just explain this theory highlighting its cosmo-logical implications, but while he was explaining, he moved the focus of his lesson to the emotional meaning that this theory may have on "all of us" (as he said to his students), under the form of music.

While talking, he started to feel "different"; a certain intense emotional state was growing in him, and as he told me: "I felt somehow inspired. It was a new, strange feeling". He spoke for 50 minutes straight, he had not realized that so much time had passed, and at the end of the hour, he felt emotional, as he said:

> An intense, warm feeling as if something really important had happened. I felt I had done exactly what I had to do, but, most of all, I felt that I exposed myself as I really am.

It was clear that one of the aspects of what had happened carried a deep sense of awe and surprise.

When he recounted to me this story, he was very moved. This feeling filled the room and myself, indicating that something "numinous" was taking place. I felt like an adept who had to get ready to hear something very important.

Another aspect of what had happened during this lesson was that, when he had finished speaking, he noticed that in the class, there was a perfect silence. All his students – 16-year-olds – were like mesmerized. Then he remembered a dream that he had dreamed 25 years before:

> I am in an amphitheater, like an ancient Roman, or Greek one. I am taking to an audience. At first, I have something like a big sausage in my hands. I do not remember what I am saying. At a certain moment something changes. The sau-sage is transformed and a blue light shines from it and fills the whole space. I feel inspired, and with pervasive, intense feeling my talking becomes something like a prophetic, visionary, religious testimony. The whole, large crowd is listening to me attentively. The general quality of the moment was uncanny and beautiful.

It took 25 years for this dream to realize itself and connect the patient's somehow dissociated, refined intellect with his heart. From this moment, the patient quickly changed. His theoretical qualities, and his language, remained permeated with those feelings and emotions that had been dissociated until then.

The fact is that the symbolic realm inhibits any real attempt for any *univocal interpretation*. If experience is symbolic, there cannot be any explanation that may completely express it, if not the individual life process itself and the infinite circumambulation around it.

Jung's ingenious, unique approach is *not* the interpretive one but the one based on amplifications; in our case, the events of the dreamer's life that the dreamer feels related to his old dream as if unfolding from it are the real amplifications of the symbols that the dream was expressing.

Such a situation regarding the role and scope of what we call "interpretation" may indeed be very frustrating, if not disconcerting. It calls for the transformation of the intellectual attempt to explaining something into *playing* with it (in Winnicott's terms). It may be disconcerting because it carries with itself the realization that knowing something through explanation implies the loss of something else – the living process of knowing. In fact, when something symbolic has fully been known, it transforms itself into a *fact* – a non-animated entity.

The other possibility is to *not* try to explain – i.e., to provide a clear-cut, cartesian idea of the Thing. This calls for another form of mourning: that of the illusion to control reality with our explanations – the power of a magic formula. Unfortunately, this is the only possible choice for an analyst – to withstand this *nigredo* of knowledge (Carta, 2020) and, while still trying to understand, to let go of every form of understanding with an ironical attitude about what one thinks to have understood.

Not only Bion, with his letting go of memory, desire *and knowledge*, is of this opinion – to recommend illuminating what is known, i.e., consciously thought, with a "light of intense darkness" – but more than anyone else, it was Jung. It is Jung that, while trying to understand, during his whole life, recommended not to avoid such a *cloud of unknowing* and to use explanations as amplifications and not as interpretations.

Therefore, the symbolic nature of experience demands that the psychotherapist describe her experience through playful explanations that, used ironically, are not meant to be interpretations but amplifications and that, for this reason, cannot but be multiple.

It is not by chance that Jung writes the following words in an essay dedicated to the empirical, experiential work of the psychotherapist with his patient within transference (hence, not on the theorization of such work):

> My business is merely the natural science of the psyche, and my main concern to establish the facts. How these facts are named and what further interpretation is then placed upon them is of secondary importance. Natural science is not a science of words and ideas, but of facts. I am no terminological rigorist – call the existing

symbols wholeness, "self", "consciousness", "higher ego", or what you will, it makes little difference. I, for my part only try not to give any false or misleading names. All these terms are simply names for the facts that alone carry weight. The names I give do not imply a philosophy, although I cannot prevent people from barking at these terminological phantoms as if they were metaphysical hypostases. The facts are sufficient in themselves, and it is well to know about them. But their interpretation should be left to the individual's discretion.

(Jung, 1946, §537)

Here, the question that may arise is this: What are these "facts" Jung is talking about? The answer is this: those that carry an affect that affects the person through a feeling which is for him *real*. This perspective clearly "abolishes psychology as a science" (Jung) to salvage experience from its explanations.

I wonder whether we might say that, while explanations, like the ones I will provide, refer to thinking, the thinking function and the support of intuition (almost indispensable for a scientific discovery) or sensation (indispensable for any scientist in the laboratory), interpretation has to do mostly with the feeling function, aided by intuition or sensation.

Feelings that derive from affects – the real *prima materia* of any life and any analysis – are the core of empirical experience. It is *from* the effectual force of the affect that the emotional subject may *then* look for the answers she needs, the meaning of her questions.

The core of any psychopathology lies in a dysfunction of the relationship between affects, feelings and emotions, such as the invasion of raw psychosomatic affects; or it is the product of the dissociation *from* emotions or from an unbalance between the two fundamental levels of human psychological reality – primary affective experience and secondary cognitive explanation.

In fact, as I already said, along with Daniel Stern, who distinguishes the "observed child" from the "clinical child" (Stern, 1985), we must bear in mind that the subject and the object of the *cognitive* approach of most infant research is foremostly the infant or child seen as an intellectual "problem solver", i.e., a scientific artifact. As we shall see, the fact of conflating such an intellectual child, or, for the matter, an adult, with the "clinical" patient to formulate a theory of human psychological functioning is a grave mistake, which carries important consequences – the misrepresentation of how human psychology works due to the scotomization of the function of affectivity and, most of all, what Jung called *numinosum*.

Having said this, I must once again emphasize that this book, as paradoxical as it seems, is an attempt to salvage Jung's descriptions of his own experiences precisely using the secondary explanatory knowledge, whose limitations I am describing. I will try to show that analytical psychology is a special form of imagination still imbued with a tremendous heuristic force, coherent with many contemporary trends deserving to be safeguarded.

As far as images are concerned, if the human soul breathes and lives by imagining, then the best language to describe our empirical psychological experience should be imaginal (Hillman, 1975), hence, stories, myths, fairy tales, dreams, etc., but also delusions or hallucinations. It should always be an "alchemical language". In this regard, not only Jung but especially Erich Neumann (1973, 2014), Edward Edinger or James Hillman are among the most rigorous "theoreticians" (as paradoxical as it may seem), as they use the language of the psyche to let the psyche explain itself.

Other forms of language, such as, for instance, Freud's or Heinz Kohut's lexicon[3] (just to make an example), seem to try to do something different. In fact, not only does psychoanalysis but also the whole language used by contemporary psychologists not speak of psychology using the imaginative emotional idiom of psychology but rather by an abstract idiom to speak *about* psychology.

For example, let's compare two styles of linguistic expressions. Heinz Kohut's uses a language that is translating into abstract categories the patient's psychological experience – an attempt related to Jasper's *verstehen*. On the other hand, Erich Neumann refers to the same kind of imaginal language that the patient's psyche autonomously produces, a language coherent to the process of *erklären*.

Kohut:

In the idealizing transference the working-through process thus concerns the following typical sequence of events: (1) the patient's loss of the narcissistic union with the idealized THERAPEUTIC ACTIVATION OF THE OMNIPOTENT OBJECT self-object; (2) the ensuing disturbance of the narcissistic balance; (3) the subsequent hypercathexis of archaic forms of either (a) the idealized parent imago or (b) the grandiose self; and, fleetingly, (4) the hypercathexis of the (autoerotic) fragmented body-mind-self.

(Kohut, 1971, pp. 97–98)

Neumann:

At the matriarchal, pregenital level, oral and anal merge with one another as life and death; the one is indissolubly bound up with the other.

In the vegetatively accented worldview over which presides the Great Goddess as mistress of all plant life – death, rot, foul-smelling corruption are not felt to be hostile to life. Because life, death and rebirth are looked upon as a continuous process and the importance of the individual is not yet overemphasized, death is not seen as an end or even as a dangerous crisis.

(Neumann, 1973)

To a naïve reader, Neumann's language may seem childish, unsophisticated – surely anti-academic – yet is an attempt to really comprehend (*verstehen*) its object (psychological affective imaginal life).

This kind of criticism will be directed towards the symbolic (i.e., unsaturated) aspect of Jung's language. In fact, Jung's terminology has been often accused of poor clarity and "confusion". The issue being whether this confusion is a sign of a sloppy mind or, instead, the only possible language to make sure *not* to explain in a saturated way its lively, experiential object – empirical psychic life. In fact, in our analytical situation as analysts, I think that we are paid more for our *incompetence* than our competence, as it is such *nigredo* of not knowing that keeps the symbol alive and lets it proceed and evolve through its own unending future.

Even if this is a general epistemological issue, the critical relationship between science – knowledge – and experience becomes utterly delicate in the case of psychology. As I already said, this critical relationship refers to the fact that no science – no scientist, no "expert" – has any legitimacy over what anyone experiences. This means that the role of the scientist, of the expert – the role I am implicitly assuming by writing these books – cannot be that of someone who tells someone else what his meaning of life should be and what should be meaningful for him. This criticism was expressed first by Max Weber (1946) and, among many others, by Foucault (for example, in Foucault, 1980) and Lyotard (1984). If this is valid for any science vs. any experience, its role becomes utterly crucial within the psychotherapeutic domain, as no psychotherapist has any right to superimpose his/her knowledge onto the patient's experience, i.e., to the empirical reality of his numinous images.

When Jung recommends relativizing the analyst's position and interpreting the analytical relationship as a relationship between two human beings, he is asking the analyst to fully participate in and experience the relationship, not to explain it.

> If I wish to treat another individual psychologically at all, I must for better or worse give up all pretensions to superior knowledge, all authority and desire to influence. I must perforce adopt the dialectical procedure consisting in a comparison of our mutual findings. But this becomes possible only if I give the other person a chance to play his hand to the full, unhampered by my assumptions. In this way his system is geared to mine and acts upon it; my reaction is the only thing with which I as an individual can legitimately confront my patient.
>
> (Jung, 1935, §2)

At the same time, this implies that the analyst's mandate will be *to go where the patient is*. The best example of this fundamental attitude is described by Marie Louise von Franz in an interview with Françoise Selhofer.

Von Franz recalled:

> Jung spoke so impressively about the reality of the soul that I, who at that time had a rather rationalistic mind, soon did not know anymore whether I'm coming or going. In the discussion at lunch C.G. Jung among other things mentioned a patient, who asserted that she has been on the moon where she had to fight a demon. So vividly was he talking as though this woman had really been on the moon. Marie-Louise von Franz, somehow irritated, objected that this young woman might have dreamed or fantasized that she was on the moon. Hereupon Jung looked at her very seriously and replied: "No, she was on the moon!"
>
> (Selhofer, 1982)

This point is coherently elaborated also by Bion, who, while admitting that outside the session the analyst may produce theoretical-explanatory thoughts (which are special forms of imagination), within the relationship, he must let go of memory, desire and knowledge (Bion, 1962). In this case, Bion's position applies not just to psychoanalysis but also to the totality of the relationship between science (epistemic knowledge) and experience (gnostic knowledge).

2.2   Bottom-Up and Top-Down Perspectives

In these books, I will resort to a bottom-up approach to complement Jung's phenomenological perspective. Jung's reflections on the bottom-up formation of the psyche – therefore, his proposal of a theoretical model to "explain" the phenomenology of human experience (the only real thing) – are interspersed throughout his collected works. Yet most of them are systematically included in volume 8. I think that an overview of Jung's own ideas on the elements and processes that form the mind might be useful to contextualize the contents of this book.

A bottom-up approach implies the attempt to reconstruct a complex whole from its antecedents and components – in our case, from the biological and neurobiological domain and from developmental psychology. My integration is due to the fact that most of Jung's writings do not deal with any real developmental theory, and Jung's clinical approach is intrinsically phenomenological, i.e., referred to the efficacy of images and to the "method" of amplification.

I will choose a bottom-up approach in using neurobiology, biology, developmental psychology and anthropology *not* to explain numinous, subjective meaningful experiences or to reduce adult life and the search for meaning, universality and the longing for infinity to their supposed causal antecedents. In fact, while I recognize the role of theories like attachment (a bottom-up theory that tries to explain the complexity of human psychology) or infant research, I refrain from referring to them to try to "explain" the level of reality that deals with the empirical contact with "religious" images and values using their causal approach. I will not refer to such bottom-up theories as the analyses of causes (for instance, attachment issues or traumatic past events) that would produce the effect of the empirical manifestation of the processes of Ego formation, i.e., of the embodiment of the Self into reality.[4] As for any dynamic complex system (i.e., a system of interacting forces in time), such processes are *irreducible* to any bottom-up theory, like attachment or, as we will see, cognitive developmental studies carried out within the Galilean framework (the classical scientific setting) of infant research.

Yet, insofar as they have a scientific validity,[5] they may, and should, be integrated within the wider perspective of the development of the Self. This means that in such a hyper-complex system as the "Self" (which, I would like to say immediately, *includes its own objects*), what are conceptualized as the "causes" from infancy and childhood when we conceptualize development as something aiming teleologically at maturity become *reasons*.

The whole point is to find a non-reductionist coherence between different levels of reality and explanation. This is why I will try to integrate findings and theories that belong to four different domains: 1) biology, especially evolutionary biology; 2) neurobiology, especially affective neuroscience; 3) psychology, especially developmental psychology, evolutionary psychology and, obviously, analytical psychology; and 4) anthropology, especially cognitive anthropology.

A bottom-up approach is necessary to study analytical psychology and use those concepts and principles that have a heuristic value and that are plausible. This is especially true for the discussion on archetypes as ready-made innate templates in the mind of all individuals of the human species.

Christian Roesler writes:

> The view, which is inherent in Jung, that there must be a template somewhere stored in the person – in the genes, brain structure or biological makeup – which is then expressed in repetitive structures, is a common fallacy. It is not necessary to assume an inherent or innate pre-configuration to be able to explain the development of similar structures in the lives of humans, in the structures of society etc.
>
> (2022, p. 69)

In my opinion, if Jung thought so, he was wrong. In fact, there is no evidence of the possibility of the existence of an innate, ready-made program, a template in the BrainMind.

The issue of the template is very similar to the radical idea of a mind made of innate encapsulated modules,[6] as described by the first important contributions by Jerry Fodor (1975) that I will discuss later. For the moment, I make mine Jean Mandler's words:

> One of the serendipities of infancy research is that a lot of things that seem obvious when you study adults become not so obvious when you study babies. The premise that one must learn a concept by hypothesis formation and test is one of these (Fodor, 1975). Although hypothesis and test is one way for students at university to learn new material, it is a highly implausible method for the newborn opening her eyes for the first time and gazing at the world. Even if we assume a moderate amount of innate machinery, newborns seem unlikely to have the wherewithal to engage in hypothesis and test. So some time ago I parted company with Fodor on what concept formation involves, insofar as he assumed that hypothesis and test is the only conceivable rational model, where irrational consists of being hit over the head
>
> (Fodor, 1975)

Ultimately, even Fodor found this view of concept formation indefensible, because to hypothesize what something is requires one to have a concept of what it is, and so when one hypothesizes that something is a dog, one must already have a concept of dog.

(Mandler, 2008, p. 208)

As I said opening this book, my intent is not to point out where Jung is right or wrong; others are doing this job. What I wish to see is whether what Jung described as a personal empirical experience of something like an archetype has a plausible ground and, possibly, some sort of explanation. This is why I have made my own path through some of Jung's concepts and some of his formulations to see whether it is in any way legitimately possible to arrive at the same or at similar conclusions about the empirical experience of, for instance, something that looks like an "archetypal image".

This is why a bottom-up approach may be helpful, and all the discussion on constraints and attractors that will keep coming up in this book is aimed at the attempt to describe how something as complex as an archetypal image may emerge, even if it were not an original template deposited in the mind – i.e., in the genes.

A rigorous indication as to how to connect "lower" causal conditions to their effects is Stuart Kauffman's principle of the "adjacent possible" and his distinction between (physical, or biochemical) causes in relation to their biological functions. The function of the heart, Kauffman says, is to pump blood, but this function is just "a subset of its causal conditions". In fact, while this function is successfully selected and realized, other adjacent, unexpected possible functions come into existence, such as the fact that by pumping blood the heart accumulates water in its pericardial sack. This *adjacent* function may become a legitimate function for another possible scenario, which could be then selected under the Darwinian principle of natural selection.

For Kauffman, between causes and functions, there is an epistemological and ontological discontinuity, as possible adjacent functions *cannot be foreseen, and their number is indefinite, therefore, non-computable* (for instance: Kauffman, 2019). Therefore, such a situation of non-foreseeability describes the wholly non-deterministic, non-reducible and virtually infinitely creative nature of life,[7] and, *still, adopting a bottom-up perspective is non-reductionist.*

Kaufman's perspective of the ontological, transcendent discontinuity between physical causes and biological functions may give us a precious indication as to how to use lower causal constraints in relation to the creation of transcendent ontologies, one of which is the ontology of the imaginal world – virtually infinite, creative, irreducible and *meaningful.*

In fact, I think that psychology should distinguish between causes, functions and *reasons* and refer only to reasons when trying to describe psychologically what happens psychologically. As there is an ontological leap[8] between the level of reality of the physical world (I should say: the physical *worlds*) and the biological worlds of life (one for each species) – i.e., the level in which life (Dionysus) enters the scene – there are further levels possible from the biological realm upward, one of which is the psychological level: the level of images and feelings. Along the same lines, the perspective of the "anthropic principle" (see footnote 7) may provide a frame to see lower-level (biological) constraints as teleologically oriented towards higher-level (psychological) formations, such as the "complex", and further, how the psychological constraints may be teleologically oriented towards social and cultural formations.

We may refer to lower constraints without reducing higher formations to them. In fact, this world is as real as the stone that Dr. Johnson kicked to respond to George Berkeley's subjective idealism. In our case, we must kick a second stone, at this point, to refute Doctor Johnson's reductive empiricist point of view, for which *only* what is material and sensorially perceived is real. Nevertheless, *sometimes without realizing it*, when we adopt a bottom-up perspective, we always run the risk of reductionism, which would radically modify Jung's paradigm. What I mean is that we *may* reject Jung's main tenets or we may even find ourselves in the position of having to do so for epistemological reasons or clinical evidence, but in such cases, *we must realize that we are doing it*. This is a consequence that some Jungian literature seems not to realize and that I will discuss in this first volume.

Notes

1 This is a typical statement that may seem confused, like some of Jung's. Perhaps it is, perhaps it is not. What I am trying to say is that *the fact* of experiencing the objectivity of my personal experience may reveal to me that everyone can. Seen from one side, this is a subjective experience; seen from another, it is universal.
2 This point will be taken up again when I will refer to the principle of co-evolution.
3 Unless, as he does in *Beyond the Pleasure Principle*, when he warns us that he has not really been theorizing but *mythologizing* – something that none of his followers ever had the courage to admit. Perhaps an exception may be that of Bion, who clearly distinguishes between the two forms of knowledge I am trying to distinguish.
4 In other words, from other semiotic worlds: The incarnation of the spirit into the *physis and, at the same time*, its emergence from the *physis* under the form of a *lumen naturae*. A different perspective of this relationship from the Christian/Western one may be found in the Amazon populations as described by Viveiro de Castro (2012).
5 As they do! In fact, I think that infant research has had the most amazing development within the field of psychology and that its research has the full intrinsic elegance and beauty of true science. The restrictions I am mentioning do not mean at all that I do not value them!
6 In cognitive science, a "module" refers to a specialized cognitive mechanism or mental processing unit that is thought to be relatively independent and specific to particular types of information or tasks. Modules are often considered as domain-specific, meaning they are designed to handle a particular type of information or perform a specific cognitive function.
    The idea of cognitive modules comes from the modularity hypothesis, which suggests that the human mind is not a single general-purpose processor but rather a collection of specialized modules evolved to solve specific adaptive problems. These modules are thought to be relatively autonomous, with dedicated processes for particular functions.
    The following are a few key points about cognitive modules:

   1. Domain specificity:
      Modules are believed to be specialized for particular cognitive tasks or types of information. For example, there might be modules for face recognition, language processing, spatial navigation and so on.
   2. Information encapsulation:
      Cognitive modules are often thought to be informationally encapsulated, meaning they operate independently of other cognitive processes and are not influenced by general knowledge or reasoning outside their specific domain.

3. Automaticity:
   Modules are typically considered to operate automatically and quickly, without conscious effort. This contrasts with more general cognitive processes that may be slower and more consciously controlled.
4. Innateness:
   Some proponents of the modularity hypothesis suggest that certain cognitive modules are innate, meaning they are present in the mind from birth and are not entirely learned through experience.
5. Evolutionary perspective:
   The modularity hypothesis is often framed in an evolutionary context, suggesting that these specialized cognitive mechanisms evolved to solve specific problems that were recurrent in the ancestral environment.

7 The astounding creativity within the biological domain is beautifully explained by Stuart Kauffman: Has the universe produced all possible atoms (therefore, at a physical level)? Yes. The atoms of the periodic table are roughly 100. Considering now the biological domain, and considering that an average protein is made of 200 amino acids (some proteins have several thousands), the question is this: Has the universe produced all such possible proteins made of 200 amino acids? The answer is no. "How long would it take to do so?" asks Kaufman. This would mean the production of 20^{200}, or 10^{260}. The question now is whether there is enough time for the universe to do so. Let's consider that the fastest time is the Planck time, which is $10{-}^{43}$ s, and that the number of existing particles is roughly 10^{80}. If every particle would be busy to produce simultaneously and in parallel those possible proteins with 200 amino acids at the rate of the Planck's time, it would take 10^{39} times the age of our universe to make all those proteins just *once*. This means that the universe above the physical level of particles is non-ergodic, non-repeating, i.e., intrinsically creative. Furthermore, we should consider that this count is not yet calculating the potential adjacent *functions* of such biological proteins.

   I cannot check Kauffman's numbers, but I rely on his authority. Yet the profound question that Kauffman is asking is this: Considering that most of possible complex things will never come into existence, why do those that exist, exist?

   This issue could bring us straight to the questions involving the "miraculous" fact that all the known universal constants (like the four main physical forces – electric, weak, strong and gravitational – but also in cosmology the cosmological constant, or the photons-baryons ratio) are precisely tuned and tuned with each other in such a way and in the only possible way that has made this universe possible. This involves the (Leibnizian) issues that refer to the strong version of the so-called "anthropic principle", i.e., that such fundamental constraints (and I will discuss the issue of constraints throughout this book) are there *so that* the universe, us included, may exist (Carr & Rees, 1979).

   In physics the amazing fine tuning of these universal constants seems to indicate the possibility of a unified, simpler theory that would explain in a unified way what today appears separate, yet the issue of an intrinsic ordering process embedded in the world (meaning what exists at every level) which determines the confines within which reality emerges seems imaginable.

   Obviously, we do not know whether these physical constraints exist for a purpose, and I think that, for reasons of parsimony, there is no need to hypothesize the existence of a Master Clockmaker that set these constants and their "miraculous" reciprocal fine-tuning for a purpose, or even for the purpose of human existence. This is not what I have in mind when I talk of teleology. In fact, even the name "anthropic" is misleading. *Nevertheless,* at this point of cosmological and physical development, these fine-tuned constants are observed, and as we humans are in this universe, this means that *this* universe, granted a certain degree of freedom, *must* be the way it is and that, from its initial, fine-tuned conditions, it "evolved" in a non-totally causal, unconstrained way, which made it probable, if not very probable, what emerged through time.

I am referring to these issues to connect the existence of these foundational constraints to other constraints at the biological and then psychological level.

8 To be precise: I do not think that there are many metaphysical realities. I hypothesize (but who knows?) that reality is unitary (infinite, creative and ultimately unknowable) and that it emerges through a plurality of ontologies (very probably infinite in number) – at least one for each animal species (see, for example: Griffin, 1976) and perhaps also for plants (see: Mancuso & Viola, 2018) and surely very, very many for human individuals and cultures. As Shamdasani writes at the closing of his *Jung and the Making of Modern Psychology*: "also the psychology of the unconscious and the very idea of an unconscious belongs to an 'optional ontology' – one from very many other possible ones, like [. . .] the increasing ascendancy of 'brainhood', to use Fernando Vidal's excellent expression for the manner in which identity has come to be located in the brain, the psychological unconscious may well be on the wane" (Shamdasani, 2003, p. 296).

I agree with R. Panikkar's vision of reality, seen as a sphere which can be known just in a contingent way, i.e., by touching it (from the Latin *cum-tangere*) in the only possible way: one touch at a time. Every being may, therefore, have an empirically true experience of reality, which is at the same time relative and absolute (Panikkar, 1989).

Regarding the cognitive domain, Boyer gives a clear example of the fact that each species has its own ontology, therefore, maintaining that ontological categories are species-specific. This converges with Jung's idea of the archetype (provided that we do not forget the role of affects as cognitive anthropologists, like Boyer seems to do):

consider this simple scene. Mary with her little lamb are resting under a tree next to a lamppost. Now imagine how this is processed in the minds of different organisms. For a human being, there are four very different categories here (human, animal, plant, artifact). Each of these objects will activate a particular set of inference systems. The human observer will automatically encode Mary's face as a distinct one but probably not the sheep's, and will consider the lamppost's function but not the tree's. If a giraffe were to see the same scene, it would probably encode these differently. For a giraffe there is probably no deep difference between the sheep and Mary (assuming that the giraffe does not identify Mary as a predator) because neither is conspecific, and a lamppost is just like a useless (leafless) tree. Now if a dog were around, it would have yet another take on the scene. Because dogs are domesticated animals, they make a clear distinction between humans and other non-dog animals, so Mary and the sheep would activate different systems in the dog's brain. But the dog would not attend to the difference between a lamppost and a tree. Indeed, both afford the same possibilities in terms of territorial marking.

So having particular ontological categories is a matter of "choice" (the world lends itself to many different ways of categorizing its contents), and the choice depends on which species you belong to (Boyer, 2001, pp. 136–137).

References

Bion, W.R. (1962). *Learning from Experience*. London: Karnac Books.

Boyer, P. (2001). *Religion Explained: The Evolutionary Origins of Religious Thought*. New York: Basic Books.

Caproni, G. (2002). *Elogio della Rosa*. Torino: Einaudi.

Carr, B.J., Rees, M.J. (1979). The Anthropic Principle and the Structure of the Physical World. *Nature*, 278, 605–612.

Carta, S. (1985). *Elogio Della Penombra. Introduction to: Edinger, E., (1985). Anatomia Della Psiche*. Milano: Vivarium.

Carta, S. (2020). Nigredo. In: *La Metafora Viva dell'alchimia*. Bergamo: Moretti & Vitali.

De Castro, V. (1998, February–March/2012). *Cosmological Perspectivism in Amazonia and Elsewhere: Four Lectures Given in the Department of Social Anthropology. Vol. 1: Di HAU Masterclass Series*. University of Cambridge.

Fodor, J.A. (1975). *The Language of Thought*. New York: Crowell.

Foucault, M. (1980). *Power/Knowledge: Selected Interviews and Other Writings, 1972–1977*. New York: Vintage Books.

Griffin, D.R. (1976). *The Question of Animal Awareness. Evolutionary Continuity of Mental Experience*. New York, NY: Rockfeller University Press.

Hillman, J. (1975). *Re-Visioning Psychology*. New York: Harper & Row.

Jaspers, K. (2000). *Psicopatologia Generale (1913–1959)*. Roma: Il Pensiero Scientifico.

Jung, C.G. (1911/1956). Symbols of Transformation. In: *The Collected Works of C.G. Jung*. Vol. 5. London: Routledge.

Jung, C.G. (1924). Analytical Psychology and Education. In: *The Collected Works of C.G. Jung*. Vol. 17. London: Routledge.

Jung, C.G. (1933). The Real and the Surreal. In: *The Collected Works of C.G. Jung*. Vol. 8. London: Routledge.

Jung, C.G. (1935). Principles of Practical Psychotherapy. In: *The Collected Works of C.G. Jung*. Vol. 16. London: Routledge.

Jung, C.G. (1946). The Psychology of the Transference. In: *The Collected Works of C.G. Jung*. Vol. 16. London: Routledge.

Kauffman, S.A. (2019). *A World Beyond Physics*. Oxford: Oxford University Press.

Kohut, H. (1971). *The Analysis of the Self: A Systematic Approach to the Psychoanalytic Treatment of Narcissistic Personality Disorders*. Chicago: University of Chicago Press.

Lyotard, J.-F. (1984). *The Postmodern Condition: A Report on Knowledge*. Minneapolis: University of Minnesota Press.

Mancuso, S., Viola, A. (2018). *Brilliant Green: The Surprising History and Science of Plant Intelligence*. Washington: Island Press.

Mandler, J.M. (2008, April). On the Birth and Growth of Concepts. *Philosophical Psychology*, 21, 2, 207–230.

Neumann, E. (1973). *The Child. The Structure and Dynamics of the Nascent Personality*. London: Karnak.

Neumann, E. (2014). *The Origins and History of Consciousness*. Princeton: Princeton University Press.

Panikkar, R. (1989). *The Silence of God: The Answer of the Buddha*. Maryknoll, New York: Orbis Press.

Roesler, C. (2022). *Development of a Reconceptualization of Archetype Theory. Report to the IAAP*. https://iaap.org/wp-content/uploads/2022/04/report-archetype-theory-roesler-1.pdf.

Selhofer, F. (1982). *Marie Louise Von Franz*. Bollingen.

Shamdasani, S. (2003). *Jung and the Making of Modern Psychology: The Dream of a Science*. Cambridge University Press.

Stern, D.N. (1985). *The Interpersonal World of the Infant: A View from Psychoanalysis and Developmental Psychology*. English edn. Karnac Books (Edizione del Kindle).

Weber, M. (1946). Science as a Vocation. In: *Essays in Sociology*, pp. 129–156. H.H. Gerth, C. Wright Mills, M. Weber (Transl. and Eds.). New York: Oxford University Press.

Chapter 3

Jung's Motivational Theory
Affects, Emotions and Feelings

As I already wrote, these books are mostly devoted to a discussion on analytical psychology within the explanatory perspective – what I also called *secondary knowledge*, i.e., the knowledge that derives from reflection, analysis and theorization. This perspective aims at finding a reflection *on* the true *prima materia – the real* object: the (analytical) experience that springs from the intersubjective encounter. In the next pages, I will briefly discuss Jung's motivational theory and his vision of the structure of the human psyche. The concepts that Jung illustrates in these pages will be helpful to show how his hypotheses on the formative processes from which the psyche is organized works and may be interpreted in a way that may shed light on their coherence within the contemporary debate and, for several aspects, so as to make of analytical psychology a unique approach within today's psychological models.

The starting point of Jung's motivational theory is inherent in his conceptualization of psychic energy, which Jung calls, like Freud, *libido*. For those unfamiliar with analytical psychology, the use of the same psychoanalytic term may be a source of confusion since the conceptualization of psychic energy is for analytical psychology profoundly different from that of psychoanalysis.

I will now briefly highlight three main founding principles: libido, affectivity, teleology.

3.1 Libido

The first principle refers to "psychic energy", or *libido*.

A useful, formal, elementary Jungian definition of psychic energy refers to the definition of energy itself. For Jung, *energy is an abstract concept of motion relations*.

> The idea of energy is not that of a substance moved in space; it is a concept abstracted from relations of movement. The concept, therefore, is founded not on the substances themselves but on their relations, whereas the moving substance itself is the basis of the mechanistic view.
>
> (Jung, 1928b, §4)

DOI: 10.4324/9781003586258-3

It is important to keep in mind this definition, which refers to "motion relations", as it will come back in a different form when I will discuss the neurobiological aspect of the "psychization" process.

Jung explicitly refers his concept of energy to the physical laws of thermo-dynamics and conservation/transformation of motion and energy. This definition should be kept in mind, as it is coherent with contemporary psycho-biological models. In fact, it contains several important implications. The first of such implications regards the concept of "*motion relations*" in reference to the development of the psyche. We will see that there is a widespread consensus among contemporary cognitive scientists,[1] neuroscientists and developmental psychologists precisely on the role of motion relations. This is one of the occurrences for which Jung's theory reveals its surprising validity, confirmed by a large body of research and findings.

In his attempt to stress the autonomy of psychology and that of the psyche, libido, or psychic energy, is an abstract concept which Jung applies to psychology, although it wholly transcends psychology. In fact, it seems to me that, at the same time, the libido is a specific psychological manifestation of a wider and more general form of energy, like the one described by the laws of thermodynamics, which appears throughout different ontological realms. Therefore, I attribute to psychic energy a *transgressive* nature for which it may pass from a psychoid realm to a psychological one, hence, expressing the idea of an abstract unitary, formal, pure force that organizes both the "material" and the "psychic" ontological realms. Seen this way,[2] the transgressive nature of psychic energy – which is, obviously, still a hypothesis – confers to it an "archetypal" quality.

The transgressive nature of such a hypothesis may at first sound implausible, or "unscientific". This impression is sometimes due not to the unscientific nature of some concepts but to a superficial knowledge of scientific hypotheses and models – to a "midcult" common-sense idea of science. This seems the case of this idea. In fact, contemporary biological research is carrying out a revolutionary perspective on the origin of life and of the morphology of living organisms. For this perspective, life is made possible already by the level of the very fabric of the *matter* that makes the living organism. I wish to directly quote Salvatore Tedesco's introduction to the work of Stuart A. Newman:

> The physical properties of organic materials, Newman argues, are comparable to those of materials such as clay, lava, rubber or gelatin, which the Nobel laureate in physics Pierre-Gilles de Gennes (1992) called *soft matter*; this means that it is possible to articulate a series of "standard behaviors" of such materials – partly examined in some fundamental articles by Newman and colleagues . . . – produce microscopic structures that are of extraordinary importance in the articulation of the organic material of both of primordial organisms as well as of the early embryonic stages of present-day organisms (I intentionally leave here in silence the question of the "evolution" of evolutionary mechanisms themselves – nevertheless central to Newman's perspective, and see again Newman, 2011).

It will thus be possible to show how the morphological structural planes (*Baupläne*) of modern organisms emerged from the physical properties of primordial aggregates.

The complexity of living organisms, then, would be accompanied by the possibility of describing, and at least to some extent predict, the emergence of such morphological features (Newman, 2003). We witness, in this sense, a mighty effort of approaching the question of the very origin of life and organic form, along a line of thought for which Newman explicitly refers to Stuart Kauffman's research; life, the main course of its own becoming and its forms would then appear as "destined to manifest itself not as an extremely improbable event, but as the expected realization of a natural order" (Kauffman, 1995, p. 35).

(Pinotti & Tedesco, 2013, pp. 188–189. My transl.)

These words express the constrained properties that make possible the emergence of life starting from its material origin. Under another perspective, while I was writing these pages, a challenging article was published, suggesting:

all evolving systems – including but not limited to life – are composed of diverse components that can combine into configurational states that are then selected for or against based on function. They identify . . . the fundamental sources of selection – static persistence, dynamic persistence, and novelty generation – and propose a time-asymmetric law that states that the functional information of a system will increase over time when subjected to selection for function(s).

(Wong et al., 2023, p. 1)

The authors argue:

the laws of motion, gravity, electromagnetism, and thermodynamics – codify the general behavior of varied macroscopic natural systems across space and time. We propose that an additional, hitherto-unarticulated law is required to characterize familiar macroscopic phenomena of our complex, evolving universe.

(*ibidem*, p. 1)

In a few words, the authors are proposing nothing less than an additional universal law (the "law of increasing functional information" based on three key characteristics of natural systems: static persistence, dynamic persistence and novelty generation), which predicts that all evolving phenomena are subject to natural processes that prioritize important functions, such as stability and novelty, thereby enabling the development of systems with increasing order and complexity.

This unique approach could help explain why a host of cosmic processes evolve over time, from stars that are more chemically enriched than their predecessors, to life-forms on Earth that are more biologically intricate than their ancestors, all the way to neural networks and artificial intelligence's architectures. In other words, it explains the dynamics through which the anthropic principle unfolds.

Like the archetypes, the meaning of such a law of increasing functional information seems to transgress the usual scientific domains thorough which we apprehend reality – such as physics, chemistry, biology, psychology and perhaps economics or sociology – as all of them seem to tend to organize themselves teleologically and anthropically as emerging consequences of complex systems.

1.2   Affectivity

For the second fundamental aspect of Jung's theory, psychic energy *appears in the psychological realm as affectivity*.

Therefore, as we will see in the next pages, a) *motion relations*, b) *perceptions* and c) *affectivity* are the three basic components of psychic life.[3]

The role of affectivity as the psychological manifestation of the libido is a fundamental aspect of my discussion. Insofar for Jung, the libido expresses itself throughout an infinite process of *transformations* of itself and, in so doing, within the psychological realm, proceeds from a symbol to another symbol, from an image to another image in an attempt that seems to be an infinite, or indefinite, process of self-revelation (Jung, 1911/1956, 1952). Through these processes of symbolization and metaphorization, the libido stands as a *tertium comparationis* between different states and organizations, whose transformations are governed by what Jung called the *principle of equivalence*.

Throughout whatever exists, the vicissitudes of the libido are virtually infinite. In fact, throughout its transmigrations, libido – transforming from one motivational system to another, progressing or regressing, becoming conscious or unconscious, expressing itself through one typological attitude or another or organizing a given phase of the individual's life – is subject to continuous transformations which, when they take on accomplished forms, are always symbolic. Thus, the energetic value expressed by a given motivation can be transformed into a *different, yet equivalent,* motivation. Such equivalence is inferred by the empirical observation that a trace of the temporally antecedent or structurally more archaic investments is always retained in such a way that the new form somehow resembles the old one or that it represents an equivalent amount of energy.

In this regard, Jung writes:

Just as we know that it is possible to repress an inconvenient desire and thus force its energy to become involved in other functions, so we also know that there are those who cannot become aware of a new idea that comes into their mind and which is far away, whose energy, as a consequence, ends up in other functions and disrupts them. I have seen many cases of abnormal sexual fantasies ceasing suddenly and completely the instant a new thought or content became conscious, or a migraine suddenly disappearing when an unconscious poem became conscious. Just as sexuality can be expressed improperly in fantasies, so too a creative fantasy can be expressed improperly in sexuality.

(Jung, 1928a, p. 134)

This process is made possible by what Jung calls the *transcendent function*.

1.3   Teleology

The third important implication is the teleological nature of psychological processes.

This implication has a more theoretical nature and regards the abstract character of the concept of energy, whereby the Jungian libido does not derive from specific substances – such as organic drive sources. In fact, here, "energy" does not indicate any specific quality – like the Freudian libido with its sexual quality (Freud, 1905/1962) – but is for Jung a purely quantitative construct that derives from quantities of motion.

Libido, in short, is in itself neither sexual, nor aggressive, nor does it designate the will to power, or attachment. To a mechanistic substantialist conception, Jung contrasts a quantitative, energetic, abstract conception, whereby in 1937, he wrote that the observer's attitude to psychic events can be either causal-mechanistic or energetic-teleological.

The mechanistic conception is purely causal and conceives the event as a consequence of a cause, in the sense that immutable substances modify their mutual relations according to constant laws.

(Jung, 1937, p. 11)

For the energetic/teleological conception, the observer conceives psychic events.

starting from the consequences to go back to the cause, in the sense [precisely] that at the basis of the modifications to which phenomena are subject there is an energy, that it remains constant precisely in these modifications, and finally that it leads entropically to a state of general equilibrium.

(ivi)

Although on a logical level, the two principles of causality and teleology mentioned previously are mutually exclusive and incompatible, for analytical psychology at the experiential level, they mutually belong together in an antinomian imbrication, as the patient *feels* that his life process is produced by causes and will tend to think of them as organizing principles of his biography. However, this biography – or to be more precise, this "mytho-biography" – cannot be wholly understandable nor can it find its real meaning only as a product of its causes. In fact, for psychology to grasp a meaning and in science in general to formulate an explicatory, comprehensive and epistemologically sound theory *of any complex dynamic system* – i.e., of any system "moving" in time, such as the "mind" surely is – the scientist cannot but approach it from a teleological perspective and observe towards which ends it seem to be "attracted". The teleological principle represents what may be defined as an "attractor" that regulates top-down – i.e., from a certain level or organization – those very processes that constitute that organization bottom-up. As we will see in the later pages, this principle is valid in all developmental domains, from biology, to psychology, to culture (Vol. 2, § 10).

I cannot emphasize enough the consequences of this teleological perspective. Its repercussions appear in every clinical moment, as every content, or every relational expression, must be thought of as both produced by a past – albeit not necessarily a historical/biographical past – and directed towards a virtual, future end.

The intimate motivational structure of analytical psychology does not neatly follow the course of linear time but describes a circuit in which the causal cause, as "aition" (αἴτιον), springs from the "structural" cause – the "archè" (ἀρχή). The archè is, therefore, a conditional, "structural" cause that, entelechially, prefigures its future goal. Therefore, for Jung, motivation, as the mover of psychic life, does not really pertain to the person's historical past (to the repressed unconscious, to childhood) with its traumatic or syntonic occurrences but is embedded within the structure of the subject-in-his-world.

The teleological perspective is not limited to psychology. It is a gnoseological principle that has been gaining more and more importance in the contemporary science of complex dynamic systems, or in the attempt to understand the behavior of objects in the real world – i.e., outside the Galilean experimental setting. Therefore, the teleological perspective is applicable also to evolutionary sciences regarding the role that the (causal) past has on the present – i.e., on the role of the bio-psychological evolutionary traces selected throughout evolution for the contemporary human.

The parallel with language theory might be helpful. We might ask: When a person utters a sentence, is this sentence caused, that is, made possible, by the phonatory apparatus and its ability to articulate a certain (very limited) number of phonemes, or is it enunciated for the purpose of conveying a meaning? The point is that *the evolutionary selection of such a phonatory apparatus would also be caused by a teleological aim* (for a further discussion: Vol. 2, §10)*: the possibility to express a meaningful message, which would have increased the ancestral speaker's chances of survival.* In fact, both approaches are valid, but they illuminate completely different realities.

The causal approach entails a *reductio ad primam materiam*, i.e., to the constitutive, elementary causes of a phenomenon. Such causes are necessarily reductive and tend towards the material and organic level, all the way down to the physical realm (thus, the mind, or psyche, would be interpreted as a side effect, an epiphenomenon caused by the somatic processes of the brain).[4] The energetic-teleological one, on the other hand, considers what is the result, the embedded purpose, the meaning of the relations that take shape over time. Thus, for Jung, motivation starts from causes but is simultaneously directed towards purposes. However, since he sees life as a developmental process (Jung, 1959), a psychology without an energetic-teleological conception corresponds to a psychology without real devel-opment, in which everything is just a mere, though perhaps disguised, repetition of the past, unconscious, unresolved problems – in a word, of childhood.

To some extent, it could be said that in analytical psychology, the ultimate and essential motivation is what Jung called the "individuation process". In fact, in its most general sense, to admit a process of individuation corresponds to admitting that (psychic) life has a direction.[5] It means looking at life, as far as possible and in a variously conflicting way, as a perilous process of potential development and to interpret a psychological symptom as a *meaningful* defect and at the same time as an attempt towards the unfolding of the teleological future.

Since Jung, many authors have written on the individuation process, on stages of development, or life cycles, so that in this respect, the teleological perspective of psychic life – in coexistence with the causal dimension – has become a commonly accepted fact. As Erik Erikson wrote, each phase of life possesses its own organiza-tion and meaning, which must be fulfilled and that is specific to that phase. It seems to me that Erikson's epigenetic approach (1994) resembles Jungian transcendental-ism, in which cause and end are mutually bound.

According to a unilaterally causal attitude, neurosis, dreams, art, culture or reli-gion all represent defensive constructions to be brought back to more elementary constructs already identified through a reductive causal process of an essentially convergent nature – i.e., to childhood. To this, Jung opposes another vision, an exquisitely symbolic one, for which the teleological nature of psychic life entails a mythopoetic openness towards the production of symbols that attempt to include the unknown and express it in the best possible way, i.e., through consciousness.

A dream, therefore, will not be moved by the tendency to produce compro-mise formations that mask a latent text. Re-establishing the dream's essential inno-cence, Jung argues instead that the dream text cannot be exhausted by breaking it down into its primary causes but that the dream – as the whole psyche – becomes fully comprehensible when it is considered as the best possible *present* attempt to express through the language of the unconscious (*per speculum et in aenigmate*), something substantially unknown to the Ego.

This language is eminently symbolic: although the dream springs from a source and a psychic authority quite different from the conscious Ego with which we all identify upon awakening, it tends to reveal, not to conceal. It is not only moved by causes, ultimately organic-infantile, but it also tends towards objectives, that is, towards an infinite construction of meaning. For Jung, therefore, what moves the psyche is the intrinsic tendency to produce new states of development through an effective production of living symbols, true transformers of mental states that can make the non-thinkable thinkable. Quite surprisingly, this intrinsic creativity of the mind, as hypothesized by Jung (who included creativity among his five basic "instincts" [*sic!*]) seems to me wholly coherent with the law of "increasing func-tional information" that I quoted before.

The teleological aspect of psychic life and its entelechial structure manifest themselves already at the very beginning of many analytical processes. In fact, it is a common experience of every analyst to come to conclude an analytic journey listening to a patient who somehow tells the same story as at the beginning but in which the same events have now been recomposed into a finally thinkable, meaningful picture. The new contents that arose during the analysis are then strangely felt as if they had always been present from the beginning. At the same time, the present, together with a new, more encompassing view of the future, carries a feeling of pacification with the past, almost an apocatastasis: a holy restoration of the origins. Then everything that was necessary is finally understood as such precisely because it has finally been given a *sense* (i.e., a meaning and an orientation).

1.4 Psychization

All the characteristics that revolve around the motivations that I have discussed so far are independent of the specific forms in which these motivations manifest themselves. Jung admits a plurality of motivational systems but does not lead us back to any one motivation to which he assigns any fundamental primacy. I will now set out what Jung sees as the main characteristics that structure psychic energy.

In "Psychological Factors Determining Human Behavior", Jung writes:

> If we started with the hypothesis that the psyche is absolutely identical with the state of being alive, then we should have to accept the existence of a psychic function even in unicellular organisms. In that case, instinct would be a kind of psychic organ, and the hormone-producing activity of the glands would have a psychic causation.
>
> But if we look upon the appearance of the psyche as a relatively recent event in evolutionary history and assume that the psychic function is a phenomenon accompanying a nervous system which in some way or other has become centralized, then it would be difficult to believe that the instincts were originally psychic in nature. And since the connection of the psyche with the brain is a more probable conjecture than the psychic nature of life in general, I regard the characteristic compulsiveness of instinct as an ectopsychic factor. None the less, it is psychologically important because it leads to the formation of structures or patterns which may be regarded as determinants of human behavior. Under these circumstances the immediate determining factor is not the ectopsychic instinct but the structure resulting from the interaction of instinct and the psychic situation of the moment. The determining factor would thus be a modified instinct. The change undergone by the instinct is as significant as the difference between the color we see and the objective wavelength producing it. Instinct as an ectopsychic factor would play the role of a stimulus merely, while instinct as a psychic phenomenon would be an assimilation of this stimulus to a pre-existent psychic pattern. A name is needed for this process. I should term it psychization. Thus, what we call instinct offhand would be a datum already psychized, but of ectopsychic origin.
>
> (Jung, 1937, pp. 115–116)

Today, the word "instinct" has been substituted with "biological predisposition". It is with this in mind that I will continue to refer to the instincts along my discussion.

Jung's position is coherent with contemporary evolutionary biology, at least for what concerns the fundamental Darwinian tenet for which *Homo sapiens sapiens* is an animal like the other animals and that he also evolved through time. Obviously, the question is *how* different *Homo sapiens* is. The fiery discussion between those who, on the basis of his neotenic, de-specialized nature, think that *Homo sapiens* is radically different from other animals and those who, on the contrary, tend to minimize such (obvious) differences by looking for (and finding) surprising continuities in the zoological world – this fiery discussion, I was saying, sometimes sounds a bit like the 1860 debate between the evolutionary Henry Huxley and the creationist Archbishop Wilberforce. In fact, the sociological repudiation of any non-sociological causes of sociological occurrences (as by Durkheim, but also by some anthropologists, like Clifford Geertz) seems like an ideological position.

For Occam's razor, we must try to resort to the most parsimonious hypotheses possible. In this case, we should look for the continuities between the human species and the rest of the living universe, pretty much as a physicist does when he extends the law of motion to terrestrial and celestial bodies without resorting to special conditions *unless anomalies occur* (like in the case of relativistic and quantistic phenomena in physics, or synchronistic phenomena in psychology – Jung's category B problems).

Hence, Jung's quote seems to me very much rooted within such a parsimonious attitude, which is the attitude of science, and quite consistent with the basic tenet of contemporary evolutionary psychology (see: Stevens, 2002):

> The human brain did not fall out of the sky, an inscrutable artifact of unknown origin, and there is no longer any sensible reason for studying it in ignorance of the causal processes that constructed it. Rather, the reliably developing cognitive mechanisms that collectively constitute the architecture of the human mind acquired their particular functional organization through the process of evolution. The evolutionary history leading to modern humans consisted of a step-by-step succession of designs modified across millions of generations, with two independent forces – chance and natural selection – governing at every point whether each new modification would be incorporated into our species-typical cognitive architecture.
>
> (Cosmides & Tooby, 1994)

Jung thinks that the complexity of the psyche derives from our interaction with the environment during evolutionary time and that such an interaction produced an innumerable series of interiorizations of the specific conditions that regulate life in such a co-evolving environment. This ancestral form of interiorization would have produced the sensory-motor patterns that would be activated by the relevant affects. Such patterns are not behavioral or sensory per se, but they must be imagined as formal dynamic structuring forces.

Throughout this book, I will keep referring to these two basic interacting psychosomatic domains: the affective one and the sensory-motor one. The affective domain expresses the emotional *quality* and the core-meaning of human (and animal) experience, while the sensory-motor apparatus confers to this qualitative aspect its proper formal organization. In my opinion, the fundamental and originary expression of affects as qualitative states is through sounds. The sensory-motor patterning will associate these affective states with another sensory domain – sight and vision – and produce visual images, so important for psychological functioning. When I will briefly discuss the complex, I will go back to the relationships between sounds, visual images and patterning organization. For the moment, I need to underscore that, as this book proceeds like a helix, these topics will reappear throughout this text until its conclusions, when I will deal with language. In fact, the same originary components of affects/sounds, sensory-motor patterning organization and visual images structure conceptual thinking and language. The affective/acoustic domain refers to the evolutionary time when "grunts" and "verses" were used by the hominids to communicate qualitative feeling states and emotions – as other animals do.

While the abstraction from visual images will become the *semantic, metaphorical aspect of language*, the acoustic domain will tend to carry our emotions (Figure 3.1). One should just think of music and of the musicality of the human voice. Fetal

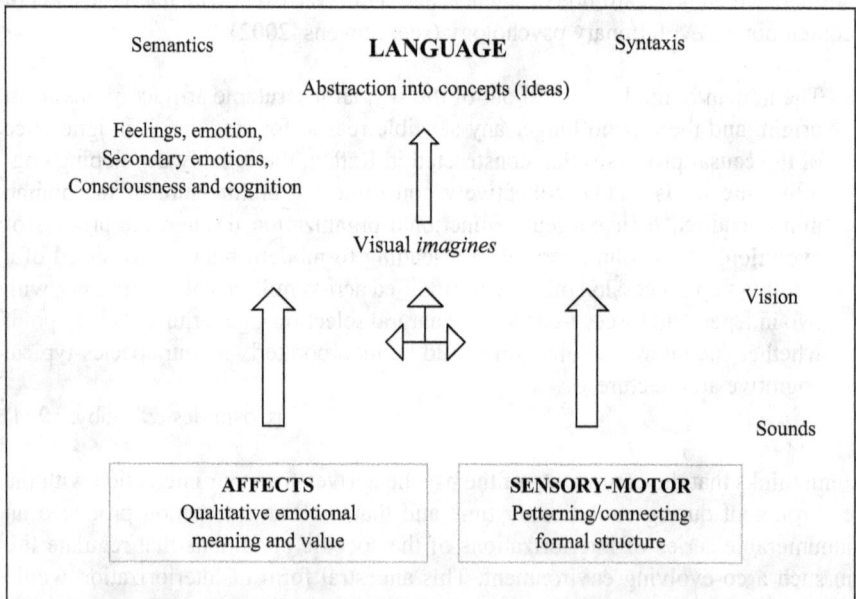

Figure 3.1 A bottom-up representation of the synergy between affects and sensory-motor schemas for the further production of thoughts and language.

hearing is a sense that matures much before vision. The infant's experience of the meaningful relationship with her mother does not begin with semantics but with the musicality of the mother's voice. It is from the acoustic realm that the feelings, coming from the acoustic pitch, volume, tone or intensity, confer the emotional essence of human communication. Rhythm, expressed by sounds and motion, has a very special place, as it confers the emotional qualitative content to diachronic time.

> the mother's face that the infant is exposed to must not be a still face, but must move, "sing" the human *phoné*, and express the mother's inner life and feelings for the infant (Tronick et al., 1978; Dixon et al., 1981; Als et al., 1980). The "still face", the petrified face of a severely depressed, *mute*, mother, makes it impossible for the infant to psychologically survive (see Green, 2001; Kohon, 1999). What I am saying here is that the importance of the face of the mother, as psychic organizer in early development, is related to something that has to do with *motion and emotion*, i.e., with what rhythms (the facial expressions and the bodily movements of the mother, synchronized or desynchronized with those of the infant, which convey what Stern [1985] calls the *vitality affects*) and sounds (the *phoné* of the mother's voice; the primal music) convey.
>
> (Carta, 2009, p. 95)

These aspects are at the center of Daniel Stern's foundation of psychological life during what he calls the *emergent developmental field*, whose basic components are (as we will see in § 10) cross-modal perception (connected to imaginal patterning, hence, to the future development of semantics and language) and Suzanne Langer's (1979) *vitality affects*, which belong to the acoustic-motor sphere.

Throughout human evolution, to the level of feeling-states expressed by sounds, the process of lateralization differentiated the use of the hands and freed the fundamental praxic nature of psychosomatic organization to be used to pattern and articulate the language of emotional singing (the human/animal verses) into a specific deep syntaxis. *This motor-related process of language patterning represents the metonymic aspect of language organization – i.e., its deep syntactic structure.* I will go back to this discussion in vol. II, § 9.3.

In the Figure 3.1, you see a bottom-up representation of the synergy between the arrow of affects and the arrow of sensory-motor schemas for the further production of images, which will be abstracted into thoughts and language. You see that language is made of syntax, derived from the sensory-motor structures, and semantics, derived from affects.

All these concepts are coherent with evolutionary theory, the only challenge being the claim that *Homo sapiens* is radically different from all other animals because he would have lost all such patterns – the archetypes in themselves – during some evolutionary mutation that led to self-reflective consciousness. I will discuss this point in many parts of this book (for example: vol. I. § 6).

Throughout the book, I will refer to the quotation from Jung's "Psychological Factors Determining Human Behavior" that I quoted at the beginning of this section as a sort of minimal compass to guide my discussion on the relationships between affects, feelings and cognition and on the hypotheses of "archetypal" – i.e., innate constraints that produce human behavior.[6]

Jung identifies five motivational systems:

- hunger
- sexuality
- activity
- reflection
- creativity.

Although these motivational systems would deserve a thorough discussion, here, I just need to emphasize the role of *creativity* and *reflection*. In my opinion, *these two motivations transgress the boundaries of psychology. They have an ontological and cosmological nature.* Within the psychological level of reality, they are the core of what Jung called *transcendent function*. In fact, the transcendent function operates by progressively transforming contents in a reflective manner from one level to a more complex and encompassing other, hence, constantly realizing a *creatio continua.* As a matter of fact, it seems to me that the creativity Jung is referring to is not only human creativity nor animal creativity but it is also the creativity inherent in nature itself (Kaufman, 2016).

As for reflection, this motivational system according to Jung has a psychoid, transgressive nature. The name that Jung gives to this motivational system and the fact that he considers it an "instinct" is due to the mind's intrinsic reflective activity, an activity that at its core is biologically predisposed and is unconscious, autonomous, compulsive and patterned.

The automatism and compulsiveness of the reflective motivation given by a deficient psychization may be found, for example, in obsessive disorders, which seem to be made of cognitive loops without an affective-motor outlet, or in severe dissociated states, as well as in the psychic defenses of rationalization and intellectualization.

Through the psychization process, the psychoid nature of life becomes progressively psychologized. This is the same line that distinguishes and connects "matter" and "spirit", or the "body" with the subjective qualitative experience of "being conscious".

We may observe this liminal territory when we face those special situations in which the deep unity of the body-mind becomes apparent, i.e., through psychosomatic disorders.

An interesting case, for its self-revealing nature, is that of a man, around 35, whose case I once supervised. He was suffering of an extreme form of ulcerative colitis for many years. When he was hospitalized he was clearly risking to die.

The hospital was specialized in microbiome research and therapy, so, the plan was to try to re-establish the intestine's proper bacterial balance.

What was very interesting was the correlation between the improvement of his microbiome, showed by medical analysis, nicely charted, and the slow but steady increase of his aggressivity. The more his colitis regressed, the angrier the patient was becoming, so much so that not only did he start to worry about what was happening to him, but also his friends and relatives (his environment), started to complain that they would have liked him better the way he was before the therapy.

My role as a supervisor had to do with the attempt to support this psychization process by finding the meaning of the aggressivity that could finally express itself, and, therefore, its teleological purpose. In this situation it becomes clear how much the transformation from a psychoid activation to a psychological expression, implies a reverberation on interpersonal and social relationships, hence reconstituting the proper environment for a human being, made of a network of embodied meaningful emotions, which ask to be consciously represented, understood and shared.

Not only do psychosomatic disorders open a breach into the psychoid realm, from which the psychization process takes place, but in my opinion, the DSM-V classification of "somatic disorders", most of all what in the 19th century was called conversion hysteria, also belongs to the psychoid realm. All these manifestations are contiguous to psychotic disorders, especially to schizophrenia.

I think that Jung's theory of psychization was derived from his experiences with the psychotic and schizophrenic patients at the Burgözli. In fact, in the schizophrenic predicament, the role of the body becomes as much enigmatic as important. The patient's unimaginable pains clearly show how much the psychization process is struggling in the attempt to transform pre-psychic "matter" into a proper psychological experience.[7] In other terms, we could say that the fundamental dissociation in schizophrenia (the schizophrenic *Spaltung*) is between the material body and the abstract mind and that it is due to the malfunctioning of the transformation (the psychization) of bodily sensations into thoughts through affects and emotions.

Therefore, *the key defect in schizophrenia would be due to the extreme dissociation of the affects arising from the pre-psychic bodily sensations (Bion's beta elements) and the abstract representations that should emerge through the psychization process.*

After all, this is the precise meaning of the word "schizo" (divided) "phrenia" (φρήν in ancient Greek is located in the chest and refers to those thoughts that involve deliberation, hence, thoughts through which affects and emotions assess the situation).

This predicament locks the patient into a form of autism (Bleuler) because his experience is derived exclusively from his own non-psychicized sensory-motor body – his nuclear self – while there is no possibility to really relate to himself and others emotionally. For the schizophrenic, the body (σῶμα) is really a prison (σῆμα).[8]

R., a 34-year-old first-rate philosopher, was slowly recovering from a persecutory psychosis with suicidal ideas of guilt and unworthiness that had paralyzed him for about two years. At the time of the session I am describing, he was already able to function well, produce very interesting philosophical writings and was completely free from delusions or hallucinations. Yet, important symptoms still persisted, such as a profound inhibition of his agency and aggressivity and a fierce interference by an ingrained, manichean moral sense against any appropriative or desiring impulse, which was immediately and mercilessly castrated with the support of phenomenal rationalizations worthy of a true specialist philosophical mind.

For the discussion that I am carrying out in this book, his most interesting symptom was also the strangest of all: a persistent and acute pain in the arm, which semi-paralyzed it, and that sometimes migrated to the shoulders, behind his neck.

During our work it became increasingly evident that one of the many meanings condensed in this somatic disorder was its relation to R.'s stubborn, highly abstract thinking, infused with "pacifist" political values which seemed to me to paralyze not just his arm, but his whole self.

A good part of our sessions was expressed in philosophical terms. Fortunately, not being unfamiliar with philosophical thinking, I was able to use philosophical metaphors to reach the dissociated and suffering parts of R., and our therapeutic alliance was very strong.

In short, I was using the language of the ego so that the Self could understand me.

R. had an ambivalent relationship with his old philosophy mentor. He was a competitive man who theorized that knowledge should not belong to anyone, hypothesizing a philosophy in which subjectivity should be completely deconstructed.

While this professor preached one thing but did the opposite – being extremely attached to the ownership of his writings – his theory justified the demolishing tendency of R.'s psychosis, which aimed at the same goal: disintegrating his legitimacy of pronouncing the pronoun "I" and the personal pronoun "my".

In this philosophy R. should literally not exist if not as a theoretical, abstract, disembodied thinking mind guided by a castrating morality. I must add that R.'s body was quite strong and that until five years old he had been a strong and impetuous child.

Thanks to the analysis of a dream, in which I defended him against this professor, it became clear that on the one hand he was dominated by an obstinate, compulsive and subject-less abstract thinking with no-body, while, on the other, by a stinging bodily pain in the arm devoid of any thought. What was missing was the possibility of anchoring himself in his own body and on the fact that pain, unlike thoughts, was felt as his own pain, his own experience. R. was caught in a fierce opposition in which his body was trying to compensate his attempt to exist as a thinker devoid of subjectivity.

Therefore, R.'s problem was to realize that he was thinking his own thoughts; that they belonged to him and that they were endowed with value, that is, with affectivity and subjectivity. That they were, in short, thoughts that belonged to him as a person, arising from the perceptions of his own sensory-motor body which produced that non-specific form of affectivity that we call anguish.

A correlation soon became evident: when R. felt pain in his arm, he could not think well. Conversely, when he was thinking and speaking well, R. did not feel pain in his arm.

What emerged was that his thinking, capable of producing refined abstractions, was subject to a form of hyper-control, along with his verbal language, which publicly expressed this functioning. Thus, the pain in his arm, private and confined in his body as it was, appeared to be an activation of the sensory-motor body that was intended to compensate for a profound dissociation.

I proposed to R. the possibility that this sensorimotor body was, as it were, hyper-critical of the hyper-abstraction of his thinking (which, in general terms was very valuable and intelligent) and that it was rebelling against it. I told him that it seemed that between the one and the other there was "something" missing – that other fundamental component of the direct expression of the body: the affects, which should subsequently be transformed into thoughts and verbal language. The link between bodily sensations and thoughts was missing.

To my comment, R. replied immediately, without hesitation:

"It is true! When I think or speak, I do not feel any emotions".

Then a thought entered my mind, and I told him:

"Perhaps, instead of talking, you should try to indulge in singing".

This strange suggestion caught him by surprise. It sounded immediately obvious and right, and it was at this point that R., the philosopher, told me that Kant's most revolutionary work was precisely the Critique of Judgement, for which thinking is essentially subordinated to affectivity, and to the imagination produced by affectivity.

"This is Kant's most revolutionary work". He told me.

"So, – I replied – perhaps you have always functioned as a subject of the Critique of Pure Reason, a pure formal subject, while instead now you may think because you feel as the subject of the Critique of Judgement".

During this session the pain in his arm disappeared, and he told me that he was feeling much better. He realized that he could finally speak much more easily – in a less controlled and more fluid way.

Now he could begin to feel free to think about the ontological legitimacy of the existence of feelings and emotions as part of a new form of reason. The possibility to generate such a thought meant that his thinking was integrating top-down with his sensory-motor body, through its psychization, into emotions.

His arm, which before was sore and semi-paralyzed, could now relax because R. could finally start to legitimize the fantasies of actively getting hold of a desired object, primarily a woman, relieved of the control of an archaic imageless castrating morality derived from his mother's "Animus".

A fundamental aspect of the psychization process is the dysregulated release (for instance, with the schizophrenic positive symptoms) or the blockage (by the

negative symptoms) of the *numinosum* feeling that I will discuss later. This relationship between release and blockage of the numinosum explains why sometimes
even very mild psychosomatic symptoms – such as a gastritis – may "encapsulate",
or "bind", in the ectopsychic body a latent schizophrenia.

It strikes me how much the importance of reflectivity, which Jung placed among
the fundamental psychological determinants of human behavior, has now been
confirmed by contemporary authors, such as Fonagy and Target (1997), who speak
precisely of a "reflective function" of the mind. On the other hand, it seems to me
that Gaddini's concept of imitation on the one hand (Gaddini, 1969) and recent
research on mirror neurons on the other always point to reflection as Jung understood it.

Reflection may be considered as a transgressive principle if we look at the tendency inherent in nature to find order through symmetry. In fact, the simplest way
to order a whole is to divide it by two symmetrical – or quasi-symmetrical – halves.
Such a reflective – symmetrical – ordering activity inherent in nature may also be at
the basis of the symmetry that exists between two *opposite* halves. If integrated with
the Jung's principle of creativity, the tension between these two symmetrical opposites may produce a third element. This is at the basis of Hegel's philosophy and
Jung's transcendent function but also of the structure of the Trinity (vol. II, § 10).

Jung's five fundamental "instincts" are articulated in six modes. The first three
are fundamentally ectopsychic (organic) but liable to psychization: sex, hereditary
predisposition and age.

> These three factors, – Jung writes – are understood primarily as physiologi-
> cal data, but they are also psychological facts, because, like instincts, they are
> subject to psychization: anatomical virility, for example, is far from proving
> the individual's psychic virility. Nor does psychological age always correspond
> with physiological age.
>
> (Jung, 1937, p. 137)

To these first three modalities, Jung adds three more eminently psychic ones: the
conscious/unconscious axis, the extroversion/introversion axis and the material/
spiritual axis.

At the phenomenological level, the intersection of the five fundamental motivations with the six modalities produces the specific unique psychological typology
of each individual, which is divided in the two symmetrical halves of introversion
and extroversion and in the four pure psychological functions: sensation, intuition,
thought and feeling.

We must consider that, differently from Jung, I am purposely using the noun
"instinct", as opposed to "drive", meaning with this term "biological predisposition". This is because I wish to underscore another distinctive feature of the Jungian thought: the constant reference to the psyche as being made not by impulses
(drives) but by formations that possess high degrees of stable intrinsic organization
produced by specific patterning impulses, which Jung calls either "drive" ("Trieb"),

or instincts ("Instinkt").[9] One may see this patterning as the "cognitive" aspect of the affective/emotional complex.

This constant reference to the *intrinsic* organization of the psyche at all levels (except in grave cases of schizophrenia or neurological disorders) makes analytical psychology a systemic-ecological psychology whose basic structural components do not have the unspecific characteristic of a drive endowed with energy without structure but instead constantly combine energy and structure, like dynamic relational fields. The integration of energy and structure describes what we may call "complex dynamic systems", i.e., complex connective formations (structures) that move (energy) through time towards a goal. For evolutionary reasons, the human mind mostly apprehends such "complexes" as visual images so that in the language of analytical psychology, they are normally called "images". Nevertheless, we should always interpret the word "image" as "*psychological pattern*", which may express itself also through any ectopsychic sensory channel (such as hearing) and movement/behavior activated by ectopsychic affects that are transformed into psychic feelings and emotions.

The distinction between visual image and pattern is important.

When Roesler writes:

in a recent German textbook on the work with symbols in Jungian psychology [. . .], Jung's assumption, that images are primary in the psyche, is repeated, without any reference to current brain research, which clearly shows that until the age of 4–6 months there are no image representations possible because of the immaturity of the neural system; the first psychic representations are embodiments, not images.

(2022, p. 91)

He seems to be conflating visual and formal patterns, such as those studied, for instance, by neurodynamics. I am not sure whether Jung thought that newborns could imagine visually, but, being interested in the productive aspect of Jung ideas, I do think that the fetuses' minds already work through dynamic patternings (what I will later also call "modules"). The specific visual content of an image is a further "filling" of such patterns, derived from the sensory apparatus. As we humans are especially visual animals, there is no surprise to notice that, after a few months, those patterns express themselves through the visual mode (but obviously not exclusively) (Bucci, 1997).

One young patient of mine remembered recurrent terrifying nightmares around the age of 4 years in which he saw geometric figures, expanding like fractals in empty space. He could connect this image/non-image with something mathematical/geometrical and told me that his panic was too great to be really expressed. My hypothesis is that these nightmares were representing a defect in the formation of this patient's mind, something like the risk to be directly exposed to something emotionally crucial and at the same time unthinkable.

Such a possibility may remind us of the beta elements in Bion's theory. Yet it is not quite like it, as these nightmarish experiences didn't just seem to describe raw primary affects, but especially the formative process that should have organized them into adequate images.

Thomas Singer directed my attention to this passage of Peter Bowles' *The Sheltering Sky*, which contains a vivid description of something similar:

> He opened his eyes. The room was malignant. It was empty. "Now, at last, I must fight against this room". But later he had a moment of vertiginous clarity. He was at the edge of a realm where each thought, each image, had an arbitrary existence, where the connection between each thing and the next had been cut. . . . It seemed to him that here was an untried variety of thinking, in which there was no necessity for a relationship with life. "The thought in itself", he said-a gratuitous fact, like a painting of pure design. They were coming again, they began to flash by. He tried to hold one, believed he had it. "But a thought of what? What is it?" Even then it was pushed out of the way by the others crowding behind it. While he succumbed, struggling, he opened his eyes for help. "The room! The room! Still here!" . . . He looked at the line made by the joining of the wall and the floor, endeavored to fix it in his mind, that he might have something to hang on to when his eyes should shut. There was a terrible disparity between the speed at which he was moving and the quiet immobility of that line, but he insisted. So as not to go. To stay behind. To overflow, take root in what would stay here. A centipede can, cut into pieces. Each part can walk by itself. Still more, each leg flexes, lying alone on the floor. There was a screaming sound in each ear, and the difference between the two pitches was so narrow that the vibration was like running his fingernail along the edge of a new dime. In front of his eyes clusters of round spots were being born; they were the little spots that result when a photographic cut in a newspaper is enlarged many times. Lighter agglomerations, darker masses, small regions of uninhabited space here and there. Each spot slowly took on a third dimension. He tried to recoil from the expanding globules of matter. Did he cry out? Could he move? The thin distance between the two high screams became narrower, they were almost one; now the difference was the edge of a razor blade, poised against the tips of each finger. The fingers were to be sliced longitudinally.
>
> (Bowles, 1949, p. 87)

The relationship between the energetic factor (the affect) and its structured representation (the image, which forms the core of the cognitive part of the psyche) is an important aspect of my discussion. In fact, the most elementary brick of Jung's psyche, its most fundamental structural element, is the *complex* "constellation" of representations organized by, or "revolving" around, an affect. Before we deal with the complex, we must first devote some thoughts to its constellating element: the affect and its relationship with the "instincts", which, on their part, describe *constrained motivational impulses*.

Notes

1 Jung's psychology has deep and pervasive cognitive implications. His theory of the unconscious is far from being based on a purely drive-discharge principle, as is the Freudian Id. As we will see, I will devote a large part of this book to the relationship between cognition, affects, feelings and emotions and about the primacy of affects on cognition and within Jung's psychology. As I hope will eventually be made clear, the role of what we call "cognition" also with regard to pre-conscious and unconscious processes will be apparent in the section on images and image-formation, for which images give form to affects and produce new forms of meaning.

2 Which may not be precisely Jung's way. I might be extending his concept of libido.

3 The deepest, most immediate psychological *perception* of the "structural" workings of *affectivity* and *motion* is music. In my opinion, music is a special form of apprehension of reality, utterly different from the visually derived conceptual knowledge. Together with conceptual knowledge, it shares an underlying mathematical structure, but differently from it, it is made essentially by the experience of the emotional flow of time. The very core of the psyche is affective; therefore, music has an uncanny primacy over semantics. In Jungian terms, the representations of the complex gravitate around a core affect; this means that images are representations of something musical.

   Before the Logos – the meanings conveyed first by the mother's language (which refers to present objects) and later by the father's language(which indicated absent objects) – while the mother's body dances, her voice is made of pure emotional music.

4 Hence, everything would be caused by biochemical causes, or, still more reductively, by organic-chemical ones, or, even more so, by *inorganic*-chemical ones, all the way down to quantum "physical" phenomena and mathematics. Yet, at this level, apparently, the most fundamental one, reductionism implodes, as in the quantistic and relativistic physics it becomes impossible to radically distinguish matter from energy. Equally, in the mathematical realm, the transgressive nature of natural numbers (which, as Jung pointed out, are at the same time invented and discovered and which he considered, for their astonishing epistemological role, the only archetype which had become fully conscious [Von Franz, 1986; Pauli, 2012]) paradoxically puts them at the bottom and not at the top of this reductionist explicatory chain, even if they have the most spiritual/psychological, immaterial nature imaginable also at this "low" level, the level of the *physis*. As Friederich Cramer, the director of the Max Plank Institute at Gottingen, wrote: Matter is full of thoughts (Cramer, 1988).

   As far as I know, Jung is the only psychologist who was aware of these issues and took them very seriously, refusing to confine his views to common-sense theories, as all the other psychological theories seem to do. With common-sense psychological theories, I refer to theories which avoid taking into consideration certain paradigmatic anomalies, such as the statute of mathematics, or of synchronistic occurrences.

   Let me make an example: knowing that reality (whatever it is) cannot be explained by Euclidian geometry (apparently, a geometry based on a common-sense sensory experience of space) nor by "Newtonian" physics, which, once again, corresponds to the way the senses perceive and organize motion (if I kick a ball, it will move; if two balls bounce against each other, they will bounce back), such a midcult scientist simply avoids and denies the existence of quantum physics and, therefore, all the transgressive quantistic phenomena that cannot be conceptualized in a Newtonian frame of reference. Since they do not fit his paradigm, they must not exist.

   In a few words, we face the typical situation described by Kuhn (1996) in which two paradigms collide in front of the complexity of empirical experience. What is sometimes slightly annoying is that when someone, like Jung himself, points to such wider and epistemologically more honest and diversified paradigm, he is treated with contempt, like a "mystic", a madman or as a naïve nonscientist.

When Louis De Broglie first proposed his law that describes the equivalence between mass and electromagnetic energy, which somehow complemented Einstein's famous equation, he was derided ("La comédie francaise!", his colleagues mocked him). Soon afterward, he won the Nobel prize for his groundbreaking discovery. Jung's position in science is quite similar.

5 For the possibility that this hypothesis might be supported by a general – if not universal – validity, see my discussion on "the roles of function and selection in evolving systems".

6 I refer just to behavior to simplify my exposition. In truth, as I hope will be clear from this discussion, "behavior" is the *last* station of a long path that originates with 1) the libido "instinctual" impulse, which represent a *primary intention*. This then 2) becomes the psychological entity that we call "affect", which 3) constellates an image/representation, which 4) finds a proper adapted way of expression within the specific *milieu* and eventually 5) produces a behavior. Without these components, we should consider the "behavior" of a ballistic missile like that of living organisms, especially humans.

7 I see something like an analogy between such a release of the numinosum that takes place when the material body is psychicized with Einstein's $E = mc^2$.

8 "Some say that the body is séma (sign, tomb) of the soul, as if it were buried in it during the present life; and again, on account of the fact that by it the soul *semaínei* (signifies) what *semaíne* (signifies), that is also why it was rightly called *séma*. However, it seems to me far more probable that the followers of Orpheus placed this name; as if to say that the soul pays the penalty of the faults it must pay, and therefore has around it, so that *sózetai* (is preserved, saved, guarded), this bodily belt in the image of a prison; and so the body, as the name itself signifies, is *séma* (custody) of the soul until it has paid in full what it must pay. Nor is there any need to change anything, not even a word" (Plato, *Cratylus*, 400c.).

9 I will come back to this in the next pages and in vol. I, § 6.

References

Als, H.E., Tronick, E., Brazelton, T.B. (1980). Affective Reciprocity and the Development of Autonomy: The Study of a Blind Infant. *Journal of the American Academy of Child Psychiatry*, 19, 22–40.

Bowles, P. (1949). *The Sheltering Sky*. London: John Lehmann.

Bucci, W. (1997). *Psychoanalysis and Cognitive Science: A Multiple Code Theory*. New York. The Guiford Press.

Carta, S. (2009). Music in Dreams and the Emergence of the Self. *Journal of Analytical Psychology*, 54, 85–102.

Cosmides, L., Tooby, J. (1994). Origins of Domain Specificity: The Evolution of Functional Organization. In: *Mapping the Mind: Domain Specificity in Cognition and Culture*. L. Hirschfeld, S. Gelman (Eds.). New York: Cambridge University Press.

Cramer, F. (1988). *Chaos Un Ordnung*. Stuttgart: Deutsche-Verlags-Anstalt Gmbh.

de Gennes, P.-G. (1992). Soft Matter (Nobel Lecture). *Angewandte Chemie International Edition in English*, 31, 7, 842–845.

Dixon, S.M., Yogman, W., Tronick, E., Adamson, L., Brazelton, T.B. (1981). Early Social Interaction of Infants with Parents and Strangers. *Journal of the American Academy of Child Psychiatry*, 20, 32.

Erikson, E.H. (1994). *Identity and the Life Cycle*. New York: W.W. Norton.

Fonagy, P., Target, M. (1997). Attachment and Reflective Function: Their Role in Self-Organization. *Developmental Psychopathology*, 9, 4, 679–700.

Freud, S. (1905/1962). *Three Essays on Sexual Theory*. New York: Basic Books.

Gaddini, E. (1969). Sulla Imitazione. In: *Scritti 1953–1985*. Milano: Cortina.

Green, A. (2001). The Dead Mother. In: *Life Narcissism/Death Narcissism*. A.Weller (Transl.). London, New York: Free Associations Books.

Jung, C.G. (1911/1956). Symbols of Transformation. In: *The Collected Works of C.G. Jung*. Vol. 5. London: Routledge.

Jung, C.G. (1928a). A Review of the Complex Theory. In: *The Collected Works of C.G. Jung*. Vol. 8. London: Routledge.

Jung, C.G. (1928b). On Psychic Energy. In: *The Collected Works of C.G. Jung*. Vol. 8. London: Routledge.

Jung, C.G. (1937). *Psychological Factors Determining Human Behavior*. In: *The Collected Works of C.G. Jung*. Vol. 8. London: Routledge.

Jung, C.G. (1952). Answer to Job. In: *The Collected Works of C.G. Jung*. Vol. 11. London: Routledge.

Jung, C.G. (1959/1969). Aion. Researches on the Phenomenology of the Self. In: *The Collected Works of C.G. Jung*. Vol. 9i. London: Routledge.

Kauffman, S. (1995). A *casa nell'universo. Le leggi del caos e della complessità*. Roma: Editori Riuniti (2001).

Kaufman, S.A. (2016). *Humanity in a Creative Universe*. Oxford: Oxford University Press.

Kohon, A. (1999). *The Dead Mother: The Work of Andre Green*. London: Routledge.

Kuhn, T. (1996). *The Structure of Scientific Revolutions*. Chicago: Univiversity of Chicago Press.

Langer, S. (1979). *Philosophy in a New Key. A Study in the Symbolism of Reason, Rite, and Art*. 3rd edn. London: Harvard University Press.

Newman, S.A. (2003). Nature, Progress and Stephen Jay Gould's Biopolitics. *Rethinking Marxism*, 15, 4, 479–496.

Newman, S.A. (2011). The Evolution of Evolutionary Mechanisms: A New Perspective. In: *Biological Evolution: Facts and Theories*, pp. 169–191. G. Auletta, Leclerc, Martinez, (Eds.). Romea: Pontificio Istituto Biblico.

Pauli, W. (2012). *The Interpretation of Nature and the Psyche*. Bronx, New York: Ishi Press.

Pinotti, A., Tedesco, S. (2013). *Estetica e Scienze della Vita*. Milano: Raffaello Cortina.

Roesler, C. (2022). *Development of a Reconceptualization of Archetype Theory. Report to the IAAP*. https://iaap.org/wp-content/uploads/2022/04/Report-Archetype-Theory-Roesler-1.pdf.

Stern, D.N. (1985). *The Interpersonal World of the Infant: A View from Psychoanalysis and Developmental Psychology*. London: Karnak Books (Kindle Edition).

Stevens, A. (2002). *Archetype Revisited: An Updated Natural History of the Self*. London: Routledge.

Tronick, E., Als, H., Adamson, L., Wise, S., Brazelton, T.B. (1978). The Infant's Response to Entrapment Between Contradictory Messages in Face-to-Face Interaction. *Journal of the American Academy of Child Psychiatry*, 17, 1–13.

Von Franz, M.L. (1986). *Number and Time: Reflections Leading Toward a Unification of Depth Psychology and Physics*. Evanston: Northwestern University Press.

Wong, M.L., Clelland, E.C., Arend, D. Jr., Hazen, R.M. (2023, October 16). On the Roles of Function and Selection in Evolving Systems. *Proceedings of the National Academy of Sciences. Biophysics and Computational Biology*, 120, 43.

Chapter 4

Jung and Affects

Affects are the a) open, b) flexible, c) undetermined, d) unconscious (more precisely conscious in an a-noetic form) and e) teleological vectors of the mind (see also, Alcaro et al., 2017).

As I already wrote, affects represent the emergence of the libido in the psychological realm and, as described in Jung's *Symbols of Transformation*, constellate, constrain and attract (teleologically orient) symbolic imagery. In this chapter, I will briefly review Jung's theory of affectivity.

I have already given a brief definition of affects in vol. I, § 1.3. The role of affects in the development of Jung's analytical psychology is clear already from the time of his association experiments, when Jung, at the beginning of his career, was busy investigating precisely the role of affects within memory and cognition. The constellating, integrating function of affects and emotions – together with their role for dissociation – was clear since the time of the association experiments at the Burghölzli.

As Paul Kugler (1982) writes, one original evidence of the affects' function (in our case, in the infant) is that they constellate words by their phonetic sound, their music, not yet by their meaning. In my opinion, this is another evidence of the connection between affects and perception, in this case, *musical* perception (i.e., the musical qualities of the mother's speech), which anticipates and makes possible the subsequent cognitive – semantic – development.

The first feature of affects that I must highlight is that affects are *dispositional and non-situational*. They do not just *react* to stimulations but try to re-establish a subjective *homeostasis* through an interpretation of the *value* – in a way, the *meaning* – of the "disturbing" stimuli.

The actual term "homeostasis" was coined several decades ago by Walter Cannon, an American physiologist, after Claude Bernard. Yet the term may be misleading, as it could be interpreted as a process meant to maintain or re-establish a *static* balance, instead of an intrinsic dynamic regulation of constant metabolic (and eventually psychological) fluctuations towards a development that we may call individuation. This transformative homeostasis pursues progressive transformed states, i.e., "metastable" states (Simondon, 2020).[1]

DOI: 10.4324/9781003586258-4

In Jungian terms, we could say that homeostasis is an *archetypal* process, as it is at the foundation of all biological life, from the first cell upward. It describes a biological and psychological principle, which must be integrated with the fact that its activity takes place within a constantly developing life process.

According to Damasio, the homeostatic process first strives for a stable, steady state. The organism tries to maintain its own integrity and optimize the chances for its survival and reproduction. Nevertheless, physiological metabolism does not proceed by thermostat-like set parameters. The organism's metabolic fluctuations have a dimensional character, which expresses shades and grades of regulation.

> This process corresponds to what is commonly experienced as feelings, and the two issues are closely related: the former, the relative goodness or badness of a given life state, is the basis for the latter, that is, feelings. On this note, it is remarkable to consider that in general we do not need to visit our physician to discover if the fundamentals of our health are fine. Nor do we need a blood test for that purpose. Feelings provide us with a moment-to-moment perspective on the state of our health.
>
> (Damasio, 2021, pp. 45–46)

Under this perspective, visceral impulses, affects, feelings and homeostasis are bound to each other, and feelings may be interpreted as the subjective experiences:

> of the state of life – that is, of homeostasis – in all creatures endowed with a mind and a conscious point of view. We can think of feelings as mental deputies of homeostasis.
>
> (Damasio, 2021, p. 25)

If feelings are connected to the conscious "emotional perception" of the state of the organism, affects may be thought of as nonconscious yet still subjective regulators of the flow of biological life from its first cellular organization. According to Damasio, feelings emerged when organisms developed a nervous system, a relatively recent development that began to occur about 600 million years ago.

One of the most crucial functions of nervous systems was to gradually enable a process that Damasio calls "multidimensional mapping" of both the world within and around them, therefore, beginning to develop what we may call "mind".

At this point, we do not yet have feelings, but their sensory precursors – for the human evolutionary phylum: smell, taste, touch, hearing and vision (for other organisms, they may be very different, like electricity for the soil-dwelling amoeba *Dictyostelium*, or sharks). As will become clear when I will discuss co-evolution, the making of minds – and of feelings in particular – is grounded on entangled interactions of the nervous system its organism and environment.

It should be clear that feelings as such are a recent development and that they inherited the homeostatic regulation that was before attributed to the senses.

Hence, amoeba do not have feelings, but they do function on an intelligent way because they are very well aware of both their internal and external milieu.

Therefore, homeostasis indicates a virtual state that, within its individuation process, the organism looks for *within* constantly dynamic, variable inner and outer (environmental) conditions. Homeostasis, therefore, does not, as Damasio seems to suggest, relate to a purely internal regulation, but it:

a) Involves the entangled situation of the organism and its co-evolutionary niche.
b) It operates to *anticipate possible events*. This principle should not seem strange. When a stimulus is integrated in a pre-existent structure, this structure will respond not just according to the nature of the stimulus but also, most of all, according to its own regulatory principles. The eye will process certain selected stimuli in a certain way, as the skin will do in its own way. Within such a systemic perspective, the concept of "anticipation" does not really include chronological time; it does not really necessarily imply an idea of a chronological future. In fact, in a synchronic structure, *like an image*, the future is represented as a more or less probable specific position in the structure. An easy analogy is this: imagine a person driving a car. From his perspective, the bridge that he will cross after five minutes is a probable event in the future. But if you are looking at this scene from an airplane, you may be able to see its synchronic configuration. From such a structural perspective, you will see both the car and the bridge. You will see *at the same time* the present of the driver and his future experience. This is an easy example of how a systemic organization (in our case, starting from the phylogenetic appearance of a core, minimal self) responds to stimuli – by including them in its own structure. Such a self-organizing structure has three characteristics that I should underscore:

i. Since it includes the future in the present, it resembles what Aristotle described as "entelechy".
ii. It is teleological.
iii. When it will develop from a a-noetic to a noetic stage, it will re-present itself as an *image*. These images are, for example, the images dreams are made of.

c) At any rate, homeostasis does not define something that looks for mere stability but metastability at a hierarchically "higher" level of organization and of reality – the (human) psychological level. It defines what Jung called *transcendent function*, in which the infinite process of pursuing a homeostatic equilibrium is attained by the progressive formation of metaphors and symbols which, for a limited amount of time (it is in the instant that the epiphany of life becomes meaningful), express a new creative composition of a previous unbalance. This disturbance is, obviously, the Mephistophelian element without which nothing could ever become.

Seeing it this way, the concept of homeostasis (related to the ever-flowing nature of the libido and, hence, comprising both its morphostatic and morphogenetic aspects) is fully coherent with Jung's concept of *compensation* or self-regulation. Further-more, including the organism's co-evolutionary niche, it defines the archetype as something-in-between, i.e., as the entangling property that realizes the intrinsic process of co-belonging of the self and its own world. Therefore, my proposal is to equate the archetype to an active pattern of information. One possible, very relevant, evidence of this may be the way the intercellular bio-electric field organ-izes the cellular functioning and the formation of the next level of embryogenetic multicellular structures, such as tissues, from its lower bottom-up constraints, the DNA.

According to Levin:

all cells, not just neurons, form electrical networks that control gene expression and cell behavior. Here, I review recent progress in the exciting emerging field of molecular developmental bioelectricity and provide a perspective on how bio-electric circuits integrate cell-tissue-, organ-, and whole-body-level information to enable morphogenesis and pattern homeostasis. Crucially, it is becoming clear that bioelectricity is not simply one more layer of mechanism that is required alongside biochemical cues and stress forces to implement morphogenesis: it enables unique, powerful information-processing capacity that facilitates scaling of cells into complex morphogenetic collectives. These aspects shed light on the evolution of multicellular forms and provide an attractive roadmap for target-ing endogenous bioelectric circuits as trac table and powerful control knobs for applications in regenerative medicine and synthetic morphology.

(Levin, 2021, p. 1973)

This electric field, which teleologically modulates genes expression, is present in the brain as an inter-synaptic organizer, as it is also present, with a less intense charge, between *all* the cells of all organisms. It should be noticed that we are now dealing with *immaterial* actions on matter, which organize it to adapt and preserve functions and/or morphology. In few words, among many other possible considerations, we are in the same domain where synchronistic phenomena may be physically admissible.

This process is one of the possible descriptions of the individuation process as the ongoing emergence of a singularity – the individual, what (also) Spinoza might have called *natura naturata* – from the collective unconscious, which may be described as a field of potentialities or, as Gilbert Simondon writes (2020), a system of "internal singular resonance" – what (also) Spinoza, referring to his God/Nature, called *natura naturans* (for a discussion on the relations between Jung's and Simondon's concept of individuation, see also: Saban, 2019).[2]

Through this infinite, emerging process of the the living organism, individual images arise and, together with them, the differentiation between inner experiences (affective sensations) and outer experiences (salient perceptions).

What is first is this system of internal singular resonance, this system of the allagmatic relation [the Greek word *allagma* can mean change or vicissitude, but it can also mean that which can be given or taken in exchange. Note by S.C.] between two orders of magnitude. In terms of this relation, there is the intrinsic and the extrinsic, but the individual is truly this relation and not the intrinsic, which is merely one of the concomitant terms: the intrinsic, the interiority of the individual, would not exist without the ongoing relational operation that the ongoing individuation is.

(Simondon, 2020, p. 50)

The individual would then be grasped as a relative reality, a certain phase of being which supposes a pre-individual reality prior to it and which, even after individuation, does not fully exist all by itself, for individuation does not exhaust in a single stroke the potentials of pre individual reality, and, moreover, what individuation manifests is not merely the individual but the individual-milieu – coupling.

(Simondon, 2020, p. 3.)

For Jung, by this process, all polarized opposites are kept in a dynamic harmonious balance through time.[3]

Although the process of becoming conscious *of the underlying unity of the opposites* is the central psychological process, these opposites may *not* be limited to just consciousness and unconsciousness but may include also the relational polarity between Subject and Object (which is the door to human social processes), or the moral polarity of Good and Bad.

For Jung's vision, one pole cannot exist without the other, and this has an important implication for his concept of individuation as a process that cannot but encompass our relational, social and cultural world.

Conscious and unconscious do not make a whole when one of them is suppressed and injured by the other. If they must contend, let it at least be a fair fight with equal rights on both sides. Both are aspects of life. Consciousness should defend its reason and protect itself and the chaotic life of the unconscious should be given the chance of having its way too- as much of it as we can stand. . . . This, roughly, is what I mean by the individuation process. As the name shows it is a process or course of development arising out of the conflict between the two fundamental psychic facts. . . . How the harmonizing of conscious and unconscious data is to be undertaken cannot be indicated in the form of a recipe. . . . Out of this union emerge new situations and new conscious attitudes. I have therefore called the union of opposites "the transcendent function". This rounding out of the personality into a whole may well be the goal of any psychotherapy that claims to be more than a mere cure of symptoms.

(Jung, 1939, §522–524)

If we agree on the fundamental role of affects (which is today gaining more and more momentum in neurobiological research) – i.e., their role for keeping a dynamic homeostasis – it derives that the individuation process itself is regulated by affectivity. Affects are biologically and functionally endogenous and express the inside of the organism. They do not just react to outer stimuli.[4]

From such a scenario, an important notion regarding the functioning of extroversion and introversion derives. In fact, for a harmonious psychological life, the introverted way of functioning describes a process for which the introverted type gains access to the object via his inner world, while the extroverted type gains access to his own subjective states via the object. The regulating "parameter" is set on the homeostatic endogenous feeling of integration, which is emotionally *felt* as a meaning that is finally, yet just temporarily, attained. This happens while the opposites of subject/object are always infinitely integrated within the introversion/extroversion circuit.

In a few words: the frequent, reductive way of interpreting life as *either* based on agency *or* on sociality is superseded in Jung's complex vision which integrates these two opposites.

Jung wrote:

Every psychic process has a value quality attached to it, namely its affective charge.[5] This indicates the degree to which the subject is affected by the process or how much it means to him (in so far as the process reaches consciousness at all). It is through the "affect" that the subject becomes involved and so comes to feel the whole weight of reality.

(Jung, 1959, §61. Modified translation by the author)

As affects, emotions and feelings are the core organizers of the psyche into complexes, they also form the foundation of all psychic activity and, therefore, the core basis of the overall organization of the Self:

Psychologists usually considered the "Self" as an object of experience appearing when the individual perceives its existence within the conscious field. In accordance with such a view, the self-representing capacity of the human mind has been related to corticolimbic learning processes taking place within individual development. On the other hand, Carl Gustav Jung considered the Self as the core of our personality, in its conscious and unconscious aspects, as well as in its actual and potential forms. According to Jung, the Self originates from an inborn dynamic structure integrating the essential drives of our "brain – mind", and leading both to instinctual behavioral actions and to archetypal psychological experiences. Interestingly, recent neuroethological studies indicate that our subjective identity rests on ancient neuropsychic processes that humans share with other animals as part of their inborn constitutional repertoire. Indeed, brain activity within subcortical midline structures (SCMSs) is intrinsically related to the emergence of prototypical affective states, that not only influence our behavior in a flexible way, but alter our conscious field, giving rise to specific feelings or moods, which constitute the first form of self-orientation in the world. Moreover, such affective dynamics play a central role in the organization of individual personality and in the evolution of all other (more sophisticated) psychological functions. Therefore, on the base of the convergence between contemporary cutting-edge scientific research and some psychological intuitions of Jung, we intend here to explore the first neuro-evolutionary layer of human mind, that we call the affective core of the Self.

(Alcaro et al., 2017)

As it often happens, Jung had a quite precise intuition of the neurobiological basis of the Self:

I have long thought that, if there is any analogy between psychic and physiological processes, the organizing system of the brain must lie subcortically on the brain stem. This conjecture arose out of considering the psychology of an archetype [the Self] of central importance and universal distribution represented in mandala symbols. . . . The reason that leads me to conjecture a localization of a physiological basis for this archetype in the brain stem was the psychological fact that besides being specifically characterized by the ordering and orienting role, its uniting properties are predominantly affective. I would conjecture that such a subcortical system might somehow reflect characteristic of the archetypal form of the unconscious.

(Jung, 1958, §582)

Once again, Jung's assumptions seem to converge with those of contemporary science and thus prove useful for analytical psychology.

Notes

1 Metastability refers to the state of a system that is stable under small perturbations but may transition to a more stable state under larger disturbances. A metastable state is one where the system is not in its lowest energy configuration, but it is trapped in a local energy minimum that it can remain in for a significant amount of time. However, given enough time or with the right stimulus, the system can transition to a more stable state, usually releasing energy in the process.
    Metastability is a concept that applies across multiple disciplines and is fundamental to understanding complex systems that do not always behave in intuitively simple ways. Jung's example of the archetype as the inherent process out of which a crystalline configuration emerges from a hyper-saturated solution (Jung, 1948, footnote, § 590) is a classical example of a metastable state.
2 From Latin: "naturing nature" and "natured nature".
3 To be precise, psychological time (Minkowski, 2013) is the *result* of this process.
4 In passing, this is a view opposite to the cognitive theorists of emotions and feelings, such as Joseph LeDoux. In fact, the role of the amygdala, on which he carried out magnificent research, is *not* that of generating affects but of connecting primary affects, which, as we will see, have a much more ancient and neuroanatomically lower locus of origin, with outer stimuli. LeDoux thinks that affects respond to the environment. I subscribe to the opposite view (together with Jaak Panksepp, or Antonio Damasio) – Jung's view of a dispositional psyche.
5 It seems to me that such a charge refers to the activation of the "libido", a principle that might remind us of the Greek *zoé* – pure life. Although it is not confined in the realm

of life, when it becomes psychologized, it is somehow translated from the *zoé* into the Greek *bios* – the life of the specific organism. It is essentially different from what will be described as the feeling of the feeling function, although the latter is also a transformation of the libido.

References

Alcaro, A., Carta, S., Panksepp, J. (2017). The Affective Core of the Self: A Neuro-Archetypical Perspective on the Foundations of Human (and Animal) Subjectivity. *Frontiers in Psychology*, 8, Article 1424.

Damasio, A. (2021). *The Strange Order of Things: Life, Feeling and the Making of Cultures.* New York: Pantheon Book.

Jung, C.G. (1939). Conscious, Unconscious and Individuation. In: *The Collected Works of C.G. Jung.* Vol. 9i. London: Routledge.

Jung, C.G. (1958). The Psychogenesis of Mental Disease. In: *The Collected Works of C.G. Jung.* Vol. 3. London: Routledge.

Jung, C.G. (1959/1969). Aion: Researches on the Phenomenology of the Self. In: *The Collected Works of C.G. Jung.* Vol. 9i. London: Routledge.

Kugler, P. (1982). *The Alchemie of Discourse. An Archetypal Approach to Language.* New York: Associated Press, Inc.

Levin, M. (2021, April 15). Perspective Bioelectric Signaling: Reprogrammable Circuits Underlying Embryogenesis, Regeneration, and Cancer. *Cell*, 184.

Minkowski, E. (2013). *Le Temps Vécu: Études Phénoménologiques et Psychopathologiques.* Paris. PUF.

Saban, M. (2019). *Simondon and Jung: Re-thinking Individuation.* In: *Holism. Possibilities and Problems.* C. McMillan, R. Main, D. Henderson (Eds.). London, New York: Routledge.

Simondon, G. (2020). *Individuation in Light of Notions of Form and Information.* Minneapolis, London: The University of Minnesota Press.

Chapter 5

Affects and Neurobiology

In his lifelong research on affective neuroscience, Jaak Panksepp individuated seven primary affects, which are a product of phylogenetic evolution in man as in mammals and, in a more limited manner, in reptiles and birds (Panksepp, 1998a, 1998b, 2005, 2010; Panksepp & Biven, 2012). They are the following:

- the SEEKING System
- the RAGE System
- the FEAR System
- the LUST System
- the CARE System
- the PANIC/Separation Distress System
- the PLAY System.

Such affects may also be called primary emotions or motivational systems.

Montag and Davis (2018) offer a very precise summary of the basic features of the primary emotional systems outlined by Panksepp (1998a,b, 2010):

First, activation of each neural network underlying a primary emotion should elicit a characteristic emotional – behavioral action pattern (such as emotional PLAY behavior usually accompanied by 50-kHz chirps in rats; Panksepp & Burgdorf, 2003). Second, activity in such an emotional neural network is initially only triggered by unconditional stimuli (such as the inborn tendency to react with FEAR to the sight of a snake). Third, these basic emotional neural networks are connected to secondary and tertiary brain levels to facilitate learning such that after learning these primary neural networks also can be activated by previously neutral stimuli. Thus, a child learns to FEAR a hot stove. Fourth, with maturity mammals exhibit stronger cortical control over the ancient neural networks underlying primary emotions. For example, most children gradually learn to better regulate their affective emotions (see also a study on the development of frontal lobe functions by Romine & Reynolds, 2005). Fifth, the emotional arousal elicited by these primary emotional systems influences sensory gating processes of the brain. This means that activation of emotional

DOI: 10.4324/9781003586258-5

neural networks can modify what information ultimately will be processed from the brain (and also in what manner). In addition, the salience of a stimulus is modified by the activity of neural networks underlying primary emotional systems: When strong FEAR is triggered a person could have difficulty shifting attention to other stimuli aside from the FEAR eliciting source. For example, when a person has a weapon pointed at him/her, they will not remember anything except the weapon ("weapon effect"; e.g., Tooley et al., 1987). Sixth, the arousal generated by activation of the neural network underlying a primary emotion persists beyond the initially triggering event. Please note our usage of the term affect generally conforms with Panksepp's rule of thumb: "Affects are the subjectively experienced aspects of emotions, commonly called feelings" (Panksepp, 2010, p. 534).

(pp. 1–2)

Subcortical function mediates affective states arising out of three categories, summarized as follows.

- Homeostatic/visceral affects: signal an awareness of internal bodily states that are perceived as moods or feelings. These visceral affects are connected to some of the homeostatic mechanisms of the body, such as the endocrine and autonomic system.
- Instinctual/emotional affects: refer to a disposition to act through avoiding or approaching certain situations. They motivate the organism towards or away from the stimulus.
- Sensorial affects: give perceptual experiences an affective value, for example, the pleasure of warmth or the unpleasantness of a startling sound. These subcortical structures include specific nuclei within the brainstem which direct motor activity.

Contemporary discussion tends to consider these primary affects as the only *real* affects, while emotions, as we have already seen, fused as they are with complex and abstract cognitive abilities, may be considered like autonomous differentiated elements of the psyche.

Affects, feelings and emotions interpret and attribute hedonic value to our subjective experience. This means that they provide the phylogenetically and ontogenetically first, basic form of meaning to subjective experience by evaluating, in a teleological manner (meaning in a way aimed at a specific purpose: metastable homeostasis), the situation in which the subject (may that be any organism) is involved. The nature of primary affects is phylogenetically rooted in the physiology, and therefore, the physiological response of an organism. This proto-mental visceral activity, which teleologically guides the organism within its co-evolutionary niche, paves the way for more evolved a-noetic affects, i.e., without feelings. Damasio posits the phylogenetic proto-mental (Jung's ectopsychic) precursors of what we call feelings and emotions in organisms as elementary and archaic as bacteria. From the origin of organic life, already very simple organisms were able to detect and respond to the stimuli from their outer environment to satisfy their inner homeostatic needs. Such interactions may be quite sophisticated and show a certain form of social intelligence. This proves once again that the co-evolutionary milieu, in which organisms and environmental conditions are entangled, must be, from the origin of life, the real protagonists. Damasio reports several experiments in which bacteria, growing in a fertile terrain, are able to afford and maintain a relatively independent life. The interesting thing is that, when the conditions change, and for instance, there is a menace, or when resources are scarce, they tend to clamp together and organize their behavious in a coordinated, "intelligent" manner.

> Bacteria can sense the numbers in the groups they form and in an unthinking way assess group strength, and they can, depending on the strength of the group, engage or not in a battle for the defense of their territory. They can physically align themselves to form a palisade, and they can secrete molecules that constitute a thin veil, a film that protects their ensemble and probably plays a role in the bacteria's resistance against the action of antibiotics. By the way, this is what goes on routinely in our throats when we get a cold and develop pharyngitis or laryngitis. When bacteria gain a lot of throat territory, we become hoarse and lose our voices. "Quorum sensing" is the process that assists bacteria in these adventures. The achievement is so spectacular that it makes one think of capabilities such as feeling, consciousness, and reasoned deliberation, except that bacteria do not have any such capabilities; they have rather the powerful antecedents to those capabilities. I will argue that they lack the mental expression of those antecedents. Bacteria do not engage in phenomenology.
>
> (Damasio, 2021, pp. 19–20)

In Chapter 10, I will look at human ontogenesis – the developmental period in which children develop the capacity to think prospectively and cooperate with others. We will see that this extremely refined competence, which obviously implies a maturation and development of cognitive abilities, apparently unique in the human species, is motivated by secondary emotional feelings. For Damasio or Panksepp, such feelings are rooted in affects. Yet, deeper down the evolutionary ladder and the anatomy and embryology of the human brain and body (as we must include the autonomic system), the ectopsychic precursors of feelings lie in *sensations* – the level activated by archaic, proto-mental mechanisms, such as those described by Damasio for bacteria based on the metabolism of proteins and other biochemical signals.

It is indeed quite striking that, already at the lowest evolutionary scale, the behavior of bacteria seems inspired by a principle of cooperation such as the one that Tomasello describes as the highest development of any species on Earth – our species (Chapter 10).

For any group to be successful, survive and reproduce, its members need to cooperate. Such cooperative behavior happens also when bacteria detect "defectors" in their group. They isolate them, as Damasio writes, *even if they are genomically related*, therefore, sacrificing a quota of their replicating advantages. According to Damasio (2021), bacteria distinguish those kin bacteria that cooperate from those that, in case of need – such as the polluting of their environment – do not cooperate with kin bacteria and will snub them. In fact, cheaters, after all, exploit energy resources and defense that the rest of the group is providing at great cost. As Damasio points out, the variety of possible bacterial "conduct" is quite remarkable (see also: Jousset et al., 2013; Kram & Finkel, 2014, 2015).

From a neuroanatomical perspective, it seems clear that affective forms of subjective experience are phylogenetically older in the BrainMind's evolution than the cognitive (and therefore, strictly "emotional") forms because they are elaborated in more medial and caudal (tailward), and hence, more ancient, regions of the brain, whereas cognitive processes involve cortical areas. An outstanding example of this is the location of the periaqueductal gray (also known as the "central gray") at the very core of the midbrain. In contrast, the discrete sensory-perceptual functions are also situated more laterally, which suggests a more recent origin.

Affects and feelings determine subjectivity and the very possibility to coalesce an organized Self. Therefore, they carry the fundamental integrative function that connects and organizes scattered elements into complexes and, in a Jungian perspective, scattered complexes into a Self. In fact, many neuroscientific authors (Damasio, 2010) maintain that early in brain evolution, a primordial neural map of the body emerged from the autonomic changes that accompany actions (Northoff & Panksepp, 2008; Panksepp, 1998b).

> Nervous systems are rich in mapmaking devices. The eye and the ear map varied features of the visual world and of the world of sound, respectively, in the retina, in the inner ear, and continue doing so in the central nervous system structures that follow them in a sequence that digs deep within the cerebral cortex. When we touch an object with our fingers, the nerve terminals distributed in the skin map the varied features of an object: the overall geometry, the texture, the temperature, and so forth. Taste and smell are two other channels for the mapping of the outside world. Advanced nervous systems such as ours fabricate, and abundantly so, images of the outside world and images of the world inside the respective organisms. In turn, the images of the world inside are of two very distinct sorts, relative to their source and contents: the old and the not so old internal worlds.
>
> (Damasio, 2021, pp. 78–79)

Therefore, the senses are extensions of the brain and act as perceptual/transformational devices that form the Ego. If we (reductively) interpret the centralized transformational system we call brain as the Self, Damasio's view is coherent with Jung's idea of the Ego as an emergence of the Self. This means that the Ego cannot be defined just as a merely perceptual structure (as in Freud) – i.e., formed by the contact with outer stimuli – but it must be conceptualized as the extension of the transformational activity of the Self (as in Jung), which integrates its "subjective" aspect with the environment *that it imagines*. We may call this body map a primitive "proto-self" (or "minimal self").

I will often refer to integration, Self and subjectivity. To proceed, it is important to distinguish what I would call the following:

1) "*structural* integration, or structural coherence" of the self (such as that which produces a personal body-schema) from the following:
2) "*meaning*-based integrity" of the self (which, for instance, will generate our body-image).[1]

While the first involves the sensory-motor apparatus, the second has to do with affects, feelings and subjective meanings. Differently from the structural integration of the Self,[2] its meaning-based integration is deeply connected to that foundational mark of subjectivity that is *agency*. This type of brain organization integrates primal experiences – such as raw sensory, homeostatic, emotional affects.

In other contributions, together with Jaak Panksepp and Antonio Alcaro, I have dealt with this emotional core-self, the primal site of unconscious consciousness and subjectivity. In fact, at this neuroanatomical functional level, this is still an a-noetic (non-representational conscious/non-reflective) affective background, a mood, a sort of atmospheric affectivity still devoid of object representations (Neumann's description of the child's primary "World of Plants" [1973] and the Winnicottian concept of the mother-environment, with the important theoretical and clinical contributions by C. Bollas on the *unthought known* [2018], are very useful).

Each Emotional Brain System – each primary affect – modifies the organism's subjective state and leads to characteristic feelings, which have impacts on learning and influence future behaviors (Panksepp & Biven, 2012). From this primary level, a-noetic forms of consciousness and subjectivity, similar to dreams and related to image-representations, will phylogenetically emerge. And finally, an auto-noetic, self-reflective form of consciousness will emerge, in which the products of the cognitive and meta-cognitive developments become crucial. In § 9, I will discuss Annette Karmiloff-Smith's work, in which she offers a very sound model that may shed light on the cognitive development towards declarative, explicit abstractions and universalization – i.e., towards self-reflective, meta-noetic consciousness.

Let's go back to Panksepp's affective, "a-noetic" consciousness – the first evolutionary step in animal subjectivity. A-noetic consciousness has been defined as an "unthinking form of experience, which may be affectively intense without being known" (Solms & Panksepp, 2012, p. 149), and as follows:

> The rudimentary state of autonomic awareness, . . . with a fundamental form of first-person "self-experience" which relies on affective experiential states and raw sensory and perceptual mental existences.
>
> (Vandekerckhove & Panksepp, 2009, p. 1)

According to Damasio, the internal milieu, the vestigial biological milieu, of the ancient organism is fundamentally concerned with homeostasis. When such an organism develops into a multicellular entity, an increasing morphological and functional complexity emerges, and the metabolism of such interior milieu will involve all its biochemical components, all its viscera, such as hearts, lungs, guts and skin, and the smooth muscles that help build the walls of blood vessels and the capsules of all organs.

> Smooth muscles are also, in and of themselves, visceral elements. The images of the internal world are the ones that we describe with such terms as "well-being", "fatigue", or "malaise"; "pain" and "pleasure"; "palpitations", "heartburn", or "colics". They are of a special kind because we do not "picture" the old interior world in quite the same way that we picture objects out in the world. There is less detail, to be sure, although we can mentally illustrate the changing geometries of viscera in the idiom of visceral sensations – the tightening of the pharynx and larynx that occurs when we are in fear, or the tightening of asthma attack; likewise, for the effects of certain molecules on varied components of the body, which often include motor reactions such as tremors. These images of the old internal world are none other than core components of feelings.
>
> Side by side with the old internal world there is also a newer internal world. This one is dominated by our bony skeleton and by the muscles attached to it, the skeletal muscles. The skeletal muscles are also known as "striated" or "voluntary"; this helps distinguish them from the "smooth" or "autonomic" variety, which is purely visceral and not under our willful control. We use skeletal muscles to move about, manipulate objects, speak, write, dance, play music, and operate machinery.
>
> (Damasio, 2021, p. 81)

Damasio continues pointing out that the imaging of the old internal world in action reflects the state of the organism's inner milieu good (i.e., assessing goodness and badness). It seems clear that in this situation, the organism is affected by such images since its survival depends on what they represent and on the information that they carry about the organism's condition and needs. Therefore, at this point in evolution, it is what will be called the "hedonic" value of feelings that will guide the organism's homeostasis: avoid what is (physiologically) bad and pursue what is good.

> This is a world of valence. The new internal world is a world dominated by the body frame, by the location and state of the sensory portals within that frame, and by the voluntary musculature. The sensory portals sit and wait within the body frame and contribute importantly to the information generated by the maps of the outside world. They clearly indicate to the organism's mind the locations, within the organism, of the sources of images currently being generated. This is

necessary for the construction of an overall organism image, which, as we shall see, is a critical step in the generation of subjectivity.

(Damasio, 2021, pp. 82–83)

For Panksepp, affects are conscious and a-noetic, therefore, unknowable if not through their noetic and meta-noetic transformations into representations (images) and self-reflectivity. Their a-noetic status means that they are perceived by a subject which is not the Ego. In a way, they resemble Bion's "untamed thoughts" in search of a meta-noetic thinker.

I would like to highlight the striking similarity, if not equivalence, between Panksepp's notion of a-noetic affects and the nature of Jung's collective unconscious as made by numinous *luminositates* – Gerhard Dorn's *caelum stellatum* – which are unconsciously conscious. A criticism to which Jung has been subjected is that he thought the collective unconscious precedes consciousness. In my opinion, this criticism may not be justified. Perhaps because Jung's language does not always differentiate what today's affective neuroscience calls a-noetic consciousness from autonoetic consciousness (which would refer to Jung's Ego-consciousness) Roesler critically writes:

Jung assumes that the primary state of the psyche is unconscious, which means that during development consciousness develops from a general primary state of unconsciousness.

(Roesler, 2022, p. 30)

Differently from Roesler's opinion, I think that for Jung, the collective unconscious is actually and paradoxically conscious, as it is dispositionally made for specific, constrained purposes (in a way, "it knows what to do because it builds its own world"). This interpretation is first of all justified on a historical ground. In his discussion of Théodore Flournoy's fundamental influence on Jung, Shamdasani writes:

Flournoy posited the existence of non-pathological and creative components of the subconscious, and stressed that automatic activity, such as the production of the trance states of mediums, need not be inferior to voluntary activity.

(Shamdasani, 1998, p. 118)

Both Frederic Myers and Théodore Flournoy inspired the view of a form of "knowledgeable" "subconscious" activity, which Jung already explored in his dissertation on the psychology of occult phenomena. Furthermore, this hypothesis of a conscious unconscious is made so clear that the Chapter 6 of an important text by Jung – *On the Nature of the Psyche* – is entitled The *Unconscious as a Multiple Consciousness:*

The hypothesis of multiple luminosities rests partly, as we have seen, on the quasi-conscious state of unconscious contents and partly on the incidence of certain images which must be regarded as symbolical. These are to be found in the dreams and visual fantasies of modern individuals, and can also be traced in historical records. As the reader may be aware, one of the most important sources for symbolical ideas in the past is alchemy. From this I take, first and foremost, the idea of the scintillae – sparks – which appear as visual illusions in the "arcane substance". Thus the Aurora consurgens, Part II, says: "Scito quod terra foetida cito recipit scintillulas albas" (Know that the foul earth quickly receives white sparks). These sparks Khunrath explains as "radii atque scintillae" of the "anima catholica", the world-soul, which is identical with the spirit of God. From this interpretation it is clear that certain of the alchemists had already divined the psychic nature of these luminosities. They were seeds of light broadcast in the chaos, which Khunrath calls "mundi futuri seminarium" (the seed plot of a world to come). One such spark is the human mind.

(Jung, 1947/1954, §6)

This view, for which there is an unconscious form of consciousness, is a product of the development of Jung's ideas and somehow a breach from his previous works. Therefore, considering this historical perspective, this is the text on which our discussions should focus, provided that we are not interested in a historical analysis of Jung's work but on its scientific cogency.

As I think that for a constructive contribution to analytical psychology, it is worth following Gadamer's suggestion to interpret the text with a faithful hermeneutic approach, I choose to think that *this* is Jung's position and that this means that he was quite ahead of his own times, provided that we interpret in a "faithful" manner those passages in which consciousness means a-noetic consciousness and when the same word refers to auto-noetic Ego-consciousness. I think that we may interpret Jung's archetypes, these luminous sparks, as specific forms of affective a-noetic apprehension and interpretation of an environment.[3] The next form of consciousness that follows such unconscious is, first of all, the noetic, pictorial form of consciousness that we experience every night when we dream (together with many species, *at least* starting from birds and reptiles), then the Ego auto-noetic (reflective) consciousness develops, and I think that on this point, all commentators agree.

What is the contemporary scientific evidence for this possibility? The experimental evidence from brain lesions that cause what is known as "blindsight" are conclusive proofs not only of the fact that animals are conscious in an a-noetic or noetic form but also that they may display very intelligent behaviors (for instance, arithmetic reasoning [Rugani et al., 2009; Wagener et al., 2018; Nieder, 2019]) without necessarily being self-reflectively *aware* of being conscious of the nature of the problem or of the stimulus (the issue of self-reflective consciousness in primates, dolphins or other animals is still quite open). The seminal observations by Humphrey (1974) showed a rhesus monkey, Helen, from whom the striate cortex was almost totally removed. Studied intensively over a period of eight years, she regained an effective, though limited, degree of visually guided behavior. The evidence suggests that while Helen suffered a permanent loss of "focal vision", she retained (initially unexpressed) the capacity for "ambient vision". This situation means that Helen was having perceptions without sensations.

A second point that regards the way we interpret Jung concerning this fundamental issue – consciousness – is that for him, consciousness (differently from Freud) is not qualitatively unitary. This is clear not only from his psychological typology but also from the related concept of individuation as a progressive[4] transformation of Ego-consciousness into Self-consciousness. Even if the latter remains a quality of the self-reflective Ego, once the unconscious conscious complexes that were latent in the unconscious are integrated in the Ego (when they become self-reflective), the Ego is not anymore how it used to be when it was dissociated from the unconscious (from the point of view of the quality of consciousness, from the inferior function). Therefore, even when Jung writes that the Ego is the center of consciousness, he is not referring to a unitary and discrete entity but to a qualitative *process* of which the Ego is the integrative center that the Self constellated. This is a process that proceeds from unconscious conscious (a-noetic) states to self-reflective ones.[5]

In its experiential, imagistic symbolic nature, the psyche represents this process in this way:

By the study of psychopathology and dream psychology, to be uncommonly probable, we are for better or worse driven to the conclusion that although the state of unconscious contents is not identical with that of conscious ones, it is somehow very "like" it. In these circumstances there is nothing for it but to suppose something midway between the conscious and unconscious state, namely an approximative consciousness. As we have immediate experience only of a reflected state, which is ipso facto conscious and known because it consists essentially in relating ideas or other contents to an ego-complex that represents our empirical personality, it follows that any other kind of consciousness – either without an ego or without contents – is virtually unthinkable. But there is no need to frame the question so absolutely. On a somewhat more primitive human level, ego-consciousness loses much of its meaning, and consciousness is accordingly modified in a characteristic way. Above all, it ceases to be reflected. And when we observe the psychic processes in the higher vertebrates and particularly in domestic animals, we find phenomena resembling consciousness which nevertheless do not allow us to conjecture the existence of an ego. As we know from direct experience, the light of consciousness has many degrees of brightness, and the ego-complex many gradations of emphasis. On the animal and primitive level there is a mere "luminosity", differing hardly at all from the glancing fragments of a dissociated ego. Here, as on the infantile level, consciousness is not a unity, being as yet un-centered by a firmly-knit ego-complex, and just flickering into life here and there wherever outer or inner events, instincts, and affects happen to call it awake. At this stage it is still like a chain of islands or an archipelago.

(Jung, 1947/1954, §6)

Affective neuroscience gives the following description of this process. Affective awareness emerges at the point of interaction between the global flux of sentience

From a neuro-biological perspective,
this phase-transition is bound to the development of cortical and Cortical-Midline-Structures (CSM),
which have a fundamental role for social communication, affective regulation and imaginative processes.

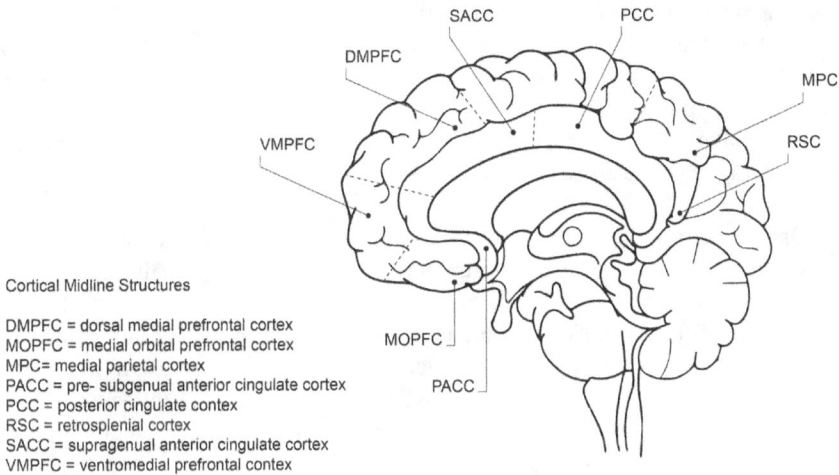

Cortical Midline Structures

DMPFC = dorsal medial prefrontal cortex
MOPFC = medial orbital prefrontal cortex
MPC= medial parietal cortex
PACC = pre- subgenual anterior cingulate cortex
PCC = posterior cingulate contex
RSC = retrosplenial cortex
SACC = supragenual anterior cingulate cortex
VMPFC = ventromedial prefrontal contex

Figure 5.1 A representation of the brain's cortical midline structures.

and certain instinctive emotional dispositions that govern essential survival and reproductive functions and that depend on the activity of neural systems located in the subcortical midline of the brain (Figure 5.1) (Alcaro et al., 2017). These instinctive emotional states orchestrate multiple coordinated responses (Panksepp, 1998b; Denton, 2006; Panksepp & Biven, 2012). For example, the RAGE System activates a cascade of neurophysiological changes (through the sympathetic nervous system) and a sequence of movements and postures that serve the animal in attack and defense.

Each Emotional Brain System also modifies the organism's subjective state and leads to characteristic feelings, which have impacts on learning and influence future behaviors (Panksepp & Biven, 2012).

To understand the biological significance of affective feelings, we should consider the possibility that the expression of the instinctive drives, as consciously experienced feelings, is a highly complex dynamic process that emerges when the activity of the subcortical midline brain circuits generates coordinated "mass action" or better, *temporal and spatial patterns of amplitude modulation in the brain and of the organism's tissues*. For Freeman, these dynamic patterns are not *representations* of stimuli but rather express the *meaning* that the nervous system of animals attributes to the lived experience (Freeman, 1999).[6]

The application of non-linear dynamic theories to neuroscience (Freeman, 1999; Brown, 2002; Llinas, 2002; Krieger, 2014), shifting the level of neurological analysis from the material-neurochemical to less readily discerned electrical fields, theoretically opens the way to shift from the physics of massive bodies to that of quantum physics and, therefore, to the level of reality in which synchronistic phenomena may be rationally admissible (Jung, 1952; Bohm, 1980/1981; Penrose, 1989; Brown, 2002) (in Alcaro et al., 2017, p. 7).

Contemporary neurodynamic theories, especially their quantistic nature, not only support the co-evolutionary paradigm but seem to converge also towards those "category B" problems that I decided not to discuss in this book – synchronicity and its relationship with the psychoid archetypes and the nature of mathematics. Silvano Tagliagambe argues:

> One of the most important discoveries of the last decades in the field of neuro-science is that the brain is an extremely dynamic organ, not only functionally but also morphologically. The "plasticity of the brain" has now superseded the concept of the brain as a "static" organ, i.e. without the possibility of further modifications, especially morphological ones, once the transition from adolescence to adulthood is over. This close relationship between the environment and the brain raises a question that is not always given due consideration. If, as a result of it, the brain modifies and differs to the point that it is now taken for granted that no two brains are identical, even in the case of monozygotic twins, because their relations with the environment obviously cannot be completely identical, this differentiation, as a result of the close link we are talking about, cannot but also involve the environment, which can no longer be understood and treated in a generic and undifferentiated way, as something that must be considered the same for everyone. It follows that the environment, which con-stitutes the reference context of our experience, must be understood as a sort of "double" of our brain and that in order to establish a correct relationship with it, copying is not enough, pure and simple "mirroring" is not enough, a creative operation is needed, a mirroring that does not concern what simply happens, the actual, but the possible, what could happen and can be seen in an alternative way. This is a fundamental crucial node that is now the focus of the conver-gent attention of neuroscience, epigenetics, quantum field theory, epistemology and aesthetics in a genuinely interdisciplinary perspective of concrete dialogue between different specialist approaches.
>
> (Tagliagambe, 2023, p. 33)

For the neurodynamic paradigm, and in line with the co-evolutionary perspective, the brain is inherently dissipative, that is, open to the world. It constructs a representation of its environment that takes the form of its own image as a double of the Self. We might say that the brain and its object-world complete each other through a dynamic process towards a transcendent unity. This proposition may perfectly fit what Jung thought individuation was (the asymptotic union of opposites) and what neurody-namic theories, based on quantum mechanics, maintain.

One crucial element that is implied in this view is the "border" between such a dissipative brain and its world. Such a border should not be conceptualized as a barrier since it works as a dividing/connecting filter between different states. In my opinion, this border is what Jung called the transcendent function itself – a function of transformation between different ontological states.

In his description of these theories, Tagliagambe writes:

[this border] produces dynamic images with an inescapable tactile component, in that they touch and touch us, that is, they operate a transfer from outside to inside, from the external landscape to the inner universe. *This is the specific function of emotions, which are a haptic means of transport, the primary and principal means of projecting out components of our body and receiving from the surrounding reality atmospheres that stir the consciousness and mobilize it.*
(Tagliagambe, 2023, p. 46. My italics and transl.)

The relationship between the brain and its world is a constant dynamic process of doubling, in which *the action observed and the action performed* are structurally equivalent (Vitiello, 2019). Thus, everything that seems static and "substantial" (the dissipative brain, its objects as "things") actually emerge as equivalences from this reciprocal, co-evolutionary mirroring dynamic process.

I would say that they are both *functions of the transformative process that neurobiologists conceptualize as a "border", or that Jung called transcendent function.*

[Vitiello's model, in this sense] refers to the results of observations obtained in the laboratory by the American biologist and neuroscientist Walter Jackson Freeman, which highlight the brain's property of accumulating experience and constructing knowledge, that is, of learning how to have "maximum grip" on the world. To this end, copying, i.e., pure mirroring, is not enough; it requires creative operation, involving the possible and not just what simply happens.

The aspect of this model that interests us here is that it, as already pointed out, considers the brain to be an inherently open system, permanently coupled with the external environment and leading to the image of a mind that lives through a continuous series of phase transitions and thus new emergent levels. Such coupling is considered "inescapable", since the mathematics at our disposal dictates that in the study of an open system, defined as system A, one must proceed to the "closure" of the system itself by considering the environment in which it is immersed. Only in this way, in fact, is the balance of the fluxes of matter, energy, etc., between system A and the environment, which we can now denote as system B, consistently obtained. For the purpose of the energy balance (and the balance of flows of any other exchangeable quantity between A and B), system B behaves like a copy of system A, in the sense that it behaves exactly like system A as far as flows are concerned, provided that their direction is reversed: in fact, what is inward for A, is outward for B, and in the opposite direction. Clearly, reversing the direction of the flows is equivalent to exchanging A for B, and vice versa. Since technically the direction of the flow is reversed by changing the sign of the time-variabile, we can say that B behaves as the copy of A for which the direction of time has been reversed (the *time-reversed* copy of A). In summary, B is the system that describes the environment as far as the balance of A's energy flow is concerned, and it is also the mirror image of A in the time mirror (the time mirror image of A). In other words, B is the *double* of A.

Indeed, brain activity requires some kind of quantum-like coherence (as assumed also by Balduzzi & Tononi, 2009) to bind a variety of information patterns into a sequence of unitary and integrated episodes in individual experience.

(Tagliagambe, 2023, p. 46. My transl. Italics in the text.)

I decided to quote this long passage from Tagliagambe's discussion because it summarizes with the minimum amount of words a cutting-edge field of research that converges in a quite surprising way with Jung's paradigm, including its most far-fetched hypothesis: synchronicity. I also highlighted the passage using italics, as it seems to converge with one of the core-issues of this book – the role of affects and emotions.

The quantum-nature of neurodynamic activity discussed by Freeman and Vitiello is at the origin of the relationship between the collective unconscious, subjectivity and consciousness (Freeman & Vitiello, 2005, 2006, 2008, 2016).

I already quoted this passage by Jung:

the immediate determining factor is not the ectoplastic instinct but the structure resulting from the interaction of instinct and the psychic situation of the moment [Sentience]. The determining factor would thus be a modified instinct. The change undergone by the instinct is as significant as the difference between the color we see and the objective wavelength producing it. Instinct as an ectopsychic factor would play the role of a stimulus merely, while instinct, as a psychic phenomenon would be an assimilation of this stimulus to a pre-existing pattern. A name is needed for this process. I should term it psychization.

(Jung, 1937, §234)[7]

From these quotes, it seems that subjective life emerges at the boundary between necessity and freedom, when the fixed, modular, domain-specific character of instincts is internalized and expresses itself in neural dynamic patterns that drive global brain activity within specific "basins" of neural activation (Freeman, 1999; Brown, 2002; Llinas, 2002; Krieger, 2014). Indeed, when instinctual drives are characterized by stereotypical and fixed action patterns, also called unconditioned reflexes (Pavlov, 1927; Lorenz, 1965; Tinbergen, 1951), they are totally procedural and unconscious, i.e., not declarative and conscious.

Another element that, on a neurobiological level, supports an integration between modularity and learning, and on which there is a general agreement, regards the modular organization of the brain (not of the mind). This refers to the principle of *degeneracy*, which, together with the fundamental action of the brain's neurodynamic activity, not only polarizes large populations of neurons but also seems to be able to activate *different* neurons to perform the *same* task. Specifically, degeneracy suggests that different neural structures or patterns can produce the same or similar outputs, providing a level of redundancy or flexibility in the functioning of the nervous system. Key points related to degeneracy in our context include the following:

1) Redundancy of function: Degeneracy allows for redundancy in neural systems, meaning that multiple neural pathways or structures can contribute to the same cognitive or behavioral outcome. This redundancy can enhance the robustness and adaptability of neural networks.
2) Flexibility and adaptability: Degeneracy contributes to the brain's ability to adapt to changes, damage or variations in inputs. If one neural pathway is compromised, another may take over to maintain functionality. This can be particularly important for recovery after brain injuries or in the face of environmental changes.
3) Structural variability: The concept of degeneracy recognizes that different individuals may have variations in the structure and organization of their neural networks while still achieving similar cognitive functions. This variability in neural structure among individuals is considered a normal and adaptive aspect of the nervous system.
4) Complex systems: Degeneracy is often associated with complex systems, where multiple elements can interact in various ways to achieve similar outcomes. The brain is a highly complex system with numerous interconnected neurons, and degeneracy is thought to be a fundamental feature of such complexity.

Therefore, degeneracy (Edelman & Tononi, 2000; Edelman & Gally, 2001; Whitacre, 2010; Chen & Crilly, 2014) is a crucial feature of the formal organization of the neural networks that constitute the modules to which I referred before vs. their structural nature. It follows the general principle of "organizational invariance" (Chalmers, 2020), for which two systems with the same precise functional organization will have qualitatively identical experiences.

From an evolutionary perspective, degeneracy can be advantageous because it provides a system with the ability to evolve and adapt to different environmental conditions without requiring significant structural changes. This implies the existence of some sort of informational functional mapping, a modularizing activity that uses neurons and neural networks. If inactive, this mapping, like an archetype in itself, seems non-existent, while it will emerge in particular conditions and, therefore, will become visible through the neurodynamic activation of the neuronal populations that it selects.

Degeneracy may *correlate (not explain)* with the possibility that a specific affectively modulated schematic image might have a *different structure* but the *same function*. On another plane, therefore, images would not need to be the same to have the same meaning, but they could express themselves as variations of an abstract organizing schema. Here, something like a mathematical organizing principle seems at work.

Once again, also for consciousness, what organizes/polarizes such hypercomplex networks is the massively pervasive activity of the value-conferring areas of the brain (Edelman & Tononi, 2000). Nevertheless, I must underscore that this fundamental principle of organizational invariance – with its somehow mathematical, platonic nature – is not enough to understand subjective conscious experience. In fact, we cannot underestimate physical and chemical properties of the cellular material that make the living organism, i.e., its "carnal" qualities (Newman, 1995).

Although individual learning may influence the expression of such automated responses (Skinner, 1935), they still maintain an unconscious nature as long as they are under the exclusive control of deterministic neural activity patterns. The same is true also for interiorized mental actions that operate beyond consciousness, leading Kihlstrom to postulate the existence of a cognitive unconscious (Kihlstrom, 1987) – a notion already subscribed to by Flournoy and then by Jung.[8]

I already wrote that primary affects are the following: open, flexible, undetermined, unconscious (more precisely, conscious in an a-noetic form) and teleological vectors of the mind. In fact, primary emotional dispositions (affects), representing affective categories, contain different manifestations and, therefore, differ from rigid behavioral automatisms since the ensemble of actions coordinated by each emotional system is organized and modulated in a flexible way. Because of this, emotions have been conceptualized as "flexible action patterns" (Llinas, 2002), which not only respond to trigger stimuli but also anticipate future events, prepare the organism to cope with uncertain situations and, with sufficient neocortex, orient its attitude towards specific intentional routes (Alcaro et al., 2017).

Notes

1 I am aware that this distinction is related to William James' distinction between *structural* and *functional* psychology. What is real is the functional one; the structural is one of its possible interpretations.

2 When I use the small "s" and write "self", I refer to the self-representation of the personality by the Ego. When I write "Self", I refer to Jung's concept of the Self.

3 As we will see, for evolutionary psychology, this environment would be the archaic environment of the Pleistocene. In my opinion, the organisms' environment at its most fundamental level refers to the entanglement of the brain's function and its *quantistic* environment. At any rate, the central issue is that such unconsciously conscious archaic collective complexes that are "within" the mind cannot not be co-evolutionarily coupled with an environment.

4 To try to avoid being too suspiciously interpreted, I wish to make clear that such a process is infinite, as "when something becomes conscious, something becomes unconscious". In a few words: Jung's attention is not on the contents but on the process. The destination of a trip is just the excuse for the voyage.

5 Two fundamental qualities distinguish the Ego-complex from all the other complexes, hence, pointing to the Ego as some sort of a fractal of the Self: the fact that, differently from the other complexes, it is meta-noetic, self-reflectively discriminative and integrative, hence, capable of reuniting in a new complex unity the plurality of the noetic complexes that make the Self. The fact that the Ego is conscious makes of it a temporalized complex, whose existence is inextricably bound to the endless nature of its own task. In

fact, as Jung wrote, when something unconscious becomes conscious, something conscious becomes unconscious.

6 There are suggestive hints in the traditional neuroscience literature for certain types of relevant synchronous oscillations within the brain, such as the 4–7 Hz rhythms in the hippocampus known as the theta rhythm, which helps animals to investigate the world (e.g., sniffing in rats) and thereby create memories in the hippocampus. The theta rhythm is the highly characteristic neural signature of the hippocampus, as it is actively processing information. This rhythm is especially evident during artificial arousal of the SEEKING system in rats, a premier information-gathering emotional system, as animals sniff and investigate their surroundings (Vertes & Kocsis, 1997).

7 Here, once again, we find the notion of "instinct" yet *not as a pattern of behavior.* In fact, it seems that, here, by "instinct", Jung has in mind something like the input from Bion's O: the *Infinite.*

8 Although its real origin in modern psychology is reported by Ellenberger (1981) and refers to the cognitive performance of the Marquis de Pyuségur's peasant Victor Race in the 18th century.

References

Alcaro, A., Carta, S., Panksepp, J. (2017). The Affective Core of the Self: A Neuro-Archetypical Perspective on the Foundations of Human (and Animal) Subjectivity. *Frontiers in Psychology*, 8, Article 1424.

Balduzzi, D., Tononi, G. (2009). Qualia: The Geometry of Integrated Information. *PLoS Computational Biology*, 5, e1000462.

Bohm, D. (1980/1981). *Wholeness and the Implicate Order*. Abingdon: Routledge.

Bollas, C. (2018). *The Shadow of the Object. Psychoanalysis of the Unthought Known*. London: Routledge.

Brown, J.W. (2002). *The Self-Embodying Mind. Process, Brain Dynamics and the Conscious Present (Il principio dell'invarianza organizzativa)*. New York, NY: Barrytown.

Chalmers, D. (2020). *Che cos'è la Coscienza*. Firenze: Castelvecchi.

Chen, C.-C., Crilly, N. (2014). *Modularity, Redundancy and Degeneracy: Cross-Domain Perspectives on Key Design Principles*. IEEE International Systems Conference Proceedings, IEEE International Systems Engineering.

Damasio, A. (2010). *Self Comes to Mind: Constructing the Conscious Brain*. New York: Pantheon Books.

Damasio, A. (2021). *The Strange Order of Things: Life, Feeling and the Making of Cultures*. New York: Pantheon Book.

Denton, D.A. (2006). *The Primordial Emotions: The Dawning of Consciousness*. New York, NY: Oxford University Press.

Edelman, G.M., Gally, J.A. (2001). Degeneracy and Complexity in Biological Systems. *Proceedings of the National Academy of Sciences*, 98, 13763–13768.

Edelman, G.M., Tononi, G. (2000). *A Universe of Consciousness: How Matter Becomes Imagination*. New York: Basic Books.

Ellenberger, H. (1981). *The Discovery of the Unconscious: The History and Evolution of Dynamic Psychiatry*. New York: Basic Books.

Freeman, W.J. (1999). *How Brains Make up Their Minds*. London: Weidenfeld and Nicolson.

Freeman, W.J., Vitiello, G. (2005). Nonlinear Brain Dynamics and Many-Body Field Dynamics. *Electromagnetic Biology and Medicine*, 24, 1–9.

Freeman, W.J., Vitiello, G. (2006). Nonlinear Brain Dynamics as Macroscopic Manifestation of Underlying Many-Body Field Dynamics. *Physics of Life Review*, 3, 93–118.

Freeman, W.J., Vitiello, G. (2008). Dissipation and Spontaneous Symmetry Breaking in Brain Dynamics. *Journal of Physics A: Mathematical and Theoretical*, 41, 1–17.

Freeman, W.J., Vitiello, G. (2016). Matter and Mind are Entangled in Two Streams of Images that Guide Behavior and Inform the Subject Through Awareness. *Mind and Matter*, 14, 1, 7–24.

Humphrey, N.K. (1974). Vision in a Monkey Without Striate Cortex: A Case Study. *Perception*, 3, 241–255.

Jousset, A., Eisenhauer, N., Materne, E., Sche, S. (2013). Evolutionary History Predicts the Stability of Cooperation in Microbial Communities. *Nature Communications*, 4, 2573.

Jung, C.G. (1937). Psychological Factors Determining Human Behavior. In: *The Collected Works of C.G. Jung*. Vol. 8. London, New York: Routledge.

Jung, C.G. (1947/1954). On the Nature of the Psyche. In: *The Collected Works of C.G. Jung*. Vol. 8. London: Routledge.

Jung, C.G. (1952). Synchronicity: An Acausal Connecting Principle. In: *The Collected Works of C.G. Jung*. Vol. 8. London, New York: Routledge.

Kihlstrom, J.F. (1987, September 18). The Cognitive Unconscious. *Science*, 237, 4821, 1445–1452.

Kram, K.E., Finkel, S.E. (2014). Culture Volume and Vessel Affect Long-Term Survival, Mutation Frequency, and Oxidative Stress of Escherichia Coli. *Applied and Environmental Microbiology*, 80, 5, 1732–1738.

Kram, K.E., Finkel, S.E. (2015). Rich Medium Composition Affects Escherichia Coli Survival, Glycation, and Mutation Frequency During Long-Term Batch Culture. *Applied and Environmental Microbiology*, 81, 13, 4442–4450.

Krieger, N.M. (2014). *Bridges to Consciousness: Complexes and Complexity*. New York, NY: Routledge.

Llinas, R. (2002). *I of the Vortex: From Neurons to Self*. Cambridge, MA: MIT Press.

Lorenz, K. (1965). *Evolution and Modification of Behavior*. Chicago: University of Chicago Press.

Montag, C., Davis, K. (2018). Affective Neuroscience Theory and Personality: An Update Personality. *Neuroscience*, 1, E12, 1–12.

Neumann, E. (1973). *The Child: The Structure and Dynamics of the Nascent Personality*. London: Karnak.

Newman, S.A. (1995). Carnal Boundaries. The Commingling of Flesh in Theory and Practice. In: *Reinventing Biology. Respect for Life and the Creation of Knowledge*, pp. 191–227. R. Birke, R. Hubbard (Eds.). Bloomington, Indianapolis: Indiana University Press.

Nieder, A. (2019). *A Mind for Numbers*. Cambridge (Mass.): MIT Press.

Northoff, G., Panksepp, J. (2008). The Trans-Species Concept of Self and The Subcortical-Cortical Midline System. *Trends in Cognitive Sciences*, 12, 259–264. https://doi.org/10.1016/J.Tics.2008.04.007.

Panksepp, J. (1998a). The Periconscious Substrates of Consciousness: Affective States and the Evolutionary Origins of the SELF. *Journal of Consciousness Studies*, 5, 566–582.

Panksepp, J. (1998b). *Affective Neuroscience: The Foundations of Human and Animal Emotions*. New York, NY: Oxford University Press.

Panksepp, J. (2005). Affective Consciousness: Core Emotional Feelings in Animals and Humans. *Consciousness and Cognition*, 14, 30–80.

Panksepp, J. (2010). Affective Consciousness in Animals: Perspectives on Dimensional and Primary Process Emotion Approaches. *Proceedings of the Royal Society B: Biological Sciences*, 277, 2905–2907.

Panksepp, J., Biven, L. (2012). *The Archaeology of Mind: Neuroevolutionary Origins of Human Emotion*. New York, NY: W.W. Norton & Company.

Panksepp, J., Burgdorf, J. (2003). Laughing Rats and the Evolutionary Antecedents of Human Joy? *Physiology & Behavior*, 79, 533–547.

Pavlov, I.P. (1927). *Conditioned Reflexes: An Investigation of the Physiological Activity of the Cerebral Cortex*. G.V. Anrep (Transl. and Ed.). London: Oxford University Press.

Penrose, R. (1989). *The Emperor's New Mind*. New York, NY: Oxford University Press.

Roesler, C. (2022). *Development of A Reconceptualization of Archetype Theory. Report to the IAAP*. https://iaap.org/wp-content/uploads/2022/04/report-archetype-theory-roesler-1.pdf.

Romine, C.B., Reynolds, C.R. (2005). A Model of the Development of Frontal Lobe Functioning: Findings from a Meta-Analysis. *Applied Neuropsychology*, 12, 4, 190–201.

Rugani, R., McCrink, K., de Hevia, M-D., Vallortigara, G.(2009). Arithmetics in Newborn Chicks, in *Proceedings of the Royal Society of London B*, 276, pp. 2451–60.

Shamdasani, S. (1998). From Geneva to Zurich: Jung and French Switzerland. *Journal of Analytical Psychology*, 43, 115–126.

Skinner, B.F. (1935). The Generic Nature of the Concepts of Stimulus and Response. *Journal of General Psychology*, 12, 40–65.

Solms, M., Panksepp, J. (2012). The "id" Knows More than the "Ego" Admits: Neuropsychoanalytic and Primal Consciousness Perspectives on the Interface Between Affective and Cognitive Neuroscience. *Brain Sciences*, 2, 147–175.

Tagliagambe, S. (2023). Un Ambiente a Misura Del Cervello. *Atque Materiali tra Filosofia e Psicoterapia*, 33–73.

Tinbergen, N. (1951). *The Study of Instinct*. Oxford: Oxford University Press.

Tooley, V., Brigham, J.V., Maass, A., Bothwell, R.K. (1987). Facial Recognition: Weapon Effect and Attentional Focus. *Journal of Applied Social Psychology*, 17, 10, 845–859.

Vandekerckhove, M., Panksepp, J. (2009). The Flow of Anoetic to Noetic and Autonoetic Consciousness: A Vision of Unknowing (Anoetic) and Knowing (Noetic) Consciousness in the Remembrance of Things Past and Imagined Futures. *Consciousness and Cognition*, 18, 1018–1028.

Vertes, R.P., Kocsis, B. (1997). Brainstem-Diencephalo-Septohippocampal Systems Controlling the Theta Rhythm of the Hippocampus. *Neuroscience*, 81.

Vitiello, G. (2019). Simmetrie e metamorfosi. *Atque*, 24, 139–160.

Whitacre, J.M. (2010). Degeneracy: A Link Between Evolvability, Robustness and Complexity in Biological Systems. *Theoretical Biology and Medical Modelling*, 7, 6.

Wagener, L., Loconsole, M., Ditz, H-M-, Nieder A. (2018), Neurons in the Encbrain of Numerically Naive Crows Spontaneously Encode Visual Numerosity, in *Current Biology*, 28, pp. 1090–94.

Chapter 6

The Problem of the So-called Instinct

Jung's reference to the instinct has raised an intense debate. In fact, many commentators – among them many Jungians – maintain that Jung's concept of the instinct is biologically outdated because, in their view, the "instinct" with its supposedly rigid behavioristic nature applies only to lower animals, and to refer it to humans, too, would be something that no biologist would agree upon today.

The correspondences between the concept of archetype and that of instinct was repeatedly underlined by Jung and his successors (see Stevens, 2002).

These commentators often quote this passage from Jung:

> In view of the structure of the body, it would be astonishing if the psyche were the only biological phenomenon not to show clear traces of its evolutionary history, and it is altogether probable that these marks are closely connected with the instinctual base. Instinct and the archaic mode meet in the biological conception of the "pattern of behavior". There are, in fact, no amorphous instincts, as every instinct bears in itself the pattern of its situation. Always it fulfils an image, and the image has fixed qualities. The instinct of the leaf-cutting ant fulfills the image of ant, tree, leaf, cutting, transport, and the little ant-garden of fungi. If any one of these conditions is lacking, the instinct does not function, because it cannot exist without its total pattern, without its image. Such an image is an a priori type. It is inborn in the ant prior to any activity, for there can be no activity at all unless an instinct of corresponding pattern initiates and makes it possible. This schema holds true of all instincts and is found in identical form in all individuals of the same species. The same is true also of man: he has in him these a priori instinct-types which provide the occasion and the pattern for his activities, in so far as he functions instinctively. As a biological being he has no choice but to act in a specifically human way and fulfil his pattern of behavior. This sets narrow limits to his possible range of volition, the narrower the more primitive he is, and the more his consciousness is dependent upon the instinctual sphere.
> (Jung, 1927/1931)

They interpret this passage as a description of human psychology and protest about a supposedly naïve and outdated position by Jung. On the contrary, like in other

DOI: 10.4324/9781003586258-6

cases, here, Jung seems, or, if you wish, may be interpreted as being in line with today's biology – so much so that he often seems to me to have been quite incredibly far-sighted.

Within the bottom-up perspective of this discussion, the clarification of the nature and the role of the original somatic motivational impulse – may that be a de-specialized drive or a rigid pre-formed instinct – is crucial.

Jung's passage that I just quoted has been widely used by many critics of his motivational theory. My opinion is that the description of the instinct that Jung uses refers to "pre-psychical" animals[1] or, to be more precise, animals that are not self-reflectively conscious, like the leaf-cutting ant. For Jung, this way of functioning applies to man only "in so far as he functions instinctively" and only when he is conceived purely "as a biological being", whose functioning is still completely at a *psychoid* – i.e., at a non-completely psychological level.

Once again, in the context of this specific discussion, I propose to interpret the adjective "psychological" as "self-reflectively conscious". In a few words, I mean that the features of a-noetic and noetic consciousness – forms of unconscious consciousness – apply to the *unconscious and not to the Ego* and, in a Jungian perspective, especially to the collective, unconscious, biologically inherited processes. As we shall see, Jung infers such an "instinctive" activity by the clinical observations on the automatic and compulsive character of his patients in psychopathology, or by the simple habitual way we all function when we do not need to be self-aware. In passing, I would like to point out that, given the psychoid nature of the collective unconscious – which deeply roots itself into the deepest strata of the bodily "matter" (Newman, 1995) – this form of unconscious consciousness might *not* be an evolutionary emergent property, like computational theories of consciousness maintain, but it may be a *fundamental* property of life from which self-reflective consciousness emerged (Hameroff, 2006; Penrose, 1994). Within my bottom-up perspective, this view of consciousness, quantistically embedded in the structure of inorganic chemistry ready to develop consciousness within organic chemistry's matter, pushes the "bottom" way, way down, towards the cosmological beginning of the beginning.

The historical roots of this theory may be referred to many authors and especially to Alfred Fouillée's theory of the *idées forces* (1911) and to Pierre Janet's theory of the *idées fixe* and of the *automatisme psicologique* (Janet, 1889; for a comprehensive discussion: Hillman, 2001). Therefore, I will argue the possibility that, while the self-reflective conscious works in a de-specialized way, the unconscious processes work through partially encapsulated modules, which Jung called complexes, at the core of which there are the instincts.

The mention of Fouillée and Janet is important also because they both focused on the relationship between affects and representations and how affects use and constrain representations, transforming facts into meanings – a theme I will deal with in the second volume. In other words, we are dealing with what Lévy-Bruhl (1910) called *representations collectives* belonging to the *mentalité primitive*.[2]

If one doesn't isolate Jung's quote that I am discussing from all the other places where he deals with the issue of the constrained nature of the collective unconscious, the interpretation of a naïve Jung as a biologist may be reversed.

To understand this, we should go back to Jung's quote that I already cited. In fact, with regard to *human* psychology, he specifies the following:

> Instinct as an ectopsychic factor would *play the role of a stimulus merely*, while instinct as a psychic phenomenon would be an assimilation of this stimulus to a *pre-existent psychic pattern*. A name is needed for this process. I should term it psychization. Thus, what we call instinct offhand would be a datum already psychized, but of ectopsychic origin.
>
> (Jung, 1937, p. 134. my italics)

So such an ectopsychic stimulus in humans (but in a lesser way, in many animals) undergoes a process of transformation, an "assimilation" of the instinctual stimulus, which Jung calls *psychization*. In fact, what Jung is describing in this passage is the *ectopsychic* factor that determines the behavior *of ants* (not humans!), i.e., in animals that Jung thought have no psychology but that function just by purely organic visceral regulation. The nervous system of the more archaic animals that Jung was thinking about is still, at most, confined to the autonomic system and the most archaic brain structures– the brainstem, the mesencephalon, the basal ganglia and a large part of the reticular substance. At this level, animals function, guided by reflexes.

Tinbergen's mechanistic, reductionist notion of instinct as a "fixed action pattern" (FAD) (Tinbergen, 1951) is not the only one. In fact, Darwin,[3] Romanes[4] or Konrad Lorenz (who distinguishes automatic reflex from non-rigid *instinct* [1965]) and, more recently, Donald Griffin (1976) speak of instincts as *endogenous dispositions which express attitudes that may be variably fixed or flexible and which already contain proto-conscious and proto-intentional nature*. These situations will be subjectively felt as an affect. This is in accordance with Jaak Panksepp's view (see vol. I, § 9) of the role of primary affects and corresponds to a basic tenet of the studies in neurodynamics.

Hence, a question arises: To what kind of "instinct" was Jung referring? To the behavioristic reflex, or to the dynamic constellating impulse?

Jung's departure point is that from evolutionary biological developments and embryology, a true psychological functioning will eventually emerge phylo- and ontogenetically. Nevertheless, this will anyway be constrained by these underpinning ectopsychic factors – the "instincts".

I would like to highlight this distinction between ants and humans, as I think that Jung had it perfectly clear in his mind. What I am saying is supported by the comparison of Jung's reference to the rigid patterns of behavior *in ants*, with the previous one, in which he discusses the role of "instincts" *in humans*. It is of paramount importance to remember that the nature of such a stimulus is, for organisms that do not function just by reflexes, that of a somatic affect. In fact, *when throughout the phylogenetic evolution, a reflex does not determine anymore a fixed action pattern (like in ants) but triggers in the organism an endogenous, teleologically constrained field of activation coupled with a specific environment, it takes the form of an affect, and eventually it will be subjectively felt as a feeling.* As we will see referring to Jacob von Uexküll and Jaak Panksepp, this form of subjectivity, which entails a whole subjective experiential phenomenology – i.e., a certain form of consciousness – does not imply self-conscious consciousness.

I will try to highlight the neurobiological characteristics of this transformative process in the next chapters, also in reference to the embryology of the brain. A notation that may be interesting is that in Jung's quotation, Jung gives us a phylogenetic account of what Bion refers to human ontogenesis under the name of "alpha function" (1967) – *the* function of human *psychization.*

Hunger, sexuality, action, reflection and creativity, as instinctive motivating forces, participate in the typical characteristics of instinct: a) automatism (which Jung identifies especially through the work of Pierre Janet, 1889), b) compulsivity, c) a high degree of intrinsic structuration endowed with d) high stability, (which manifests itself in patterns of behavior), as well as e) the relationship to a highly specific *Umwelt* (as we will see in the next chapter).

I would like to emphasize the coherence of the Jungian motivational framework, in which the instinct is a motivating force that actually pushes-specifically-for-something, i.e., an extra-psychic force which, *when it enters into relation with the subjective psychic environment*, is modified, i.e., psychicized, producing the *embryonic* form of the most archaic psychic layer of the mind – something like a constrained affective field, which we may call "complex". In this case, such complexes would be still pre-conscious and species-specific and will constrain their own future development all the way to the emergence of what Jung describes as "archetypal images".

In turn, this peculiar, embryonic, highly organized affective structure effectively corresponds to a teleological motivation coupled with an environment, i.e., a force-for-something-specific. Through psychization, what was an extra-psychic, automatic and compulsive instinct accedes to self-representation (today, we would say "becomes mentalized"), becomes more flexible and rooted in the specific psychic situation – it identifies itself – and metaphorizes itself into a potential multiplicity of symbolic representations[5] all gravitating around an affective energetic value still constrained and derived from the original "sense of the specific instinctual force". Eventually, this activity will lead to and determine self-reflective consciousness and the structure of the Ego.

As we will see later when we will deal with metaphors, the "instinct" of "hunger", when psychicized, can transform and metaphorize itself into intellectual greed or emotional insatiability. Of course, flexibility, personalization, mentalization and metaphorization increase as the motivating force of the instinct is integrated into consciousness and subjected to the influence of will and discrimination.

These notations are connected with Fordham's construct of the "de-integrated". As Rosemary Gordon points out (Gordon, 1985), the manifestation of the archetype, which can reach enormous levels of imaginal and meaningful complexity, may be linked with the progressive development of the reintegrated (psychoid) elements as they move towards consciousness. Archetypal processes, therefore, would be hybrids made by psychoid reintegrated elements on the one hand and by lived experiences (including, for example, linguistic and semantic structures) at various levels on the other. Thus, unlike the extra-psychic – i.e., organic – instinctual baggage that is typically rigid and compulsive, becoming psychic through psychization involves an unfolding of that typically hermetic and protean transformativity, variability and metaphorization processes that prelude to the becoming specific individuals. I see a very close similarity between these processes and Bion's transformation in O within what he described, along with the schizo-paranoid and the depressive positions, as the "transcendent position" (Bion, 1965; Grotstein, 1996).

Therefore, from Jung's previous quote, it should be clear that he might *not* be referring to instincts as "fixed action patterns" (FAP). We all agree that an instinct defined as such cannot be referred to human behavior, but it may be referred – with various degrees of freedom – to other animals, *if we exclude certain human behavioral categories such as psychopathological rituals and their similarity with religious rites.* In fact, there is the possibility that these behaviors indicate a layer of the human psyche which may function compulsively as archetypes (I will discuss these issues in vol. II, § 7).

This discussion on the meaning and role of the instinct is further complicated by two facts: the imprecise translation from German into English within Jung's works, where "Instinkt" is very often translated as "drive" (apparently, never the other way around), and by the fact that Jung himself did not seem to bother too much about such a terminological distinction. On the contrary, this distinction is crucial in Freudian psychoanalysis, in which the original (phylogenetic and ontogenetic) "Instinkt", made by four intrinsic components – its somatic source, its economic force, its aim towards motor release and a specific object (originally, for the baby, the mother's milk) – is transformed into a "Trieb" (Freud's "drive") because of the loss of the fourth component, the Object, around the third month of life (Freud, 1962).[6, 7]

In fact, Jung seems not to *lexically* distinguish between "*Instinkt*" and "*Trieb*", although he clearly *conceptually* differentiates very well the issues involved in the presence, absence and degree of the various characteristics involved in these terms.

This passage is quite revealing:

Although, in general, instinct is a system of stably organized tracts and consequently tends towards unlimited repetition, man nevertheless has the distinctive power of creating something new in the real sense of the word, just as nature, in the course of long periods of time, succeeds in creating new forms. Though we cannot classify it with a high degree of accuracy, the creative instinct is something that deserves special mention. I do not know if "instinct" is the correct word. We use the term "creative instinct" because this factor behaves at least dynamically, like an instinct. Like instinct it is compulsive, but it is not common, and it is not a fixed and invariably inherited organization. Therefore, I prefer to designate the creative impulse as a psychic factor similar in nature to instinct, having indeed a very close connection with the instincts, but without being identical with any one of them. Its connections with sexuality are a much-discussed problem and, furthermore, it has much in common with the drive to activity and the reflective instinct. But it can also suppress them, or make them serve it to the point of the self-destruction of the individual. Creation is as much destruction as construction.

To recapitulate, I would like to emphasize that from the psychological standpoint five main groups of instinctive factors can be distinguished: hunger, sexuality, activity, reflection, and creativity. In the last analysis, instincts are ectopsychic determinants.

(Jung, 1937. §245–246)

This passage is interesting for several reasons.

1) We can see that the distinction between drive and instinct is not precise, as it is in Freud's works, where he refers to the "Instinkt" just a handful number of times, while he constantly speaks of "Trieb(en)".
2) Jung is referring to the "Instinkt" while talking about creativity. This seems a real contradiction if we were to refer to the behavioristic notion of Instinkt, with its rigid procedural structure, which Jung describes in the famous example of the leaf-cutting ant.
3) It shows that Jung did not intend "Instinkt" in a behavioristic manner, but he referred to it as a dispositional patterning impulse which would produce *specific affective-behavioral and cognitive tendencies*, in line with Romanes' or Lorenz's meaning of "Instinkt".

   If this description is too abstract, an easy analogy – if not a true example – might be the fact that the impulse that is triggered by the release of dopamine in a particular area of the brain will constellate *specific* fields of affective activation (for example, Panksepp's PLAY provided the right level of testosterone and psychostimulants) or, more specifically, the release of brain opioids, or perhaps the insulin-like growth factor-1 (IGF-1 [Panksepp & Biven, 2012, §10]). If, on the contrary, the impulse is produced by adrenaline, the activation will constellate a specific, very different affective field.
4) It shows that Jung, on the basis of his clinical experience, uses "Instinkt" in reference not to a rigid pattern but for the following:

   a) its dispositionally dynamic nature, and
   b) its compulsive aspects, features that may be also attributed to a "drive".

Therefore, in this passage, Jung is excluding the main feature that differentiates a *behavioristic* "Instinkt" from a "Trieb" because, in my opinion, *he is not referring to ants but to humans* (I suppose he would also refer to mammals in general), in which the impulse triggers a vastly more complex and plastic probabilistic field of affective activation.

As we will see in vol. I, § 6, for Jung, humans (and surely, mammals) function quite differently, precisely because of the non-behavioristic theory of the instinct. Therefore, although the term is overly loaded with history and ambiguities, we may still call such a stimulus "instinct",[8] provided that for "instinct", we refer to the role of a "stimulus" as a dispositional impulse, a trigger constellating and activating – as Jung wrote referring to the complex – a potential state of readiness for a certain response.

Jung's concept of both instinct and drive is radically different from the idea of a non-specific, objectless drive (like Freud's theory as in the *Three Essays*), for which humans seem to be completely de-specialized animals.

As Sonu Shamdasani rightly says, in Jung, "the affect is always incorporated into the image".[9] Such an intrinsic unity of image and affect has great theoretical and clinical consequences, as it explains, for example, why dreams have no latent text and, therefore, why their images represent themselves, or, better said, the affects that they "imagine". In my opinion, this idea makes great sense, but if we approach analytical psychology from a bottom-up, evolutive perspective, it needs to be better explained.

I think that already at the dawn of ontogenetic life, the infant is endowed with a series of highly specialized sensory-motor patterns of behavior regulated by affects, quite like behavioral instincts. They emerge and become more complex in a way analogous to what Piaget described discussing his pre-operatory stage because they constellate *fields* of activation.

At this starting point, affect, sensory-motor pattern and the target-object – for instance, the nipple in the rooting "reflex" – form an innate unbreakable whole (if not in severe cases of neuropsychological deterioration). Nevertheless, already from this moment, the infant's psycho-biological maturation expresses new and evolving dispositional affective needs, beyond these already-established instinctual "patterns of behavior".

At the starting point, the triggering factor of these new more complex needs is an affective impulse (something like a "drive") that looks for its proper image in its relational environment (something like an instinct).

This presupposes the existence of a "holding" situation (Winnicott), which is, by the way, an innate, species-specific situation in which the mother's and the infant's affects are "loosely coupled" (Sander et al., 2014). What is happening is a transformation, through experience, of the impulse's affective latent pattern into an adequate representation – an image. Whenever this happens (and it happens all the time), affect and image tend to converge. From the moment that an image is "found", it will form an unbreakable whole with the constellating affect, where affect is dispositionally incorporated into the image.

It should be clear that this perspective implies that the "right" object-world is a world that is dispositionally "good to be imagined" by the child, i.e., a world that satisfies the requests of the child's Self, which are activated by the instinct as an affective patterning impulse.

All this implies that the first factor that is activated is an affect, which tends towards a dispositional, specific, patterned field of activation. While the infant interacts in the holding situation, his mind is activated in a patterned way and will look for the right "object". This object may be anything that represents the embodiment of the affect's teleological purpose and forms the imagistic representation of the affect itself.

We may, therefore, say that it is not the affect that is incorporated into the image but that it is the image that is incorporated into the affect. The point is that this process, phylogenetically and ontogenetically triggered by an affect, happens immediately and automatically, and from the moment it has taken place, it will be impossible to dissociate image from affect. *This is why any psychotherapy must work with and through images since they are the representations of the affective core-self.*

I hope that throughout this book, it will be clear that this developmental process is not confined to infancy or childhood but that it begins at the beginning of life and ends when a person (psychologically) dies because it is *not* aimed towards forming an Ego but towards the integration of the Self into consciousness.

This view seems coherent with the theory of the "archetype" as an emergent dynamic structure and with Saunders and Skar's (2001) hypothesis of the archetype not as a form but as a process which generates similar patterns that follow a process of self-organization both at a neurobiological level and at a psychological level. In another context, this is also the position of Gilbert Simondon (2020).

Referring to a complex dynamic system perspective – one with which I agree[10] – the authors argue that once a pattern is established, further information will be filtered and processed according to such a pattern. I will try to illustrate that these initial patterns are formed because of innate constraints and that they will then act as attractors for further information, which will anyway follow the original constraints that formed such patterns all the way to what Dan Sperber calls "susceptibilities" (see vol. II, § 5.1), which translate psychological representations into socio-cultural ones.

This process may be well called "transformation", where something essentially constant (a theme) will variate within a specific basin of activation and organization into differentiated expressions (the variations of a theme). Bion's discussion on the relationship between a view and the painting of this view may be useful to elaborate this issue (Bion, 1965).

To better understand the difference between archetypes as forms or templates deposited in the minds and archetypes as processes – fundamentally *affective* processes – that happen between individuals, we could refer to the following statement by Skar:

When we employ a dynamical systems view of development, we no longer need the archetype-as-such to explain the formation of complexes. In fact, we could do without it altogether and still have the same basic psychological system that Jung proposed.

(Skar, 2004, p. 247)

We can and must do without the archetype-as-such postulated as a template, or as an innate form, but we may save this term to describe the "abstract" organizing principle – somehow the mathematical-like information – that organizes something into a pattern.

Hence, this non-behavioristic notion of "instinct" means that the "archetype" should not be thought of as producing an automatic and inflexible behavior or mental activity – like a reflex – but as an affective impulse triggering the need for a constrained yet "non-fixed representation of the impulse itself ",[11] a field of probabilities made possible by the activation of the *Default Mode Network* and its imaginative "mind-wondering".

This is another passage in which Jung tries to distinguish between archetype-in-itself and archetypical images, where the archetype in itself:

> Preforms the crystalline structure of the mother's liquid, although it has no mate-rial existence of its own. The first appears according to the specific way in which the ions and molecules aggregate. The archetype in itself is empty and purely *for-mal*, *nothing but* a facultas preformandi, a possibility of representation which is given a priori. The representations themselves are not inherited, only the forms, and in that respect, they correspond in every way to the instincts, which are also determined in form only. The existence of the instincts can no more be proved than the existence of the archetypes, so long as they do not manifest themselves concretely. With regard to the definiteness of the form, our comparison with the crystal is illuminating inasmuch as the axial system determines only the stereo-metric structure, but not the concrete form of the individual crystal.
>
> (Jung, 1948, footnote §155)

I think that in this passage, Jung means that the archetypes in themselves are ectopsychic formative factors and that in such a way, they cannot be represented directly, except through the very process of psychization that they trigger and regu-late and that emerges under the form of emotional patterns/images.

Jung's analogy of the crystal is perhaps the most important analogy used by Gil-bert Simondon, a philosopher that should be taken in more consideration in the Jun-gian world, whose thought is veritably strikingly coherent with Jung's (Saban, 2019). My view of the archetype as a function-in-between and that of Simondon's are also very compatible.

> it is necessary to reverse the search for the principle of individuation by con-sidering the operation of individuation as primordial, on the basis of which the individual comes to exist and the unfolding regimes and modalities of which the individual reflects in its characteristics. The individual would then be grasped as a relative reality, a certain phase of being which supposes a pre individual reality prior to it and which, even after individuation, does not fully exist all by itself, for individuation does not exhaust in a single stroke the potentials of pre

individual reality, and, moreover, what individuation manifests is not merely the individual but the individual-milieu coupling.[12]

We will begin by attempting to present physical individuation as a case of the resolution of a metastable system on the basis of a system state, like that of supercooling or supersaturation involved in the genesis of crystals.

. . .

We would then understand the paradigmatic value of the study of the genesis of crystals as processes of individuation: [so to] to grasp on the macrophysical scale a phenomenon that depends on system states which belong to the microphysical domain and which are molecular and not molar; we would grasp activity that is *at the limit* of the crystal in its formation. Such an individuation is not the encounter of a preliminary form and the preliminary matter existing as previously constituted separate terms, but a resolution emerging within a metastable system rich in potential *form, matter, and energy preexist in the system.*

(Simondon, 2020, pp. 5–6. His italics)

Once again, such ectopsychic factors should not be conceptualized as forms but as innate "informational rules" for the formation of dynamic affective patterns (perhaps I should use Winnicott's typical gerundives: holding, object presenting, handling, going-on-being, etc.). Hence, we should not speak of patterns but of a process of patterning that preserves an original footprint. One way to describe how the archetype-in-itself works would be analogous to $y = ax^2 + bx + c$. Its informational nature would be the informational activity of operators "+" and the square relation in ax^2, together with their position in the equation, while the patterned outcome (an image, a behavior, etc.) would be the corresponding parabola. Spinoza's concepts of *natura naturans* and *natura naturata* also seem to me to refer to such a relationship.

Furthermore, Jung's passage is interesting for its coherence with contemporary biology and neurobiology, which interpret the "instinct" precisely as a trigger for a latent dispositional patterned functioning. I have already quoted two authoritative biologists who share such an idea – Lorenz and Griffith.

Under this respect, Anthony Stevens rightly highlights the following:

Professor Robert Hinde of Cambridge made the useful suggestion that, rather than wasting time arguing about which behaviors are learned and which are innate, the progress of science would be better served if we conceive a continuum of behaviors ranging from those which are *environmentally stable*. It has relatively little influence by environmental variations and those which are *environmentally labile*. Hinde's suggestion was wholeheartedly adopted by Bowlby, who never argued that human instinctive behavior patterns where themselves innate. "Instinctive behavior is not inherited", he wrote: "what is inherited is the potential to develop . . . behavioral systems, both the nature and form of which differ in some measure according to the particular environment in which development takes place".

(Stevens, 2002, p. 58)

Stevens' reference to Bowlby is important, as it is coherent and confirms Jung's point of view of one of the most relevant contemporary psychological theories, surely, one of the better operationalized ones and one wholly grounded in biological science (yet reductively so) – attachment theory.

I would like to return for a moment to Jung's reference to the process of the emergence of the crystal from a supersaturated medium. First of all, such a medium seems to be the scientific description of the Gnostic *Pleroma*, which, in this case, would be the equivalent to those intuitions that Pauli referred to as belonging to an "hintergrund-physik" (the "ancestral physics" to which some images belong, like those in dreams or imaginative states, and that are then proven scientifically viable after centuries. One example is Heraclitus' idea that everything is "fire", which Einstein validated 2,600 years later) (Pauli, 2012). I would like to notice two aspects. First, the cata-strophic process (*natura naturans*), through which the potential crystal in a metastable state comes into existence (*natura naturata*), is described by molecular biologists as an analogue of the way the DNA replicates. Just as the crystal molecules in the solu-tion find each other when an anomaly occurs, tilting its homeostatic state towards metastability, after the double DNA helix unravels to ignite replication, like keys in their locks, the DNA nucleotides will chemically pair in such a way that a new (almost) identical DNA double helix will be built, precisely like a crystal (Noble, 2008). Therefore, Jung's example of the crystallization process was much deeper than a mere analogy but a fitting description of the process through which archetypal forms emerge out of the prepotential psychoid medium that he called collective unconscious.

The second interesting aspect is that the process that disturbs homeostatic stabil-ity, and that is intrinsically related to life (in fact, the emergence of a crystal can be referred to the inorganic domain; what interests us here is the process), is *necessarily triggered by* a disturbance, which will tilt the prepotential, pleromatic state that is potentially "ready" to respond (and here, I would like to remind you of the definition of the complex as a readiness to respond). I think that the role of such a disturbing element is precisely that of the environment, Jung's "situation of the moment":

the immediate determining factor is not the ectoplastic instinct but the struc-ture resulting from the interaction of instinct and the psychic situation of the moment. The determining factor would thus be a modified instinct. The change undergone by the instinct is as significant as the difference between the color we see and the objective wavelength producing it. Instinct as an ectopsychic factor would play the role of a stimulus merely, while instinct, as a psychic phenom-enon would be an assimilation of this stimulus to a pre-existing pattern. A name is needed for this process. I should term it psychization.

(Jung, 1937, § 234)

I will develop the issue of the relationship between the organism and its environment, quoted by Hinde, when I will deal with the concept of co-evolution, hence, with the view of the archetype as the entangling function, the something-in-between the organism and its environment.[13] This eco-psychological perspective is the view that has inspired the four volumes by Dennis Merritt's "The Dairy Farmer's Guide to the Universe" (2012). In a clinical setting, the archetype would connect and pattern the many potential developments of the relationship between the analyst and her patient within the transferential field as Jung described in his *Psychology of Transference* (1946).

At this point, it is once again important to recall that such an organizing dispositional trigger *has an affective nature* that will determine its meaning and that what such an instinctive trigger organizes are representational and behavioral *patterns*, which Jung called "complexes", which, as we will see, represent, within a cognitive, representational and abstract fashion, precisely the feelings that constellate them. (For a specific discussion on the neurobiological implications of this perspective: Alcaro et al., 2017; Alcaro & Carta, 2019, and for the psycho-neurobiological description of such a reflective process from sensory-motor and affective primitive dispositions to images, thoughts and, ultimately, language, see the discussion of Jung's dream of the four-layered house in Carta & Alcaro, 2022.)

Another quote may confirm that the idea of a purely behavioristic interpretation of the instinct is far from Jung's idea of how *human* psychology works. Jung tells us that the pattern of behavior would represent the *biological* – not yet mentalized – emergence of the organization of the unconscious and of its expression when emotionally activated. Its *psychological* counterpart is the image:[14]

Just as we have been compelled to postulate the concept of an instinct determining or regulating our conscious actions, so, in order to account for the uniformity and regularity of our perceptions, we must have recourse to the correlated concept of the factor determining the mode of apprehension. It is this factor which I call the archetype or primordial image. The primordial image might suitably be described as *the instinct's perception of itself*, or as the self-portrait of the instinct, in exactly the same way as consciousness is an inward perception of the objective life process.

(Jung, 1919, p. 136. Jung's italics.)

In a previous article, written with Antonio Alcaro and Jaak Panksepp (Alcaro et al., 2017), we defined the archetype as activated by something like an "'instinct' of imagination" (see also Bucci, 1997), like an inherited disposition to imagine (i.e., represented via the organization of material borrowed from the senses by exaptation),[15] a cluster of representations gravitating around a characteristic meaning. Such a meaning corresponds to an affective state, triggered by inner and outer conditions which it will *dispositionally interpret* to re-establish a dynamic homeostasis (i.e., "metastability", Simondon, 2020), i.e., to creatively solve a problem.

The implication of such a perspective is decisive. Beyond the mere responses based on reflexes – Tinbergen's "fixed action patterns", i.e., once a core-self is phylogenetically stabilized – the organism will respond to the inner and outer stimuli to *anticipate possible events* (Sprevak, 2024). I will return to this concept later, but it is important that the reader always frames my discussion on the way organisms, and most of all, *Homo sapiens*, process information and develop a phenomenological experience.

I think it is now sufficiently clear that Jung's words which refer to the ant cannot be equated to the ones that I just quoted, which once again refer to the transformation of an ectopsychic factor into a proto-psychological content. In fact, here, Jung differentiates "instinct" and "image", saying:

> There are, in fact, no amorphous instincts, as every instinct bears in itself the pattern of its situation. Always it fulfils an image, and the image has fixed qualities.
> (Jung, 1927/1931, p. 201)

Like in other cases, I think that we could constructively interpret Jung in a way that would be in line with today's research.

As I already wrote, Jung is often accused of being confused and contradictory. In fact, if Jung was not scientific enough, at least sometimes it seems so not because he was wrong but because science had not yet progressed enough. For example, Panksepp and Damasio seem to agree not only with Jung's theory of the role of affects – Panksepp being the one to claim not only their importance but also their dispositional perspective, later agreed upon by most neurobiologists, Damasio included. One other example, that I have already discussed, is the issue about unconsciousness and consciousness and the analogy between a-noetic affects and Dorn's *caelum stellatum* that Jung quoted from his alchemical studies.

To summarize the issue of the instinct as a pattern of behavior, the quote that deals with the ant's behavior has often been interpreted as a description of *human* psychism, while I argue that, on the contrary, such a pattern of behavior refers to the *ectopsychic* factor – something that belongs to the collective, i.e., species-specific psychoid unconscious not yet "psychologized" – that I have quoted previously.[16] In fact, Jung differentiates "instinct" and "image", saying that "every instinct bears in itself the pattern of its situation. Always it fulfils an image, and the image has fixed qualities".

This sentence may be interpreted as an expression of two meaningful and bio-psychologically sound hypotheses:

1) The instinct as a trigger is embedded in a co-evolutionary milieu (a "patterned situation", as we will see contemporary biologists, such as Richard Lewontin, describe). As we will see, Jung's very definition of what is a complex implies such a reciprocity of endogenous, innate constraints and environmental factors.
2) It aggregates a potential, latent *image*, which – and this is implied in all of Jung's reference to consciousness, symbolization and individuation – will express

itself throughout infinite variations-on-the-theme.[17] In fact, the compulsiveness and the recurrent nature of emotionally species-specific triggered patterns (may they be representational or behavioral) take place "in so far as he [the person] functions instinctively".

The obvious anthropological diversity between human cultures and the psychological diversity between individuals is not under discussion. It is directly connected to the biological principle of our de-specialization, our neotenic nature, which no one denies. The question is whether such differences (the variations of the theme) wholly exclude or, on the contrary, may coexist *together with* archaic modes through which fixed structural (quasi) universal patterns emerge (the theme of the variations) – a hypothesis coherent with contemporary research.

Notes

1 I am using an expression that Jung might have used.
2 It might be worthwhile to connect the role of Lévy-Bruhl as one of the bridges from psychology to anthropology, especially to the psychology of the unconscious and, therefore, of the *numinous* – to the way people think and behave in the social domain. Nevertheless, in recalling Lévy-Bruhl's role, we should reposition his idea of a primitive mentality as belonging to primitive peoples (like also Jung, unfortunately, did) and, instead, refer it to the primitive way the mind of *Homo sapiens* works when it functions unconsciously. This is Lévi-Strauss' version of this issue, when he refers (in his own way and often surprisingly misunderstanding Jung's position) to a *Pensée Sauvage* (1967). For Lévi-Strauss, there are no savage people, just a savage way the mind works.
3 In the *Descent of Man and Selection in Relation to Sex*, Darwin described his fascination with a male *Chiasognathus grantii Stephens* (*Coleoptera, Lucanidae*), a stag beetle species with enormous mandibles – just as Wallace in his book *The Malay Archipelago* recorded his enchantment with a male *Euchirus longimanus L. (Coleoptera, Scarabaeidae)*, a "chafer" species with "immense forearms" (tibia or femora). These are examples of intraspecific mutations, proofs of phenotypic plasticity, later transmitted in the genome.
4 Romanes: 7 March 1881: "Does the animal learn by its own individual experience? [. . .] If [. . .] it could be shown by experiment [. . .] that a particular earthworm admits of being taught by experience how best to manipulate unknown leaf, [. . .] there could no longer be any question as to the action being in the full sense of the word intelligent" (pp. 261–262) (Schwartz, 2014, p. 260).
   In his "*The Formation of Vegetable Mould through the Action of Worms*", Darwin (1882) used Romanes' opinion (Darwin's letters, 16 April 1882) for which *worms* (!) express an intelligent behavior (learn from experience within their ecological niche), therefore, showing the plasticity of its *reflexes* and the co-evolutionary interaction between phenotype and its proximal environment.
5 Here, I am directly referring to Jung's definition of consciousness as "differentiation", which not only involves the differentiation of the individual mind but also the emerging of cultural differences. It is obvious that in both cases, once a differentiation has been reached – once I become sufficiently myself and different from you – I will act again in an unconscious, automatic way yet in an unconscious way that I may bring back to consciousness through reflectivity.
6 This process would happen following Hackel's principle for which ontogenesis recapitulates phylogenesis.

7 The original bio-psychological Object – the milk – will be metonymically displaced into the Breast and metaphorically transformed into all the Objects of introjection and, later, of identification (Laplanche & Pontalis, 1974).

   The radical neotenic interpretation of humans and such a theory of the Object-loss misled all psychoanalysis until the works of Fairbairn (1994) and, after him, Bowlby (1991). Analytical psychology simply never needed to painstakingly correct such a wrong interpretation of the motivational structure of humans; therefore, I was never impressed by Bowlby's (whom I had the pleasure to meet and talk to as a young student) "revolution".

8 Once again, not as a fixed action pattern.

9 Personal communication.

10 My reading of Jung is that of a precursor of complex system theory and cybernetics. I interpret his theory like this because of his view of the Self as a unity of opposites and his fundamental regulatory principle of *compensation*, which today, we may also call *feedback*, his view of the psyche as composed of an indefinite number of autonomous complexes interacting at different levels (conscious, unconscious, personal, collective, etc.) and his idea of the transcendent function as something that may lead to transcend *opposites* – like organism/environment or inner/outer. This interpretation of mine (or if you wish, choice) of Jung's perspective may reveal a deep similarity between him and Gregory Bateson.

11 Something like Karmiloff Smith's implicit or explicit unconscious [E1] levels of cognitive representational redescription.

12 Simondon's "pre-individual reality" may correspond to Jung's collective unconscious and, in my opinion, to the Gnostic *Pleroma*. The ontogenetic ongoing emergence of the living *individual – the individuation process* – from such a pre-individual reality filled with potentials is very beautifully and convincingly described by Simondon as the emergence of a "singularity".

13 This is not a very original idea. I think that it is intrinsic in Jung's idea of the archetype in itself as a pure, empty, active catalytic relational structure, as it is described already in *Symbols of Transformation* (Jung, 1911/1956).

14 I will discuss the theme of the image in the second volume.

15 Exaptation occurs when a trait or feature that evolved for one function is later co-opted for a different function. In other words, a structure or behavior that originally had a specific purpose is later adapted to serve a new and different purpose. This idea contrasts with the notion of adaptation, where traits evolve under natural selection to perform a specific function that enhances the organism's fitness in its environment. Exaptation recognizes that some features may have originated for one purpose but have been repurposed or co-opted for another function over time. A classic example often cited is the evolution of feathers. Feathers likely originated in the lineage of theropod dinosaurs for insulation or display purposes. Later, in the lineage leading to birds, feathers were exapted for flight, providing a completely new function.

16 We are now mentioning "behavior". If we describe it as something that the organism is doing, *this* would be the manifestation of the latent patterning process – a motor manifestation. A pattern of behavior may be found in fetuses and infants; the rooting schema is one example. Obviously, such patterns are very, very far from anything like an archetypal image, yet we find such motor patterning at the other end of human behaviors, the cultural end – in religious rituals. I also find a similarity to such patterned behaviors in symptoms like compulsions and in the way the "hysterics" in Charcot's time moved their bodies. In the next chapter, I will mention the surprising observation by Aby Warburg that the overextended postures of these "hysteric" patients expressed the same "dynamogram" as the Greek images of the nymphs (Didi-Huberman, 2017).

Another perhaps just curious but potentially relevant fact is the apparent relationship between mathematical thinking and the motor centers of the brain: when a subject is involved in mathematical thinking, the areas of the brain that control movement patterns are activated (Lakoff & Nuñez, 2001). Regarding this phenomenon, the relationship between mathematics and patterning stop being just an analogy.

17 The usefulness of the concept of variation-on-themes in human ontogenetic development will be discussed later in reference to the works by Daniel Stern.

References

Alcaro, A., Carta, S. (2019). The "Instinct" of Imagination. A Neuro-Ethological Approach to the Evolution of the Reflective Mind and Its Application to Psychotherapy. *Frontiers in Human Neuroscience*, 12, 422481.

Alcaro, A., Carta, S., Panksepp, J. (2017). The Affective Core of the Self: A Neuro-Archetypical Perspective on the Foundations of Human (and Animal) Subjectivity. *Frontiers in Psychology*, 8, Article 1424.

Bion, W.R. (1965). *Transformations*. London: William Heinemann. (Reprinted London: Karnac Books, 1984).

Bion, W.R. (1967). A Theory of Thinking. In: *Second Thoughts*. London: Heinemann. (Reprinted *International Journal of Psycho-Analysis*, 43, 4–5, 1962).

Bowlby, J. (1991). *Attachment and Loss*. 3 Vols. Dublin: Penguin.

Bucci, W. (1997). *Psychoanalysis and Cognitive Science: A Multiple Code Theory*. New York: The Guiford Press.

Carta, S., Alcaro, A. (2022). Una casa di 3 piani + 1. Il Sogno di Jung e le Omologie Archetipiche Cervello-Mente in una Prospettiva Evolutive. *Studi Junghiani*, 28, 1.

Darwin, C. (1882). *Viaggio di un Naturalista Intorno al Mondo – Lettere (1831–1836)*. Milano: Feltrinelli (1982).

Didi-Huberman, G. (2017). *The Surviving Image: Phantoms of Time and Time of Phantoms: Aby Warburg's History of Art* (trans. Mendelsohn Harvey). University Park: Pennsylvania State University Press.

Fairbairn, W.R.D. (1994). *Psychoanalytic Studies of the Personality*. London: Routledge.

Fouillée, A. (1911). *L'Évolutionisme des Idées-Force*. 5th edn. Paris: F. Alcan.

Freud, S. (1962). *Three Essays on Sexual Theory*. New York: Basic Books (1905).

Gordon, R. (1985). Losing and Finding: The Location of Archetypal Experience. *Journal of Analytical Psychology*, 25, 3.

Griffin, D.R. (1976). *The Question of Animal Awareness. Evolutionary Continuity of Mental Experience*. New York, NY: Rockfeller University Press.

Grotstein, J.S. (1996). Bion's Transformation in "O", the "Thing-in-Itself", and the "Real": Toward the Concept of the "Transcendent Position". *Melanie Klein & Object Relations*, 14, 2, 109–141.

Hameroff, S. (2006). Consciousness, Neurobiology and Quantum Mechanics. In: *The Emerging Physics of Consciousness*, pp. 192–251. J.A. Tuszynski (Ed.). Springer Science & Business Media.

Hillman, J. (2001). *Emotion: A Comprehensive Phenomenology of Theories and their Meanings for Therapy*. London, New York: Taylor and Francis.

Janet, P. (1889). *L'Automatisme Psychologique: Essai de Psychologie Expérimentale sur les Formes Inférieures de l'Activité Humaineœ*. Paris: F. Alcan.

Jung, C.G. (1911/1956). Symbols of Transformation. In: *The Collected Works of C.G. Jung*. Vol. 5. London: Routledge.

Jung, C.G. (1919). Archetypes of the Collective Unconscious. In: *The Collected Works of C.G. Jung*. Vol. 9ii. London, New York: Routledge.

Jung, C.G. (1927/1931). The Structure and Dynamics of the Psyche. In: *The Collected Works of C.G. Jung*. Vol. 8. London, New York: Routledge.

Jung, C.G. (1937). Psychological Factors Determining Human Behavior. In: *The Collected Works of C.G. Jung*. Vol. 8. London, New York: Routledge.

Jung, C.G. (1946). The Psychology of the Transference. In: *The Collected Works of C.G. Jung*. Vol. 16. London: Routledge.

Jung, C.G. (1948). Apsychological Foundation of Belief in Spirits. In: *The Collected Works of C.G. Jung*. Vol. 8. London: Routledge.

Lakoff, G., Nuñez, R. (2001). *Where Mathematics Comes from: How the Embodied Mind Brings Mathematics into Being*. New York: Basic Books.

Laplanche, J., Pontalis, J.-B. (1974). *The Language of Psycho-Analysis*. New York: W.W. Norton & Company.

Lévi-Strauss, C. (1967). *The SavageMind*. Chicago: Chicago University Press.

Lévy-Bruhl, L. (1910). *Les Fonctions Mentales dans les Societes Inferieures*. Paris: Les Presses Universitaires de France.

Lorenz, K. (1965). *Evolution and Modification of Behavior*. Chicago: Chicago University Press.

Merritt, D.L. (2012). *The Dairy Farmers Guide to the Universe*. 4 Vols. London, New York: Routledge.

Newman, S.A. (1995). Carnal Boundaries. The Commingling of Flesh in Theory and Practice. In: *Reinventing Biology. Respect for Life and the Creation of Knowledge*, pp. 191–227. R. Birke, R. Hubbard (Eds.). Bloomington, Indianapolis: Indiana University Press.

Noble, D. (2008). *The Music of Life: Biology Beyond Genes*. Oxford: Oxford University Press.

Panksepp, J., Biven, L. (2012). *The Archaeology of Mind: Neuroevolutionary Origins of Human Emotion*. New York, NY: W.W. Norton & Company.

Pauli, W. (2012). *The Interpretation of Nature and the Psyche*. Bronx, New York: Ishi Press.

Penrose, R. (1994). *Shadows of the Mind: A Search for the Missing Science of Consciousness*. Oxford: Oxford University Press.

Saban, M. (2019). Simondon and Jung: Re-Thinking Individuation. In: *Holism. Possibilities and Problems*. C. McMillan, R. Main, D. Henderson (Eds.). London, New York: Routledge.

Sander, L., Amadei, G., Bianchi, I. (2014). *Living Systems, Evolving Consciousness, and the Emerging Person. A Selection of Papers from the Life Work of Louis Sander*. London, New York: Routledge.

Saunders, P., Skar, P. (2001). Archetypes, Complexes and Self. *Journal of Analytical Psychology*, 46, 2, 305–323.

Schwartz, J.S. (2014). *The Life of Letters of George John Romanes*. Literary Licensing LCC.

Simondon, G. (2020). *Individuation in Light of Notions of Form and Information*. Minneapolis, London: The University of Minnesota Press.

Skar, P. (2004). Chaos and Self-Organization: Emergent Patterns at Critical Life Transitions. *Journal of Analytical Psychology*, 49, 245–264.

Sprevak, M. (2024). Predictive Coding I: Introduction. *Philosophy Compass*, e12950. https://doi.org/10.1111/phc3.12950.

Stevens, A. (2002). *Archetype Revisited: An Updated Natural History of the Self*. London: Routledge.

Tinbergen, N. (1951). *The Study of Instinct*. Oxford: Oxford University Press.

Chapter 7

Affects, Feelings and Co-evolution

All the discussion so far has been centered on what happens within the organism or, in other words, within a person's BrainMind. Such a perspective was necessary to illustrate a series of principles and phenomena, yet it is an empirically abstract and nonrealistic way to look at any organism, least of all, the human being. In fact, this perspective isolates the organism from its environment, creating the illusion that such a state of affairs really exists. But it does not.

Let's go back once again to Jung's quote on the psychization process. We might remember that it involves the "assimilation" of the biological "instinct" (rooted in the structure of the body and the autonomous, peripheral and central nervous systems) to the individual psychic environment. As I pointed out, the immediate determining factor is not the "ectopsychic instinct" but the structure resulting from the interaction of instinct and the psychic situation of the moment. The determining factor would thus be a "modified instinct" (Jung, 1937).

All this takes us to the concept of co-evolution. In fact, if we admit that the teleological structure of motivation is derived from those constraining ectopsychic impulses (the "instincts"), we must necessarily admit, in accordance with biology, that the motivating affects, endowed with energy and archetypal structure, *include* in its target what Jacob von Uexküll called the *Umwelt* (literally: "surroundings"), just as the instinct does in animals (like ants). The organism is entangled to its environment.

Von Uexküll's concept of *Umwelt*, with its corollary – co-evolution – are pivotal concepts that we should always keep in mind in reading this book. Von Uexküll, distinguishing between physiology and biology and reinterprets the latter in terms of a *subjective biology* (*subjective Biologie*, Von Uexküll, 1907) – a science by which one subject studies another subject.

Considering that each animal is entangled in its own specific Umwelt, the living universe may be imagined as a compound of interacting a priori forms of space and time, the variety of which eventually coincides with the number of animal species.

All animals, from the simplest to the most complex, are fitted into their unique worlds with equal completeness. A simple world corresponds to a simple animal, a well-articulated world to a complex one.

(Von Uexküll, 1934, p. 11)

DOI: 10.4324/9781003586258-7

Depending on the constraints imposed on it by its "structural plan" (*Bauplan*), each organism is endowed with receptor organs that *select* innumerable stimuli from the environment, taking in only part of those that may have a "meaning" for the organism itself. Once selected, this portion of the overall natural background is then analyzed according to the nature of the organism's receptors.

According to von Uexküll, although different animal species, including the species *Homo sapiens*, may share the same world, each of them will experience it as its own environment – its Umwelt – in a specific manner *inaccessible to all others* because the organism is conditioned by its own organization, which matches the perceivable world as a lock does against its own key. Every animal organism is endowed with "locks" in its own sensory structures that perfectly match the "keys" of certain external perceptual "signs".

Yet the receptive moment is only one side of the coin of the *Umwelt*: *the* face corresponds to the world of perception (*Markwelt*); the other side is the *operational world* (*Wirkwelt*), which the organism constantly modifies through its effector organs. Therefore, perception and motion are two inextricably coupled moments of the subjective life of each and every organism (Von Weitzsächer, 1940). Thus, the relationship between subject and its own *Umwelt* is made by a reciprocal action – *a unitary functional circuit* (*Funktionskreis*). In vol. II, § 4, I will refer again to the importance of movement for the distinction between outer perceptions and inner sensations and the emergence of noetic consciousness.

As von Uexküll writes, each organism is in a constant, active interaction with its environment, made up of the receptive signs that it perceives. A wasp, in short, will perceive "wasp-like" things, and it will act on them in a circular relationship or, better said, a *spiral* relationship, in which it is the action of the phenotype that changes the genotype and not the other way around. Such a perspective, for which it is the ontogenesis that determines the phylogenesis (Müller & Newman, 2003; Callebaut et al., 2007; Pigliucci & Müller, 2010; Müller, 2013), revolutionizes the vision of the central role of the genes as the agents of all evolutionary changes and of the selection mechanism. This idea, for which the gene is the deterministic center of all (for instance in Dawkins, 1976, 2015; Dawkins & Ward, 1997) is today replaced by a multicausal theory for which the specific intrinsic developmental characteristic of the organism may not be totally genetically programmed by a random selective process but may teleologically interact with the genome (Gould, 2002; Noble, 2008) and, therefore, set up a circular – better say a *spiral* – relationship teleologically oriented towards the organism's survival. Biologically speaking, this spiral process means that that while the genome constrains higher processes and forms, these may interact with the genome to pursue specific goals.

We need to see that the success of a gene lies in its involvement in the expression of high-level function. This, after all, is what enables a given organism to be favoured in the selection process. The logic for explaining the success of a gene therefore does not lie in its DNA code; it lies in how that code is interpreted and in how the results of that interpretation fit into the overall successful logic of life. Fundamental questions like "What is a gene?" need to be re-addressed. The answer is not so obvious when we have to take account of modular coding regions that form parts of many genes, of genes that code for many different proteins, and of genes that completely change their function as one species evolves from others. This raises the question whether a gene should be defined by its coding or by its function.

[Nature] has serendipitously explored possible functional combinations. Only a very tiny fraction of these actually make sense at a higher level. And it was at this higher level that success or failure was determined. Looked at from the systems-level perspective I am advocating, genes and proteins are rather like the building blocks of a child's toy such as Lego. They are elements that can be arranged in many different ways, with the same elements playing different roles depending on how they are arranged to interact with other elements. That is why I lay stress on gene expression patterns. The same genes expressed in a different pattern can produce a quite different physiological function.

(Noble, 2008, p. 16)

If the barycenter moves from genes' coding to genes' expression, then the genome needs to be read through the phenotype, not the other way round. Hence, the DNA code has a functional meaning only within its environment (within an organism, which is within an outer environment); it has no sense unless it is interpreted functionally,

first by the cell/protein machinery that initiates and controls transcription and post-transcriptional modifications, and then by the systems-level interaction between proteins that generate higher-level function. A gene can do nothing without this interpretation by the system.

(Noble, 2008, p. 21)

This perspective enshrines a precious new vision of biological life, for which evolution is not pushed by its causes from the "lower" level of genes but is pulled by the embedded teleology of higher systems – like cells, or the whole organism, all the way up to the outer environment in which the organism lives – which *uses* the random coded mutations for their survival.

Jung's idea that an accumulation of ancestral experiences interacted with the archetypal domain has often been mocked as a naïve Lamarkian theory *against* the Darwinian theory of a random natural selection, although Darwin himself, together with Romanes, devoted his last ten years to prove precisely such a "pseudo-Lamarkian" teleological top-down causation (from the phenotype to its genome), which may explain sudden mutations, grafting and new breedings or, during embryogenesis, the preservation of the same morphology through new, unexpected pathways of cellular reproduction. Once, this was Darwin's theory of the passing of "gemmules" from the organism – its cells – down to what later would have been discovered is the genome. To emphasize its importance, Darwin even called this theory his "beloved child" (Ross, 2004). Today, there has been an impressive accumulation of evidence of the existence of such top-down teleological interactions, in which RNA, pieces of DNA, large chunks of proteins, etc., pass from the organisms to the DNA to pursue a certain goal (for example: Deisseroth et al., 2003).

The implications of such a perspective are huge, as they dethrone the neo-Darwinian theories (Julian Huxley's "Modern Synthesis", 1942), for which evolution is only wholly caused by a random bottom-up process and introduce already at the molecular biological level a co-evolutionary principle for which the DNA's environment (i.e., the organism itself and its own environment) *teleologically* interacts top-down, in a fashion similar to Lamark's (Colvis et al., 2005; Jablonka & Lamb, 2005). A groundbreaking example of such a situation is the cellular regeneration of the kidneys' tubular epithelium. If during the embryogenesis (of a salamander) one modifies the cellular sizes of the layers that form such epithelium, the number of the cells also modifies so to retain its morphology. Even when just one single giant cell is left, it will fold itself to secure the same tubular morphology. This is a striking evidence that there is a developmental inherent plan that teleologically guides top-down what has been encoded in the DNA in ways that are *not* encoded in the genome (for a general discussion: Levin, 2021).

This implies the following important considerations:

1) *Jung's archetypes do not correspond to the biological genome but, as co-evolutionary functions-in-between, are at a functional higher degree of abstraction, as they regulate the spiral interaction between the genome and its environments.*

2) *It is much more efficient to intervene top-down at the highest possible level of organization than at the lowest one, as it is the higher level that informs and organizes the lower one. If this is valid for biology, it is even more valid for psychology, where the non-reductive top-down action at the highest possible level, that of* meaning – *the level that I will discuss in the second volume – may be the most efficient one, as it would inherently involve all the other lower levels, out of which it has emerged.*

Hence, it is a complexity of factors at many levels that contributes to the development of life. The organism (starting with the cell's cytoplasm), acting as the environment in which the DNA is placed, causally interacts top-down with the genome, while the genome phylogenetically *stabilizes* (not *determines*) the organism's features. In this regard, the groundbreaking research carried out by Michael Levin on the planarian are extraordinarily interesting (Levin et al., 2019). Thus, the genes are not conditions, or causes, but *followers*, whose role is to ensure stability at a genetic level for those interactions that are expressed by the organism's development and that do not derive from them (Callebaut et al., 2007). Therefore, in each animal, it is its specific structural plan that guarantees the possibility of perfect *adequacy* between organs, receptors and perceptual signs on the one hand and effector organs and operational signs on the other. In fact, Von Uexküll argues against a certain Darwinist reductionism since we should now speak of the organism's evolutionary *adequacy*, and not anymore of "*adaptation*", for, if one were to accept the idea that the organisms must progressively "adapt" to their environment, one would conceive of them as fundamentally inadequate to it, at least at an early stage, and compare them with an abstract idealized idea of adaptation.

The spiral relationship between the organism and its environment described by this functional circuit follows a principle well described by Rasskin-Gutman (2005, p. 330): "Produce the parts, reproduce them, modify them". As I said, it seems that this circuit has a dispositional barycenter in the organism's structural plan, hence, in its subjective experience.

Indeed, is it true that the environment selectively acts on the organisms in the way described by the standard evolutionary theory, but it is also true that *the environments change and co-evolve along with the organisms*. This gives rise to the fundamental concept of "ecological inheritance" (Odling-Smee et al., 2003), which is one of the most significant outcomes of the niche construction theories.

For psychology, von Uexküll's subjective biology represents a radical turn from a machine-like, wholly reductively physicalist *behavioristic* view of living organisms. It paves the way for a paradigm in which biology and psychology converge on the common ground of the organism's subjective *internal, dispositional states*, together with their co-evolutionary entanglement with the environment, the *Umwelt* (for the emergence of subjectivity on a neurobiological perspective, see: Alcaro et al., 2017).

> According to the behaviorists, man's own sensations and will are mere appearance, to be considered, if at all, only as disturbing static. But we who still hold that our sense organs serve our perceptions, and our motor organs our actions, see in animals as well not only the mechanical structure, but also the operator, who is built into their organs, as we are into our bodies. We no longer regard animals as mere machines, but as subjects whose essential activity consists of perceiving and acting. We thus unlock the gates that lead to other realms, for all that a subject perceives become his perceptual world, and all that he does, his effector world. Perceptual and effector worlds together form a closed unit, the Umwelt.
>
> (Von Uexküll, 1934, p. 6)

From an "externalist" perspective, wholly focused on the pressure of natural selection and the adaptive response of the organisms to a conception that may be called "internalist", it is possible to theorize the reciprocity in co-evolution of the organisms and their environments, along with their effectual subjective experience. Along this line is the theory of the construction of the ecological "niche"

(Odling-Smee et al., 2003; Laland et al., 2000), conceivable first and foremost as a mode of action peculiar to all living organisms – humans included.

I wish to underscore the fact that the concept of the *Umwelt* has to do with the same issue of Jung's psychization. Starting from Ernst Heinrich Weber and Gustav The-odor Fechner's initial psychophysics to von Weitzsächer's pivotal contemporary contributions, this issue, which has to do with the transformation from a *perception* (what happens, objectively, out there) into a *sensation* (what happens, subjectively, to me), is one of the central themes of biology *and* psychology (see vol. II, § 4).[1] Such a transformation from a perception into a sensation means nothing less than the advent of the possibility for a *subjective experience* (sensation), which evolu-tionarily paves the way for an "unconscious consciousness" and, eventually, for self-reflective consciousness.

I will get back to the issues of unconsciously conscious processes and the role of the movement shortly. Now I would like to point out that, *while these biologists (like von Uexküll) posed the issue of psychization focusing on the sensory-motor apparatus because they were mostly focusing on the extroverted process of the perception of outer affectively salient objects (especially objects of touch), Jung's dispositional introverted perspective put at the center the inner images (images that cannot be touched) that present themselves to the mind not because they "exist out there" but because they are affectively salient*. The primary motivational factor that makes a particular stimulus salient for an organism is the affect. Therefore, to these two elements – the sensory apparatus and the organism's agency, identified by Weitzsächer – we must add the affect, which is not only inseparable but is also what triggers the whole living process.

As I said, the notion of the *Umwelt*, together with its accompanying concepts – like co-evolution, or ecological niche – is a pivotal concept. I will indicate just a few of the relevant implications of these concepts:

• The fact that a specific stimulus activates a receptor implies that, for the organ-ism, this stimulus is affectively salient. Hence, affects are at the base of the existence of any organism's subjective *Umwelt*, and of subjectivity itself.
• The *Umwelt* presupposes a dispositional interpretation of life and its organization in those discrete entities that we call organisms. This is quite coherent with Jung's notion of the organismic nature of the complex and, most of all, of the Self.
• As in Jung, the *Umwelt* is based on the *dispositional nature of the living organ-isms*. At the same time, these discrete dynamic entities are in a mutual rela-tion with their environment so that the perception from the environment and the motor action towards it are two sides of the same coin. This fits quite well with Jung's paradigm, for which any differentiation represents the emergence of a "twoness" (hence, also that between world and organism) derived from an intrinsic fundamental unity – the original "oneness".
• These concepts directly apply to the human predicament. They are very clear in specific situations, such as the relationship mother-child, which seems to per-fectly fit into the description of the ecological niche.

- Last, but not least, the analytical situation as Jung conceived it also follows the same structure as the non-human *Umwelt* and may be interpreted as an ecological niche.

Throughout the developmental, affect-laden process by which the *Umwelt* becomes more mentalized and abstract and the dispositional sensory-motor nature of its constraints changes, the original *Umwelt* is transformed into an inner-outer environment made also by specifically human primary, secondary and tertiary emotions, representations and specifically human cognitive inferential systems. The images that emerge at this level will not be perceptual anymore but imaginative.

Taking into consideration the fundamental notion for which the *Umwelt*, like the psyche, has a dispositional nature, what happens is that from the beginning of ontogenetic life, the psyche, functionally integrated into the world, actively *imagines its own perceptions* so that, as von Üexkull writes, the specific signs of its sensory organs are projected outside, and when looking at the sky, the blue sign that the organ dispositionally produces becomes a cue for the "blueness" of the sky "out there". As development proceeds, this archetypal apparatus for imagination (von Uexküll's *Bauplan*, or the Jungian Self) expands its horizons towards the creative apprehension of other aspects of its own *Umwelt* made of more universalized, spiritual contents.

In his anthropological masterpiece, discussing the four ontologies that organize human cultures – totemism, animism, analogism and naturalism – Philippe Descola makes an explicit reference to von Uexküll's subjective biology, thus building a direct bridge between ethological biology and social anthropology.

> Let us generalize a little more. At first sight, animism seems to result in a relativistic approach to knowledge, not so much because of the origin of the viewpoint expressed on it – it is always that of humans that prevails, since it is they who speak for non-humans – but because of the conditions that make it possible: to each type of physicality corresponds a type of perception and action, hence of *Umwelt*, hence of relationship with things that are not definable by means of absolute properties and, rather, by means of perceptions and uses that vary according to the types of subjects that have to do with them, and the possibilities they offer for their own objectification by these subjects.
>
> (Descola, 2021, pp. 324–325)

Von Uexküll's "structural plan" seems to be homologous[2] to those sets of constraints that from the collective unconscious make the emergence of a specific Ego possible. To this process, the specific fundamental developmental characteristic of us humans – that of developing a meta-noetic consciousness – expands the perceptive-motor human *Umwelt* into a representational and symbolic one. In this perspective, the miraculous quality of science (and eventually mathematics) makes it possible to gain a (theoretical, not perceptual) access to other alien *Umwelten* – the world of other animals – and to alternative ways to grasp the nature of the world through different hypothetical perspectives.

I wrote that in the lower animals' kingdom, the motivational impulses are emotionally triggered by inner and outer perceptions – the "innate release stimuli", which the animal "interprets" and towards which it performs a certain behavioral response (an "elicited motor pattern"). The examples of instinctive behavior in the non-human biological world would be innumerable, and there is no need to dwell on them. Now, however, if the environment is for the animal a natural place, for the individual, it becomes a *world* – a cultural milieu. Here, the motivation inherent in the individual soul, the individual's *subjective* experience, must also include the world in which we humans are involved. From a strictly bottom-up perspective, this issue has to do with what genes are and what they actually do – whether they really can determine how a phenotype is going to be in relation to its genotype, or whether, as is probable, they *stabilize* what empirically occurs during ontogenesis. Our bottom-up perspective is important to decide whether, how and how much Jung's idea of the archetype is acceptable or not.

Richard Lewontin, in discussing the biological metaphor of development as an unfolding program completely predetermined by the organisms' genes, writes:

> The trouble with the general scheme of explanation contained in the metaphor of development is that it is bad biology, if we had to complete the DNA sequence of an organism and had unlimited computational power, we could not compute the organism, because the organism does not compute itself from its genes. . . . Of course, it is true that lions look different from lambs and chimps from humans because they have different genes, and a satisfactory explanation for the differences between lions, lambs, chimps, and us needs to involve other causal factors. But if we want to know why two lambs are different from one another, and a description of their genetic differences is insufficient and for some of their characteristics may even be irrelevant. Even a very faulty computer will be satisfactory if one of these is only interested in calculations to an order of magnitude, but for accuracy to one decimal place a different machine is needed. There exists, and has existed for a long time, a large body of evidence that demonstrates that the ontogeny of an organism is this consequence of a unique interaction between the genes it carries, the temporal sequence of external environments through which it passes during its life, and random events of molecular interactions within individual cells. It is these interactions that must be incorporated into any proper account of how an organism is formed.
>
> (Lewontin, 2000, pp. 11–12)

My opinion is that the unspecific form of environmental plasticity and the rigid genetic predetermination are both abstractions. Looking from a complementary perspective, both the specific, "unique" individual and the environment are at the same time inherited (predetermined by, or better said, *through* evolutionary laws) and yet also unique and specific. Therefore, I think it might be fruitful to imagine the function of archetypes as if they are *something-in-between* the individual organism and its environment.

The famous sentence by Winnicott:

There is no such thing as a baby. . . . A baby cannot exist alone but is essentially part of a relationship.

(Winnicott, 1960, p. 88)

Is not only valid for just a baby[3] but it is also so for *any* organism since every organism is encompassed by and encompasses (through interiorization) its environment. Therefore, from now on, we should keep in mind that the individual organism, its body, brain and psychology I referred to until now must be seen where they belong: within its/his/her environment. To do so, it is necessary to explain the principle of co-evolution.[4]

The co-evolutionary perspective that I am now dealing with corrects two ideas. First, that the struggle for life and its unfolding are based on competition. Darwin's theory has been unilaterally bent towards the notion of competition and applied to what is known as "social Darwinism", not on a biological basis but on ideological ones aimed at rationalizing human violence. Nevertheless, Darwin himself always resisted such cultural interpretation of his biological theory, i.e., the direct application of the survival of the fittest to social life. An example may be read in his letters (Darwin, 1982).[5]

Darwin spent his last years studying how the variation found among orchid species could have resulted from interactions with pollinators, providing us with the first model of a co-evolutionary process. Therefore, it is from Darwin himself that the concepts of commensalism, amensalism, symbiosis and co-evolution developed.[6] For the purposes of our discussion, this point is important since it connects with the birth of the human's psychological capacity for fairness and cooperation that I will discuss in vol. I, § 10.1.

The second idea that co-evolution corrects is the opposition between disposition and situation, or between what is biological and what is socio-cultural. If we do not split the levels of analysis and reality and accept that humans are animals, the environment may be seen just as much as the product of evolution as are the genes themselves.

This point might provide an answer to Merchant's criticism of Goodwin's position about the interaction between genetic/innate factors and the environment, as if the two could be ever completely distinguished. The issue is, therefore, on pre-formationism and the idea of the autochthonous revival of archetypes. According to Merchant:

However, such a gene-environment coaction aspect of genetic research gains minimal attention in Goodwyn's (2020) paper, no doubt because his focus is more on the genetic background rather than any environmental foreground.

(Merchant 2021, p. 134)

Here, Merchant refers to those bio-psychological constraints that will, from the bottom-up, pave the way for a further process of metaphorization throughout learning and experience. He is right in being suspicious if we admit the possibility that anything as complex as a full-grown archetype – let's say the Trinity – could emerge with its whole complexity already unfolded out of the genome. Yet my feeling is that Merchant is still looking at the innate/learned components as mutually excluding one another and considers the environment (or for us humans, the symbolic, social and cultural world) as radically split and autonomous from any factors. Later, I will discuss this issue within the field of cognitive anthropology and evolutionary psychology. For the moment, let me quote Roesler:

> Goodwyn then provides a list of examples: Cold = social isolation, Heat/ fire = intense emotion, Light and dark = states of knowledge and safety, The Centre = the "important" part, Water = the hostile unknown or the mysterious, Size/Up = power, Symmetry = conceptual harmony, round shape = wholeness.
> Critique of Goodwyn's position.
> I have already pointed out above that such associations as Goodwyn provides as examples for archetypal elements can come about reliably through experience in the life of humans, and there is no need to assume any biologically preformed pattern of association. Goodwyn argues that similar mental structures are the result of self-directed learning, but he oversees the possibility that these similarities come about through experiences with comparable conditions in the world outside. It is not necessary to have a pre-formed category of above and below, because there is no way of getting around the experience of gravity. It is also not necessary to have a pre-formed pattern for a circle, as there are perfect circles in nature, e.g., the sun, the moon etc. and, as I have pointed out above, the circle is in itself a perfect shape, so it is no wonder that it was associated with perfection and completeness in different cultures.
>
> (Roesler, 2022, p. 106)

First, Roesler's claim of the absence of bottom-up constraints and top-down attractors and that the idea that archetypal elements (i.e., emotionally charged constrained representations) may arise through experience is unfounded and incorrect. This presupposes the existence of a general, non-specific form of intelligence and the absence of modular diversity.

Secondly, Roesler seems to mistake the mere sensory data which contribute to the formation of an image, with the same image (for instance, the sun) that is triggered and organized by the underpinning dispositional affect. Yet the idea, advanced by Swadesh (Swadesh, M., 1955) that human concepts are determined by universal conditions derived from the feature of the human environment is untenable. The issue is not that we have all seen perfectly round objects by perception; it is that such an image may be dispositionally acquired and interpreted by the mind to shape and represent a specific affect and, hence, that is transformed from a perception into a sensation/meaning. Language does not reflect the world directly; it reflects human conceptualizations derived from the human interpretation of the world. On example of such a radically dispositional-interpretive nature of our way of functioning is given by Anna Wierzbicka:

> For example, the Eastern Aztecs in Central America don't have a special word for the side of the body – they only distinguish between the thorax and the abdomen – so that when a bible translator wants to say the Jesus was pierced in the side, he must decide whether he was pierced in the side below the ribs or between the ribs, because there is not general word for "side".
>
> What holds for body parts holds also for the features of our physical environment. For example, not all languages have a general word for wind. They may distinguish several kinds of wind, such as "zephyrs", "tornadoes", "hot winds of the desert", and "freezing winds", without having a general word for "wind".
>
> (Wierzbicka, 1992, pp. 7–8)

Thirdly, Roesler does not consider that also the physical environment and, as we will see, also the *cultural* environment are in direct or indirect ways (like in the case of the cultural world) products of evolution.

This quote may help to explain this idea:

> To understand why this is so, one needs to distinguish "the environment" in the sense of the real total state of the entire universe – *which, of course, is not caused by the genes or the developmental mechanisms of any individual* – from "the environment" in the sense of those particular aspects of the world that are rendered developmentally mentally relevant by the evolved design of an organism's developmental adaptations. It is this developmentally relevant environment – the environment as interacted with by the organism – that, in a meaningful sense, can be said to be the product of evolution, evolving in tandem with the organism's organized response to it. The confusion of these two quite distinct senses of "environment" has obscured the fact that the recurrent organization of the environment contributes a biological inheritance parallel to that of the genes, which acts co-equally with them to evolutionarily.
>
> (Barkow et al., 1992, p. 84)

In the classical interpretation of Darwin's theory, variation among organisms results from an internal process – what is now known as gene mutation and recombination – not responsive to the demands on the environment. The variants that are produced are then tested for acceptability in an environment which has come into being independent of that variation.

In describing the classic paradigm of Darwin's evolutionary theory, Lewontin argues:

> Many metaphors have been invoked for this relation between independent environment and organism. The Organism proposes and the environment disposes.

> The Organism makes conjectures and the environment refutes them. In the most popular current form in the technical literature of evolutionary studies, the environment poses problems and the organism throws up random solutions. In such a conceptual structure the metaphor of adaptation is indeed appropriate. Adaptation is literally the process of fitting an object to a pre-existing demand.
>
> (Lewontin, 2000, p. 43)

Yet the situation of contemporary biology is not exactly that of Darwin's times, and there is a correction to be made to the "standard" evolutionary theory. In the following lines, Lewontin introduces the first and the most general principle of this correction:

> Just as there can be no organism without an environment, so there can be no environment without an Organism. There is a confusion between the correct assertion that there is a physical world outside of an Organism that would continue to exist in the absence of the species, and the incorrect claim that environments exist without species.
>
> (Lewontin, 2000, p. 48)

As von Uexküll also argues (2013), the organism chooses within the general environment the stimuli that are specific to it and turns its relations to certain characters of the things around it, understanding them in a web that leads to its own existence. Jung seems to share the same paradigm when he defines the fundamental elements upon which the psyche is built – the complex. I will quote now, for the second time, Jung's definition:

> In my studies of the phenomena of association I have shown that there are certain constellations of psychic elements grouped around feeling-toned contents, which I have called "complexes". The feeling-toned content, the complex, consists of a nuclear element and a large number of secondarily constellated associations. The nuclear element consists of two components: *first, a factor determined by experience and causally related to the environment; second, a factor innate in the individual's character and determined by his disposition.*
>
> (Jung, 1928, §18, my italics)

Clearly, Jung's description of the structural synergy of organism and environment is an "introverted" one, as it describes the "inner" scene of the same paradigmatic co-evolutionary situation.

What I am describing is a clearly systemic paradigm, in which all parts are interconnected in a developmental pattern similar to a helix (although mentioning "parts" may lead us to a substantialist perspective. In reality, such parts are also actually stabilized emergent processes in time) and in which the *active agent is the living organism.*

Within this systemic frame of reference:

1) The organism determines which parts of the environment will be put together to make its own specific environment.
2) The organisms actively *constructs* their own world, their environment.
3) This represents a constant, active process of alteration of the world to sustain the living process. The easiest example of this is that every living organism consumes and produces.
4) The organism can constantly modulate and regulate the statistical properties of its environment throughout time. This property shows the beautiful, deeply meaningful inherent intelligence of life.
5) Each organism selects and interprets in peculiar ways the physical signals that it perceives. It is the organism's setup that determines the existence of a specific world and not another. This property means that not only we humans but that all biological life also has a dispositional nature and that each species on the planet inhabits a partly or wholly different world (Lewontin, 2000; Lewontin et al., 2017; Yong, 2022).

Therefore, if we transpose the co-evolutionary perspective to a human psychological environment, we may say that it is the child herself that maintains, molds and modifies her caregivers. It is much truer that it is the son and the daughter that make the parent and not the other way around. This is an easy example that shows that any human co-evolutionary niche is, at the high levels of the helix I have been referring to, also a *social* one and that, therefore, we are not just dealing with a biological description, but we are referring to what Laland et al. (2000) calls an "eco-cognitive perspective", while I would refer to an eco-*emotional*-cognitive perspective, or "eco-*psychic* perspective", because, as the reader may guess, the word "cognitive" is a reduction of the more pervasive "psychic" that I would use since, at the bottom, the cognitive aspect of such complex niches is, firstly, affective.

From what I wrote so far, it should be clear that the general biological principle of co-evolution, valid from the beginning of cellular life all the way up to human psychology, indicates that the organism's *agency* within a proximal environment (like the caregiver for the child) does not have to just *adapt* to the environment and is not a passive-reactive nature but has a dispositional, teleological nature.

Within such a systemic paradigm, it could be more fruitful and correct to think of archetypes (or something like archetypes) not as something in the organism's mind, or body-mind, but as helix-shaped functions of the relationship between not only the organism and its environment but, due to their transgressive nature, also between all the parts of such a system at every level of complexity.

According to Catherine Lutz (1988), the Ifaluk of Melanesia do not think of emotions as something that happens within an individual subject but as a relationship between different people, in which emotions exist independently and outside the personal psyche. This seems to me a beautiful way to imagine both emotions and archetypes – as species-specific, relational, creative, dynamic functions based on affects. This process acquires an indefinite number of different ways of social expression, function and organization. This definition could work just as well if related to cultural complexes.

For Thomas Singer:

1) A cultural complex expresses itself in powerful moods and repetitive behaviors – both in a group as a whole and in its individual members. Highly charged emotional or affective reactivity is the calling card of a cultural complex.
2) A cultural complex resists our most heroic efforts at consciousness and remains, for the most part, unconscious.
3) A cultural complex accumulates experiences that validate its point of view and creates a store house of self-affirming ancestral memories.
4) Cultural complexes function in an involuntary, autonomous fashion and tend to affirm a simplistic point of view that replaces more everyday ambiguity and uncertainty with fixed, often self-righteous, attitudes to the world. The thinking of cultural complexes is black and white, admitting of little subtlety or any gray areas.
5) Cultural complexes have archetypal cores – that is, they express typically human attitudes and are rooted in primordial ideas about what is meaningful, making them very hard to resist, reflect upon and discriminate.
6) Not all are pathological but in fact add in a positive way to a group's identity.

On the other hand, the peculiar relational feature of the notion of the archetype that I am introducing entails that it would have at least three characteristics:

1) A tendency to be deeply stable.
2) A function that defines those parts that are bound by it as a common category. In our case, what makes all human individuals really human would be this kind of transpersonal archetype.
3) A feature for which a change in the specific relational property of such an archetype would cause a second-order, non-linear transformation. Such second-order transformations have four characteristics. They are:

   a) Discontinuous (all-or-nothing, they are non-linear leaps).
   b) Unpredictable (as to when they will occur).
   c) Irreversible.
   d) Creative (it cannot be predicted what the transformation will produce).

I would like the reader to keep in mind this hypothesis of such a "relational" archetype, as it would be the "co" prefix of "co-evolutionary".

One of the greatest achievements we owe to structural anthropology as well as to the pioneering work of Gregory Bateson, found even in those who pretend to ignore its origin, is the awareness of the interest of considering social life from the point of view of the relationships that make up its fabric, but a choice that implies recognising a greater stability and structural regularity to what it connects than to the contingent actions of the connected elements. Whatever the sphere organised by these relationships – kinship, economic exchange, ritual activity or the ordering of the cosmos – their possibilities of variation are, by logical necessity, much more limited than those of the infinitely diverse entities they connect. Thus emerges the possibility of a reasoned systematisation of the diversity of relations between existents, the aim of which would consist, firstly, in establishing a typology of possible relations with the world and wih others, human and non-human, and, secondly, in examining their compatibility and incompatibility.

(Descola, 2021, p. 110, my transl.)

Following Lévi-Strauss, anthropological structuralism in general, but also the same sources of research on ontogenetic developmental processes, Descola (2021) expresses himself in a manner compatible with Jung's view. Relating to the role of structural relations, bound to a restricted number of combinations possible with all the in(de)finite production of particular cultural forms, they write:

Every child bears at birth, in the form of sketched mental structures, the entirety of the means humanity has had from eternity to define its relations with the world and with others. But these structures are exclusive. Each of them can only integrate certain elements, of all those that are on offer. Each type of social organisation thus represents a comma choice that the group imposes and perpetuates.

(Lévi-Strauss, 1949, p. 108. My transl.)

Provided, however, that it is made clear that these "means that mankind has had since eternity" are not merely reduced to innate mental structures, but constitute above all of a small number of internalised practical schemes that synthesise the objective properties of every possible relationship with humans and non-humans.

(Descola, 2021, p. 112, my transl.)

Now, going back to the co-evolutionary scene, in psychological terms, we may refer to the way Winnicott describes it when he writes that the "True self acts, while the False self reacts" (Winnicott, 1965, pp. 37–55) since it is the infant's True self that, through the guidance of affectivity, selects and transforms its own environment (the mother's responses) while the mother holds the infant's ways of doing so in viable, adaptive ways. Here, Winnicott seems to essentially agree with Jung's view of the Self.

Therefore, already from the beginning of ontogenetic life, at the start of cognition, the protagonists are the two distinct domains of the perceptual-motor and the affective systems, in which the affective system gives value and meaning to the perceived experiences and builds a specific *Umwelt*. This is why we should refer to the field within which cognition and emotions develop as a "co-evolutionary field". For us humans, this is *an intersubjective and social field*,[7] which expresses top-down attractors, social constraints and, as we will see, "susceptibilities" (Vol. II, § 5.1).

Taking into consideration, through a misunderstood idea of individuation, only the subjective and, therefore, solipsistic aspect of subjectivity, Jung's thought is often interpreted as one that excludes the object, the interpersonal experience and the political or the social domains. Already starting from Jung's motivational theory, this is a serious mistake since psychic energy itself is generated by the tension between opposing polarities, among which there is the polarity between the so-called internal/subjective and the so-called external/objectual worlds. Jung's human motivational teleology – a product of the tension of opposites rooted into affects – includes the group and the cultural world.

This quote should suffice to emphasize Jung's far-sighted view of psychiatry, 60 years before the birth of social psychiatry (Basaglia, 1968; Ruesch et al., 1957), when he was still working at the Burghölzli, at the time still a Foucaultian "total institution" (Goffman, 1961; Foucault, 2006). Following Bleuler's footstep in the dismantling of the nosology of *dementia praecox* into that of *schizophrenia*, Jung wrote:

> As regards the apparently destructive and degenerative traits of dementia praecox, I must call special attention to the fact that the worst catatonic states and the most complete dementias are in many cases products of the lunatic asylum, brought on by the psychological influence of the milieu, and by no means always by a destructive process independent of external conditions. It is a well-known fact that the very worst demented catatonics are to be encountered in badly administered and overcrowded asylums. It is well known also that removal to noisy or otherwise unfavorable wards often has an unwholesome influence; the same applies to coercive measures or forced inactivity. All the conditions which would reduce a normal person to a state of psychic misery will have an equally baleful effect on a patient.
>
> (Jung, 1919, §472–473)

The importance of the environmental conditions is so much valued by Jung that he interprets a patient's catatonia as "a pathologically exaggerated emotion, brought on by being confined in a lunatic asylum" (Jung, 1919, §475).

I wanted to quote these lines because they express three important aspects of Jung's theory that are relevant for my discussion:

1) The cultural and social environment is crucial for the development and interpretation of psychopathology: "To be crazy is a social concept". Obviously, this sheds a light on the positive side of the Persona.
2) The only criteria to define "madness" is when the person is not able to make himself understood.
3) There are "Negro psyches", i.e., the psyche is differentiated by the belonging to a biological (pseudo)categorization.

If the first two points are real jewels within Jung's psychology, the third is a very problematic one, to say the least. It is an idea that I strongly disagree with, for which I do not have much hesitation to denounce Jung's racist cultural positivism, together with his idea of the underdeveloped "non-European psychologies".[8]

> If you are all alienists and I present to you a certain case, then you might say that the man is insane. I would say that that man is not insane for this reason, that as long as he can explain himself to me in such a way that I feel I have a contact with him, that man is not crazy. To be crazy is a very relative conception. For instance, when a Negro behaves in a certain way, we say, "Oh well, he's only a Negro", but if a white man behaves in the same way we say, "That man is crazy", because the white man cannot behave like that. A Negro is expected to do such things, but the white man does not do them. To be crazy is a social concept; We use social restrictions and definitions in order to distinguish mental disturbances. You can say that the man is peculiar, that he behaves in an unexpected way and has funny ideas, And if he happens to live in a little town in France or Switzerland, you would say, "He is an original fellow, one of the most original inhabitants of that little place"; but if you bring that man into the midst of Harley Street, well, he is plumb crazy.
>
> (Jung, 1935, §72)

7.1   De-specialization vs. Specialization?

The issue of the possibility that some images have a universal character, i.e., that they are a product not of the individual ontogenetic development but of the phylogenetic evolution of the species directly involves the more general discussion on archetypes.

The obvious anthropological diversity between human cultures and the psychological diversity between individuals is undeniable. This is normally attributed to the biological principle of humans' "neotenic" nature. Therefore, the real question is whether such individual and cultural differential modes of existence (the variations of a theme) wholly exclude or, on the contrary, may coexist *together with* the existence of archaic modes through which fixed structural patterns emerge (the theme of the variations).

The possibility that constrained patterns (in Jung's collective unconscious) may coexist with metaphorized symbolic expressions (in Jung's consciousness) is coherent with contemporary research. The issue of the possibility that some images have a universal character (i.e., that they are a product not of the ontogenetic development of the individual but of the phylogenetic evolution of the species) directly involves the more general discussion on archetypes and on the ancestral triggers that constellate their patterned nature – the affects. As a matter of fact, the debate between the phylogenetically inherited, domain-specific modularity (archetypes) vs. the individual non-specific networks constructed and learned through experience seems to overlap with what ethologists call *precocial vs. altricial species* – i.e., "specialized" and "de-specialized species".[9]

Precocial species are more rigidly modular, while altricial ones are more open to learning thanks to a non-specific, general device to create hypercomplex, plastic neural networks while the organism interacts with the environment, i.e., something like a general, unconstrained intelligence factor.

While I have no doubts that the human species shows a marked neotenic, plastic, de-specialized nature, it is quite noticeable that, as it often happens, Jung's answer to this question whether humans are de-specialized or not is neither a "yes" nor a "no". According to Jung:

Although the existence of an instinctual pattern in human biology is probable, it seems very difficult to prove the existence of distinct types empirically. For the organ with which we might apprehend them – consciousness – is not only itself a transformation of the original image but also its transformer. It is therefore not surprising that the human mind finds it impossible to specify precise types for man similar to those we know in the animal kingdom.

(Jung, 1947/1954, §399)

In simple words, what Jung is saying is that while consciousness is de-specialized (altricial) the collective unconscious is specialized (precocial). Were this theory right, it would mean that *within the same species*, in this case, *Homo sapiens*, the two opposite versions of the psychological debate (evolutionary psychology and cognitive psychology) could find a common ground.[10]

In more general terms, the debate on the relationship between "nature" and "nurture", which involves the biologic relationship between the genome and the epigenetic – phenotypic – effects (all the way up to the symbolic and social sphere of learning, creative adaptation, relational structures, esthetics and ethics), would find an integration.

It seems that, in principle, Jung was right. In fact, in a 2002 article (Weir et al., 2002), the ethologist Jackie Chappell described a New Caledonian crow who repeatedly made hooks from straight pieces of wire and used them to extract a bucket of food from a vertical glass tube. In ten trials, this crow, which the researchers named Betty, had made usable hooks in at least four significantly different ways, suggesting that something more was going on than merely acquiring food.

The presence of such intelligent, flexible (obviously non-declarative) learning has been found in several other species so that the ethologist Aaron Sloman and Jackie Chappell (Chappell, Sloman, 2007a,b; Sloman Chappell, 2005, 2007) later suggested that the basic distinction is not between precocial and altricial species but between precocious and altricial *competences* (2007).

For Giorgio Vallortigara, one of the leading Italian neuro-ethologists, one strong evidence of the possibility that constraining, precocial structures may be associated with altricial learning and discriminating processes is evident already from the ethology of chicks (Vallortigara & Andrew, 1991, 1994; Vallortigara, 2021):

When evaluating a novel stimulus, an organism . . . on the basis of previous experience it must estimate the degree of novelty of the stimulus and, in order to do so, it must recall stored memories then process them for future use. Secondly, it must use certain properties of the stimulus, despite variations in many other properties, to try to assign it to a category, and then decide what type of rapid response, if any, should be provided.

. . . In order to classify events or stimuli, the organism must recognise and memorise those features of an experience that recur as invariants in different episodes or stimuli [a precocial competence, SC], ignoring or discarding unique or peculiar variable features that do not recur and are therefore not essential for learning. This allows the organism to regularly and possibly automatically enact skilled motor behaviour in response to certain invariant features of episodes or stimuli. Conversely, in order to detect novelty and construct a detailed record of episodic experiences, the organism must pay attention to contextual aspects that uniquely mark individual experiences, i.e. it must recognise variations between episodes rather than invariance [an altricial competence].

(Vallortigara, 2021, pp. 39–40)

Vallortigara then proceeds to explain:

The construction and transfer of memories in the hours following imprinting is an example of this need to separate functionally incompatible types of analysis. Immediately after exposure, in the *Intermediate Medial Medipallium*, a description of the object of imprinting is formed in the left hemisphere as a general category of social partner (based on the invariant properties of stimuli). This allows for quick responses based on all-or-nothing categorisation /"Is it a social partner or is it food?"). Discrimination within the category is instead made possible by making use of variable properties of the stimuli, i.e., by detecting those unique and characteristic aspects that make a particular chick different from any other ("Is it the same chick I was exposed to before or is it a new one?"), thus enabling individual recognition through the use of right-hemisphere neural structures.

(*ivi*)

The recognition of general perceptual categories through constrained elaboration processes is at the base of the emergence of what we call "ontological categories" (Vol. I, §9) and seem to be the structure of the archetypal functioning of the psyche, which can learn precisely *because* it is endowed with innate general ordering categories.

Sloman (2021) compares Betty's behavior with the process of representational redescription described by Annette Karmiloff-Smith, as both seem to be problem-solving tasks. Could Betty desire to explore alternative solutions to an already solved problem? Certainly, in both the learning process in children and in Betty's, a fairly deep knowledge of alternative possible spatial arrangements and rearrangements of objects was used. But there are still many unanswered questions. How do brains represent sets of possible alternatives? How do they identify some combinations as impossible? Recognizing and eliminating impossibilities from a search for solutions is an important aspect of intelligence, as it saves enormous amounts of wasted effort, which would otherwise produce what is known as "combinatorial explosion".

> with each new degree of freedom added to a system, or with each new dimension of potential variation added, or with each new successive choice in a chain of decisions, the total number of alternative possibilities faced by a computational system grows with devastating rapidity. For example, if you are limited to emitting only one out of 100 alternative behaviors every successive minute (surely a gross underestimate: raise arm, close hand, toss book, extend foot, say "Havel", etc.), after the second minute you have 10,000 different behavioral sequences from which to choose, a million by the third minute, a trillion by six minutes, and 10^{11} possible alternative sequences after only one hour-a truly unimaginable number.
>
> (Barkow et al., 1992, p. 102)

For Chappell and Sloman's theory, humans also have both altricial and precocial competences. The first refers to the helpless and immature nature of infants and children, the second to important precocial competences, including the ability to obtain nourishment by sucking and swallowing, which requires complex coordination of a collection of muscles. The very concept of *Umwelt* presupposes the interaction of precocial and altricial competences.

A second implication of Jung's idea is that in a brain that is at the same time precocial and altricial, *the more we become conscious of something unconscious, the less it is possible to appreciate and reveal its modular origins, precisely because we are learning from it and through it*. It is something a bit like it is not possible to appreciate the colors of a Sony TV if we are looking at them through a Philips one.[12]

To tackle the issue of the relationship between altricial and precocial competences in the same species, Sloman writes:

> Our claim was that some genetic specifications are *parametrized*, with information gaps that can be filled given parameters during gene expression. Obvious examples include genetically specified physiological structures, such as bones or muscles, the change in size, weight, strength, and other features during individual development, in coordination with changes in associated mechanisms, including neural control mechanisms. For example, larger bones will usually require larger, stronger muscles. We extended this kind of variability from genetically specified *physical* structures to genetically specified *competences*, including sucking, chewing, swallowing, grasping, and various forms of sensory information processing.
>
>   ... *Preconfigured* competencies are genetically specified, and any change in parameters they need are either intrinsically generated or continuously derived from the changing developmental environment, including other parts of the developing organism.

... In contrast, *meta-configured* competences result from abstract, parameterized, genetic specifications that may be activated at different stages of development, using parameters that depend on information acquired during earlier gene expression. ... Human language development is an example of such multilayered meta configured gene expression, including spectacular cases of later developments. Substantially re-organizing the information gained in earlier phases of language development, including coping with exceptions to previously learned syntactic regularities.

[Therefore,] a meta-configured genome can produce meta configured competences that are parameterized by information acquired using results of earlier gene expression influenced by the environment.

(Sloman, 2021, pp. 79–81)

For Sloman, this theory represents a biological description of the mechanism of representational redescription – both of which might be, in my opinion, manifestations of the same transgressive principle (an archetype) that Jung called "reflection". This theory, that I find useful, hypothesizes how a complex archetypal image, belonging to the domain of symbols, might arise from the subsequent parametrized development triggered by original somatic constraints and that those constraints emerge during the lifetime within a co-evolutionary environment.

7.2 A Parametrized Process Towards Complex Concepts and Images

A representation of this heuristic hypothesis may come from the analogy between biological homologies within the context of evolutionary biology as described by D'Arcy Thompson in his groundbreaking 1917 work, *On Growth and Form*.

In Chapter 17 of his magnum opus entitled "On the Theory of Transformations, or the Comparison of Related Forms", applying for the first time mathematical analysis to biology, Thompson describes what he calls "morphological transformations".

Key aspects of D'Arcy Thompson's theory include the following:

1. *Mathematical transformations*: Thompson applied mathematical transformations to demonstrate how one form could be transformed into another through processes like *scaling, rotation* and *deformation*. He showed that these transformations could explain the similarities in form observed across different species.
2. *Physical forces and constraints*: Thompson emphasized the role of physical forces, such as tension, compression, and growth patterns, in shaping biological forms. He believed that the constraints imposed by physical forces played a significant role in determining the shapes of organisms.
3. *Unity of biological forms*: Thompson argued for a unity of biological forms, suggesting that underlying mathematical relationships and physical principles could account for the similarities seen in different organisms. He used examples from various organisms, including plants, animals, and shells, to illustrate his points.

The images from Thompson's book that I am showing are among the most compelling and beautiful images in the history of science and describe the aspect of evolution, change and morphological continuity within the evolutionary process that must include specific biological developmental constraints, which seem to limit the possible alternatives and combinations of evolutionary changes. This is the fundamental problem that involves the relationship between evolutionary theories and developmental theories (the so-called "Evo-Devo" theories).

Biologists assumed that an organism was a straightforward reflection of its component genes: the genes coded for proteins, which built the organism's body. Biochemical pathways (and, they supposed, new species) evolved through mutations in these genes. Yet this elegant theory could not explain embryology (Scott, 2003). Had Evo-Devo's insights been available, embryology would certainly have played a central role in the synthesis.

The turning point came when in 1961, Jacques Monod, Jean-Pierre Changeux and François Jacob discovered the *lactose* operon (in genetics, an operon is a functioning unit of the DNA) required for the transport and metabolism of lactose in the bacterium *Escherichia coli* (Monod et al., 1963). This was a cluster of genes arranged in a feedback control loop so that its products would only be made when "switched on" by an environmental stimulus. One of these products was an enzyme that splits a sugar, lactose; and lactose itself was the stimulus that switched the genes on.

This seems to show that the interaction between the organism and its co-evolutionary environment not only is fundamental to understand biological life (and then psychological life) but also that this does not imply that the organism will change in a completely free and unconstrained way.

Developmental biology is a branch of biology that studies the process by which organisms grow and develop. It encompasses a wide range of biological processes, including fertilization, embryonic development, tissue regeneration and aging. The goal of developmental biology is to understand how a single-celled zygote, formed by the fusion of egg and sperm, gives rise to a complex multicellular organism with specialized cell types and tissues.

Key topics within developmental biology include the following:

a) Embryonic development, which involves the series of events that occur from fertilization to the formation of the adult organism. It includes processes such as cell division, cell differentiation and morphogenesis (the shaping of tissues and organs).
b) Cell differentiation, which refers to the process by which cells become specialized into specific cell types with distinct functions. Differentiation is essential for the formation of tissues and organs.
c) Pattern formation, which establishes spatial, morphological organization in tissues and organs. This includes the formation of body axes (e.g., anterior-posterior, dorsal-ventral) and the positioning of structures within these axes.

d) Morphogenesis: the process by which tissues and organs acquire their three-dimensional shapes. This involves cell movements, cell shape changes and tissue rearrangements.

e) Genetic control of development, which refers to the role of genes in controlling the developmental processes. This includes the action of regulatory genes, such as homeobox genes, which play a crucial role in specifying body patterns.

f) The study of stem cells with their ability to differentiate into various cell types. Stem cells play a crucial role in development and tissue repair.

As we have already seen, together with *evolutionary* biology, evolutionary *developmental* biology (Evo-Devo) examines the developmental processes to understand how organisms have evolved and mutated over time. This perspective is necessary to produce a model that explains how simple constraints may produce complex images. A second crucial moment in the history of developmental biology is based on the discovery of the "Homeobox genes" – a group of genes that play a crucial role in the early development of animals, including humans. These genes encode proteins called "homeodomain-containing transcription factors". Homeobox genes were first discovered in the fruit fly *Drosophila melanogaster*, where mutations in these genes were found to result in dramatic transformations of body segments. Subsequent research revealed that similar genes exist in many other organisms, including vertebrates like humans.

The main function of homeobox genes is to c*ontrol the body plan and the formation of body structures during embryonic development.* They act as master regulatory genes that determine the identity of different body segments and tissues. In fact, their main function is to c*ontrol the body plan and the formation of body structures during embryonic development, therefore,* acting as master regulatory genes that determine the identity of different body segments and tissues (McGinnis et al., 1984, pp. 428–433). The homeobox genes control a process through which something more complex is built from something less complex. This possibility seems to me coherent with the existence of the fine-tuned anthropic constants that make possible the existence and development of the psychical world.

Homeobox genes are often organized on chromosomes into clusters, and the order of genes within these clusters corresponds to the order in which the genes are activated during development. The presence of such a mechanism to control development, and its stable and ancestral presence in the biological world, is the base for a formulation of a rational hypothesis for the existence of a general mechanism that constraints the whole development of an organism, and also of humans, so that the further abstraction and combination of constrained conceptual primitives, which exist to give form and thinkability to affects, may be regulated and directed too.

Regarding this hypothesis, one thing must be clear: such a developmental process leaves a huge margin for individual variations, as it takes place in tandem with a co-evolutionary environment.

The discovery of the homeobox genes and the related perspective of developmental biology (which integrates evolutionary biology) makes it possible to extend the anthropic principle to the psychological developmental process. In fact, within the bottom-up perspective that I am using to justify the extension of the anthropic process all the way to psychology and to the universal features of cultural symbols, we need to hinge the whole process on the biological innate dispositions from where I started my whole discussion – like Panksepp's motivational system and the genotypically determined sensory and motor structure. *In other words, since the existence of innate complex images or concepts is not acceptable, we need to hypothesize the existence of constrained, parametrized* processes *that preside to the emergence of complex archetypal images from the simple affective and sensorimotor modular original constraints. Some of such processes may be triggered even before birth, while some others after birth throughout a person's life (an example in puberty and adolescence, when a massive reorganization and increase in complexity occurs). In any case, such parametrized processes would guide the development towards complex images the same way a complex system organizes itself, or the way Winnicott's object presenting proceeds.*

This parametrized process doesn't work as a fixed, predetermined genetic constraint (as in Dawkin's "selfish gene" theory) but happens like in the crystallization process, which is triggered by a situational factor which tilts a prepotential field into a process in which a new state is actualized. One easy biological example is the tilting of the infantile body-psyche into that of an adolescent triggered by the accumulation of bodily fats, which are precursors of the hormone leptin. In a way, the puberal new being was latent in the child, but situational factors are needed to realize a new form. As I already said, this situational factor may be the global state of the organism, or the outer environment (or both); hence, it would modulate the parametrized process top-down. Modifying the theme in an indefinite number of possible variations.

At a genetic level, the presence of a wholly new virus (like the Coronavirus) against which the organism's immune system has no immunoglobulins will cause the organism to, first of all, inhibit DNA replication reparation mechanisms and so *promote a huge increase in random, casual mutations from which the organism will then select the useful one to produce a wholly new set of immunological organismic conditions.* What I wish to underscore is that, for a formation of a new structure – in psychology, a thought, a feeling state, an image, etc. – the coexistence of a parametrized process and an environmental input is needed.

The discovery of the class of homeobox genes that I have mentioned makes it possible not to exclude a constrained nature of the whole developmental process itself ("from biology to culture"), which would be anthropically constrained towards an attempt to subjectively imagine or grasp the meaningful unity of reality – something that the human mind is able to do through dreams, art or the "unreasonable effectiveness" (Eugene Wigner) of mathematical thinking, which, according to Jung, is based on the anomaly of the archetypal yet *conscious* nature of natural numbers. When I write "anthropically constrained towards an attempt",

I do not refer to any sentient mind that has devised a teleological plan but to the emergence of specific conditions out of a necessary constrained process. This is the same structural architecture of the system that determines its own development and differentiation – obviously, following the principle of "theme with variations" that I mentioned before and always in a dialectical relationship with a salient environment.

Evo-Devo biology deals with how evolution and development takes place (Minelli, 2007) – i.e., with the relationship between the Darwinian genotypic principles of evolution based on natural selection and exaptation, together with the expression, constraints and mechanisms within the phenotype. Evo-Devo received a phenomenal impulse from the findings of molecular biology and embryology.

A famous example has to do with the number of legs of a centipede:

When it emerges from the egg, the little centipede is equipped with 21 pairs of legs and that number it will retain even as it grows, through a series of molts reminiscent of those by which a butterfly caterpillar grows.

Are there ever exceptions to this rule? The answer is positive. In fact, a not-insignificant minority among the centipedes does indeed possess 23 pairs of legs and segments, but these are different species (only in a rare South American species do individuals with 21 pairs of legs and individuals with 23 seem to coexist). That the number of segments (and of legs and segments) is invariable within each species is an interesting fact. It suggests that the (genetic?) machine responsible for producing these segments must be very precise. The most unusual aspect of the matter, however, is the total absence of centipedes with 22 pairs of legs and segments.

The same issue concerns the geophiles, a group of small animals akin to centipedes in which the very elongated and sometimes vermiform trunk bears a greater

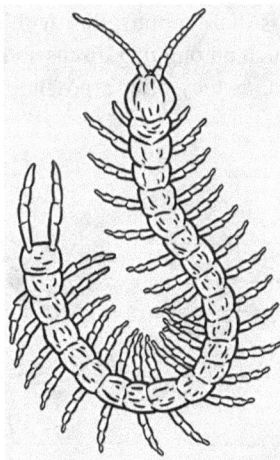

Figure 7.1 The centipede.

number of pairs of legs, from a minimum of 27 to an ascertained maximum of 191. These two numbers (27 and 191) are also odd numbers, as were 21 and 23. Even numbers are also totally forbidden in geophiles, just as they are in centipedes.

> In geophiles, however, there is an even more paradoxical situation. On the one hand, within some species we still find perfect constancy in the number of segments, even though these are, for example, 45, or 49. On the other hand in most species the number of trunk segments in this zoological group is variable but again even numbers are absolutely forbidden. The fact that an animal can produce exactly 49 segments without a single individual being mistaken in the count makes unlikely the hypothesis that in these animals the segments are produced serially and one after the other. What counting-segment device could a geophilus possibly have to rigorously arrest its production always at the same level?
>
> . . . In fact, it is likely that individuals with an even number of trunk segments do not exist for the simple reason that they cannot be constructed. If this is the case, natural selection does not eliminate them at all; it simply never encounters them just as it does not encounter butterflies with six wings, or with eight. Which means that the explanation for the fact that geophiles or centipedes in general always have an odd number of pairs of legs is not to be found in the greater probability of survival, (i.e., ultimately, in the greater reproductive success) of odd-segmented individuals over even-segmented individuals, but rather in the fact that nature knows how to produce the former but, apparently, does not know how to produce the latter.
>
> (Minelli, 2007, pp. 21–22. My translation)

Now I present a few images from Thompson's work (Figures 7.2–7.11). I must say that, while their compelling beauty and the elegance is beyond discussion, what is still under scrutiny is their applicability within general evolutionary theory. Knowledgeable about such an ongoing discussion within the Evo-Devo field, I wish to share these images, as they offer a possible analogy to the issue of the

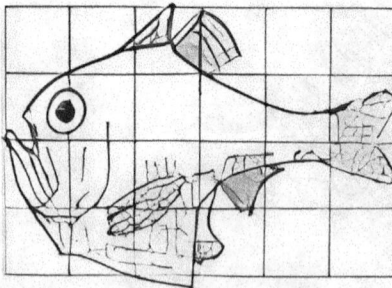

Figure 7.2 Argyropelecus olfersii.

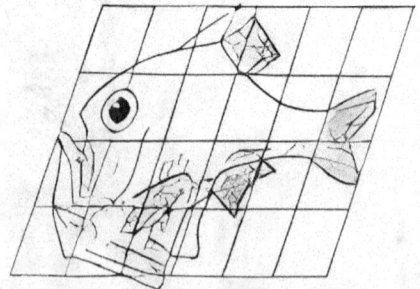

Figure 7.3 Sternoptyx diaphana.

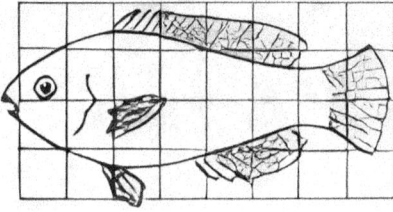

Figure 7.4 Scarus sp.

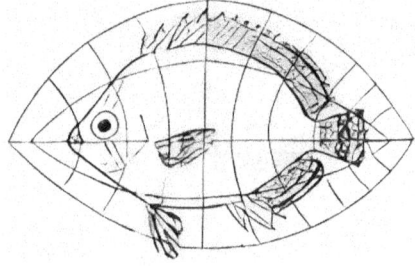

Figure 7.5 Pomacanthus.

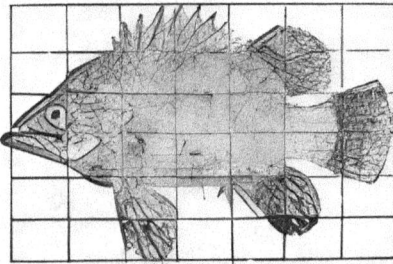

Figure 7.6 Polyprion.

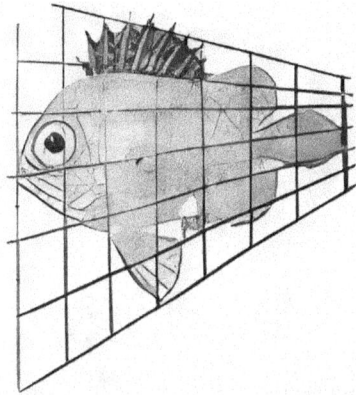

Figure 7.7 Pseudopriacanthus altus.

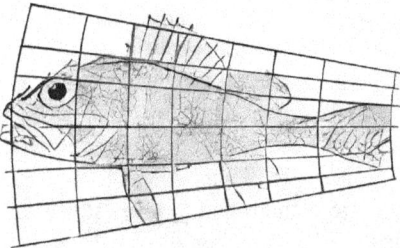

Figure 7.8 Scorpaena sp.

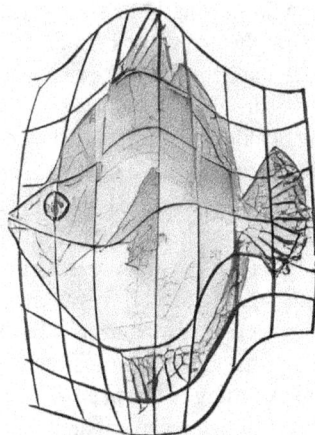

Figure 7.9 Antigonia capros.

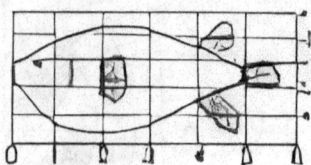

Figure 7.10 Diodon.

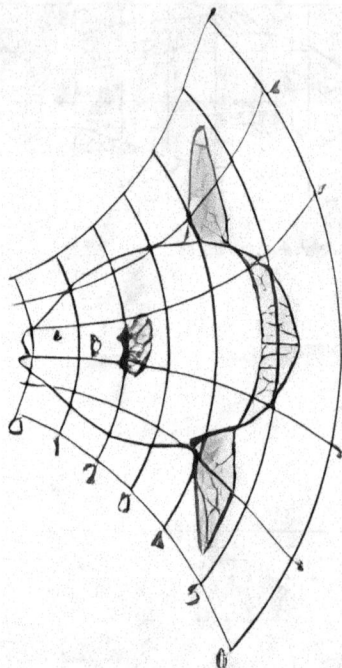

Figure 7.11 Orthagoriscus.

ectopsychic-organizing archetype-in-itself and the many, yet constrained, images that emerge through time and place. The numbering of the images is the original contained in D'Arcy Thompson's *on Growth and Form* (1917. Courtesy of *Project Gutenberg*).

What is striking in these images is that what at the same time constraints, regulates and, therefore, makes possible phenotypic variability and change is a latent, abstract, mathematical-like rule, analogous to the ectopsychic functioning of Jung's archetype in itself. If this has to do with the biological domain, it is possible to add a further analogy between these biological homologies and Aby Warburg's *Nachleben and Pathosformeln* in the cultural and symbolic domain of art (Warburg, 2021).

In his research on the Florentine art of the 1400s, Warburg discovered how Ghirlandaio, Botticelli and his patrons inferred antiquity from the texts they read and focused on the persistence of antiquity and its influence on Florentine art, investigating the relationship between works of art and poetic texts, in which he finds described in words the scenes he sees transposed into images by Botticelli, who, probably, listened to the instructions of some learned humanist. Moreover, from this work emerges the need to ground a historical anthropology of gestures that can examine the technical and symbolic constitution of bodily gestures in a given culture (for a discussion on gestures and universals, see vol. II, § 9.3).[13]

Figure 7.12 A typical posture of a 19th-century hysteric patient.

Source: Paul Marie Louis Pierre Richer (1881). *Études Cliniques sur la Grande Hystérie ou Hystéro-épilepsie.* 2. éd., rev. et Considérablement augm. Études cliniques sur la grande hystérie ou hystéro-épilepsie, 2. éd., rev. et Considérablement augm. Paris: Adrien Delahaye et Emile Lecrosnier

Figure 7.13 Charcot hypnotizes a hysteric patient, who seems to be mimicking the woman painted in the painting in front of her, at the other side of the room.

Source: A. Brouillet, *Une lecon de Clinique a la Salpétriere*, 1887 (*Musée d'histoire de la médecine de l'Université Paris Cité*)

Figure 7.14 The posture of two menads in an ecstatic dance.

Source: Terracotta relief. Around 27 BC–68 AC. Metropolitan Museum, New York (12.232.8a)

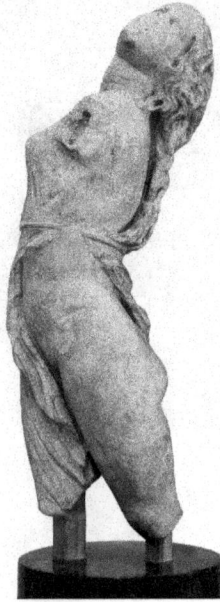

Figure 7.15 Skopas (335–330 BC), *Dancing menad.*
Source: Staatliche Kunstsammlungen, Dresden

For Warburg, the relevance of his work on Botticelli lies not only in the comparisons between works of art and literary texts but especially in having traced an anthropological principle whereby body movements, gestures, greetings and attitudes are traces of a natural unity between word and image, *Wort und Bild*. This organization around these "survivals" (*Nachleben*) informs the artist of the Renaissance, who seems to be attracted towards specific, similar forms that return throughout history.

In Botticelli's works, Warburg observes those "intensified movements", *gesteigert Bewegung*, those traces of antiquity that give the rendering of movement and are often understood as dance.

In a few words, these highly cultural and symbolic images seem to reveal an underlying texture that organizes them and makes of homologues, as the representation of the patterns of transformation in evolution does in the biological domain. This might indicate something like the emergence of the process of *parametrization* that Sloman is hypothesizing – a process that develops bottom-up from biology to culture. As Marsilio Ficino would have said, here, the link between biology and culture is the *anima copula mundi*. I will discuss the role of psychology in this context when I deal with anthropology and representations.

The Figures 7.12–7.15, with the clear identity between the pathosformel of the 18th-century hysterics and those of the Greek menads, would be enough to

Figure 7.16 The nymph reenters the Reinassance scene.

Source: Artist from the circle of Domenico Ghirlandaio (or one of his imitators), Bearer of Fruit (copy of the Doge from the *Birth of St. John the Baptist*). Detached fresco, late 15th–early 16th century. Chiesa di Santa Maria Novella, Firenze[12]

reinterpret hysteria under an archetypal perspective, in which the patriarchal definition "penis envy" could have been immediately corrected. In fact, those "hysterics" were the first line of a Dionysiac revolution in which Western women were reclaiming not Adam's rib, nor his penis, but *their own* body and its absolute freedom against the patriarchal Pentheus' phallic oppression and control.

Myth always precedes and informs history, and the first irruption of an archetypal mytheme sometimes happens through psychopathology – the numinous discourse of the psyche. The implosion of myth into tragedy – of the numinous in the human sphere and its history – takes time and painful psychological and social labor. This has also been the case for Western women in their psychohistorical process to transform the mythical Dionysian's liberating call of the 19th century into the feminist psychology and politics of the 20th century. Hence, no envy, rather, revolution.

A process of parametrized development implies that not all the latent structure – such as that which informs these images – must emerge immediately nor always or everywhere. They may emerge through time. This is well described by Winnicott's paradigm of the object-presenting (which I will discuss in vol. I, § 10). This ingenious paradigm, connected to the principle of the self-organizing nature of complex systems, describes something like a virtual teleological top-down attractor that step-by-step leads the subject towards its own self-realization. From the "right" moment to sleep, wake up, suckle at the mother's breast, etc., to the right choice of a partner or of a job, to the right word to say . . . this paradigm describes the possibility to coherently build constrained complexities from elementary constraints.

Once again, processes of parametrized development may be hypothesized already from the teleological *anthropic principle*. If you recall, the existence of irrational natural constants, finely tuned with each other, has "miraculously" made it possible for our physical universe to exist. Such constants are fundamental constraints within which existence is possible; outside of which neither the physical universe nor our species, which discovered these constants, would exist (Vol. 1 § 2.1). The hypothesis of the existence within the psychoid realm of one or more anthropic principles that make possible the coherent formation of *complex* recurrent patterns starting from simple constraints is not untenable.

Due to environmental conditions, some latent possibilities will never emerge,[14] some will emerge throughout the organism's maturational process; yet both processes may be constrained (by genes and mathematical conditions, which probably, in the end, are the same thing).

I think that it is possible to extend the anthropic principle (i.e., the fact that there are constraints at every level of reality) to the psychological developmental process since the discovery of the homeobox genes. In fact, in this perspective an anthropic principle would constrain the whole psychological trajectory, from the biological to the cultural level, as it would regulate and take place in a co-evolutionary environment with a limited degree of freedom determined by its own constrained origins. This implies that the emotional and cognitive responses would *also* be constrained and would be produced creatively as "variations on themes" before the constraining effect of internal conditions, such as maturation, aging and illnesses, or external conditions, like belonging to the co-evolutionary environment. It should be noted that the external conditions obviously also constrains development but within a situational perspective.

If we remember that the birth of developmental evolutionary theory took place to explain some aspects of embryology and morphology that the sole Darwinian evolutionary perspective could not explain, then the question as to why the prefrontal cortex must mature later than subcortical structures and why the brain keeps changing throughout life might receive an answer that does not exclude a parametrized ("archetypally" constrained) perspective.

A second possible implication of Warburg's "survivals" is connected with the issue of mental susceptibilities and culture that I will discuss in vol. II, § 5.

Let's now imagine that while the altricial competences relate to self-reflective consciousness and involve the neocortex with its massive neurodynamic processes involving prefrontal, parietal and temporal regions, the precocial functions/competences of the BrainMind, which might be located in subcortical areas, involve the foundation of those higher cognitive acquisitions. The nature of precocial competences is both procedural, automatic, domain-specific and, as far as at least the sensory-motor is concerned, modular, *while it is dynamic and vectorial for what concerns affects and feelings*. For this view, we must finally underscore that not only subcortical sensorimotor coordination[15] but also primary *affects* located, as they are, deep in the brain might well be involved in some form of patterned – modular – activity and might bottom-up influence further mental processes.

Jung's precocial unconscious, therefore, seems to correspond to the site of (primary) affects – the origin and organizing forces of the psychic life of Panksepp's contemporary neuro-affective sciences. This hypothesis, for which the unconscious processes are located in subcortical strata of the brain, was endorsed by Jung, although he was not the first one to do so. Certainly, the neuroanatomist Theodor Hermann Meynert, who was one of Freud's teachers, was of the same opinion (Sulloway, 1979). McLean's view of the brain as a morphologically stratified brain (1985, 1990) (*not* his theory about a supposed "reptilian" brain, as humans do not descend from reptiles) is obviously an important reference to this whole discussion on the presence of both precocial and altricial competences.

It should be clear that such a precocial unconscious, if it exists, refers *not to* the individual subject – the Ego – but belongs to the *Homo sapiens* species. Therefore, it has a collective nature and follows Darwinian principles, which apply not within an individual context but in an epidemiological, collective one.

In Jungian terms, this relationship between precocial and altricial competence would represent a possible answer to Fodor's problem of the relationship between inherited modularity and learning (Fodor, 1983, 2000) through ontogenetic, relational and cultural development, like the transformation of an archetype per se – polarized by affects, modular and procedural – into a complex and, most importantly, to the Ego (for a more detailed discussion, see: vol. 1 § 9).

In this view, the Ego might be defined, accordingly to Jung's theory, as the least bound to domain-specific tasks and patterns, while, at the same time, connected to the *global and synthetic* functioning of the BrainMind. Such an Ego-consciousness, as an expression of a "global workspace" (Dehaene, 2003), or of what Edelman and Tononi (2000) describe as the "dynamic nucleus", would represent the conscious emergence of a part of the unconscious Self.

If we now recall my discussion on the role of the "instinct", not as a "fixed activation pattern" but as a top-down attractor/stimulus-trigger of a field of possibilities, we may complete this description by saying that in *Homo sapiens*, such a trigger belongs to the phylogenetically *inherited* psychoid, a-noetic[16] strata of the affective unconscious, while the responses that it elicits, remaining confined within the "basin of activation" of the affective trigger,[17] are flexible, varied, specific and learned during ontogenesis. Therefore, this neurodynamic polarizing function of affects would belong to the most ancient precocial strata of the brain, where it is highly probable that modularity prevails.

In a somehow elegant design, affects:

a) Confer *value* to the sensory-motor networks which seem to be involved in generating proto concepts and may be thought to shape them in specific procedural patterns ready for a further conscious declarative processing, without which the human organism would perish.
b) Confer value and organize experience and learning within an environment where humas co-evolved, both in "natural" and "cultural" ways. In this second case, the interaction with such an environment, "interpreted" and "organized" affectively, takes place through the sensory-motor system and its peculiar neuronal patterns and modules, both learned and inherited.

Notes

1 Although the real, fundamental level has to do with quantum physics since the sensory organs are receptors and transformers of bio-electric impulses.
2 Homology: (1) A degree of similarity, as in position or structure, and that may indicate a common origin, a correspondence of structure. (2) (*evolutionary biology*) A state of similarity in structure and anatomical position but not necessarily in function between different organisms indicating a common ancestry or evolutionary origin.
3 Although it is constantly violated through diagnosing the child as a wholly differentiated unit, or even by prescribing drugs as if his brain was not meant to extend itself into its environment – what Jung would have called the Great Mother.
4 I will limit myself to a concise description of one of the many implications of this principle, which is useful for the purposes of this general discussion.
5 Here, the perspective by Kropotkin, as a proponent of the centrality of cooperation in the biological realm, is important.

Commenting Darwin's *Origins*, he wrote:

"While he [Darwin] himself was chiefly using the term in its narrow sense for his own special purpose, he warned his followers against committing the error (which he seems once to have committed himself) of overrating its narrow meaning. In *The Descent of Man* he gave some powerful pages to illustrate its proper, wide sense. He pointed out how, in numberless animal societies, the struggle between separate individuals for the means of existence disappears, how struggle is replaced by co-operation, and how that substitution results in the development of intellectual and moral faculties which secure to the species the best conditions for survival. He intimated that in such cases the fittest are not the physically strongest, nor the cunningest, but those who learn to combine so as mutually to support each other, strong and weak alike, for the welfare of the community. 'Those communities', he wrote, 'which included the greatest number of the most sympathetic members would flourish best, and rear the greatest number of offspring' (2nd edit., p. 163). The term, which originated from the narrow Malthusian conception of competition between each and all, thus lost its narrowness in the mind of one who knew Nature".
(Kropotkin, 1890, p. 524)

6 Symbiosis (from Greek συμβίωσις, *symbíōsis*, "living together", from σύν, *sýn*, "together", and βίωσις, bíōsis, "living") is any type of a close and long-term biological interaction between two biological organisms of different species, termed symbionts.

A commensal relationship occurs when one species benefits from a close prolonged interaction, while the other neither benefits nor is harmed. Amensalism is a nonsymbiotic, asymmetric interaction where one species is harmed or killed by the other and one is unaffected by the other.

7 Among the many authors that have studied the impact of such an eminently emotional co-evolutionary relational field for the molding of the brain, see: Siegel, 1999.

8 I will go back to this point which concerns the relationships between whatever biology is and whatever psychology and cultures are in the introduction to my discussion on culture and archetypes (vol. II).

9 Technically, altricial: species in which the young are relatively immobile after birth or hatching and must be cared for by adults. Precocial: species in which the young are relatively mature and mobile soon after birth or hatching.

10 At any rate, evolutionary biology seems to be progressively eroding the idea that *Homo sapiens* is radically different from other species and the rigid distinction between precocial and altricial species. Among the plethora of cognitive competences that humans share with non-humans, an interesting example is the presence of what was thought to be a cognitive feature *unique* in humans (Tulving, 2002; Suddendorf & Corballis, 1997) and strictly related to self-reflective consciousness: the capacity to foresee future episodes (episodic prospection), which is a part of episodic memory (Tulving, 1972). The surprising finding is an example of convergent evolution (in which identical evolutionary pressures selected the same competence in animals belonging to far taxa). In fact, a series of controlled experiments demonstrated that western scrub-jays do remember what types of food caches they hid, in which spatial locations and how long ago (Clayton & Dickinson, 1998). Moreover, the birds form integrated memories about "what happened, where and when" rather than encoding each of these three pieces of information separately (Clayton et al., 2003) (for a review of some of these issues: Haun et al., 2010).

Obviously, this does not mean, nor imply, that the human species does not have specific and perhaps unique characteristics. It just calls for great prudence about the uniqueness of such specific qualities. The book by Griffin (1976) is a useful reference for this discussion. It deals with human's apparently most *unique* characteristic – language – hinting at the possibility that the presence and development of such a competence is mostly a matter of quantitative evolutionary changes and that human's uniqueness, although real, is just a bit less unique.

Once again, Jung's position (or the way I wish to interpret him) is convergent with contemporary biology:

"As we have immediate experience only of a reflected state, which is ipso facto conscious and known because it consists essentially in relating ideas or other contents to an ego-complex that represents our empirical personality, it follows that any other kind of consciousness – either without an ego or without contents – is virtually unthinkable. But there is no need to frame the question so absolutely. On a somewhat more primitive human level, Ego-consciousness loses much of its meaning, and consciousness is accordingly modified in a characteristic way. Above all, it ceases to be reflective. And when we observe the psychic processes in the higher vertebrates and particularly in domestic animals, we find phenomena resembling consciousness which nevertheless do not allow us to conjecture the existence of an ego. As we know from direct experience, the light of consciousness has many degrees of brightness, and the ego-complex many gradations of emphasis. On the animal and primitive level there is a mere 'luminosity', differing hardly at all from the glancing fragments of a dissociated ego".

(Jung, 1947/1954, §387)

11 Mark Johnson, one of the authors of the seminal book *Rethinking Innateness* (Johnson, Elman, Bates, Karmiloff-Smith, Parisi & Plunkett, 1996), writes:

"In the conclusion to chapter 5 of *Rethinking innateness*, we discussed the relevance of then- current developmental neuroscience to the key concepts of architectural and chronotropic constraints on the emergence of representations. It was argued that while representational nativism (genetically encoded prewiring of detailed patterns of connectivity) was potentially a feature of some midbrain systems, the cerebral cortex is best viewed as an organ of plasticity in the sense that its intrinsic connectivity patterns were more malleable (albeit that the overall architecture of cortex provides constraints and limits on the nature and types of representations that are generated)".

"Despite much debate over the ensuing decades as to the extent to which the differentiation of cortex into distinct structural and functional regions is activity dependent, the general view of the cortex as a machine evolved to generate and manipulate representations remains plausible today. The general models of cortical function available at the time of *Rethinking innateness* were largely based on feedforward networks in which greater abstraction away from sensory input was achieved through hierarchical stages of re-mapping (re-representation) [. . .]. This hierarchical progression of abstractions of representations has a sequential temporal element, (a constraint according to *Rethinking innateness*) – with representations closer to the sensory being required to be established before more abstract or integrative representations are formed".

(Johnson, 2021)

My interpretation of these words is the development of higher, conscious, cortical functions, based on archaic modular, subcortical structures.

12 The Santa Maria Novella Church in Florence, specifically the Cappella Tornabuoni, is property of the *Fondo Edifici di Culto*, administered by the *Direzione Centrale degli affari dei culti e per l'amministrazione del Fondo Edifici di Culto* of the Italian Ministry of Interiors.

13 Volume 2, A Jungian and Evolutionary Approach to Psychology and Culture: The Infinite Ladder.

14 It might be worthwhile emphasizing that this "environment" acts as a triggering stimulus if it is salient for the organism, in our case, for a human. In fact, there exist as many environments as there are biological species. The notion of a "universe" is wholly misleading. We should always refer to a multiverse made of a potentially infinite number of environments. The specific, salient nature of a specific triggering environment means that the latter is already meant-to-be for the specific organism. The discussion within developmental evolutionary biology is meant to study the specific endogenous constraints that make a generic environment "the" selected environment for a specific organism.

15 Something Jean Mandler considers for the basis of proto-concepts.

16 For Panksepp, "a-noetic" consciousness is the first evolutionary step in animal subjectivity. It has been defined as an "unthinking form of experience, which may be affectively intense without being known" (Solms & Panksepp, 2012, p. 149).

17 As described by Freeman (1999) and Llinas (2002) within a neurobiological perspective.

References

Alcaro, A., Carta, S., Panksepp, J. (2017). The Affective Core of the Self: A Neuro-Archetypical Perspective On the Foundations of Human (and Animal) Subjectivity'. *Frontiers in Psychology*, 8, Article 1424.

Barkow, J., Cosmides, L., Tooby, J. (Eds.). (1992). *The Adapted Mind: Evolutionary Psychology and the Generation of Culture*. Oxford, New York, Toronto: Oxford University Press.

Basaglia, F. (1968). *'L'istituzione Negata: Rapporto Da Un Ospedale Psichiatrico*. Torino: Einaudi.

Callebaut, W., Muller, G.B., Newman, S.A. (2007). The Organismic Systems Approach: Evo-Devo and the Streamlining of the Naturalistic Agenda. In: *Integrating Evolution and Development. From Theory To Practice*, pp. 25–92. R. Samson, R.N. Brandon (Eds.). Bradford, PA: Bradford Books.

Chappell, J., & Sloman, A. (2007a). Contributions to WONAC: International Workshop on Natural and Artificial Cognition Two ways of understanding causation: Humean and Kantian. International Workshop on Natural and Artificial Cognition. Pembroke College, Oxford. June 25 and 26, 2007. http://www2.cs.arizona.edu/projects/wonac/

Chappell, J., & Sloman, A. (2007b). Natural and artificial meta-configured altricial information-processing systems. *International Journal of Unconventional Computing, 3*(3), 211–239.

Clayton, N.S., Dickinson, A. (1998). Episodic-Like Memory During Cache Recovery by Scrub Jays. *Nature, 395,* 272–274.

Clayton, N.S. et al. (2003). Can Animals Recall the Past and Plan For the Future? *Nature Reviews Neuroscience,* 4, 685–691.

Colvis, C.M., Pollock, J.D., Goodman, R.H., Impey, S., Dunn, J., Mandel, G., Champagne, F.A., Mayford, M., Korzus, E., Kumar, A., Renthal, W., Theobald, D.E.H., Nestler, E.J. (2005). Epigenetic Mechanisms and Gene Networks in the Nervous System. *The Journal of Neuroscience,* 25, 45, 10379–10389.

d'Arcy, T. (1917). *On Growth and Form.* Kidke edn. Project Gutenberg.

Dehaene, S., Sergent, C. and Changeux, J.-P. (2003). A neuronal network model linking subjective reports and objective physiological data during conscious perception. Proc. National Academy of Science (USA) 100. 14: 8520–8525.

Darwin, C. (1982). *Viaggio di un Naturalista Intorno al Mondo – Lettere (1831–1836).* Milano: Feltrinelli.

Dawkins, R. (1976). *The Selfish Gene.* Oxford: Oxford University Press.

Dawkins, R. (2015). *The Blind Watchmaker: Why the Evidence of Evolution Reveals a Universe Without Design.* New York: Norton.

Dawkins, R., Ward, L. (1997). *Climbing Mount Improbable.* New York: W.W. Norton.

Deisseroth, K., Mermelstein, P.G., Xia, H., Tsien, R.W. (2003). Signaling from Synapse to Nucleus: The Logic Behind the Mechanisms. *Current Opinion in Neurobiology,* 13, 354–365.

Descola, P. (2021). *Oltre Natura e Cultura.* Milano: Cortina.

Edelman, G., Tononi, G. (2000). *A Universe of Consciousness: How Matter Becomes Imagination.* New York: Basic Books.

Fodor, J. A. (1983). Modularity of Mind. Cambridege (Mass): MIT Press.

Fodor, J. A. (2000). The Mind Doesn•t Work that Way: The Scope and Limits of Computational Psychology. Cambridge (Mass): MIT Press.

Foucault, M. (2006). *Psychiatric Power: Lectures At the Collège De France, 1973–1974.* Palgrave Macmillan.

Freeman, W.J. (1999). *How Brains Make Up Their Minds.* London: Weidenfeld and Nicolson.

Goffman, E. (1961). *Asylums: Essays On the Condition of the Social Situation of Mental Patients and Other Inmates.* New York: Doubleday.

Goodwyn, E. (2020). Archetypes and the 'Impoverished Genome' Argument: Updates from Evolutionary Genetics. *Journal of Analytical Psychology,* 65, 5, 911–931.

Gould, S.J. (2002). *The Structure of Evolutionary Theory.* Cambridge, MA: Belknap Press of Harvard University Press.

Griffin, D.R. (1976). *The Question of Animal Awareness. Evolutionary Continuity of Mental Experience.* New York, NY: Rockfeller University Press.

Haun, D.B.M., Jordan, F.M., Vallortigara, G., Clayton, N.S. (2010, December). Origins of Spatial, Temporal and Numerical Cognition: Insights from Comparative Psychology. *Trends in Cognitive Sciences,* 14, 12.

Huxley, J. (1942). *Evolution: The Modern Synthesis. With a New Foreword by Massimo Pigliucci and Gerd B. Müller.* Definitive edn. Cambridge, MA: MIT Press.

Jablonka, E., Lamb, M.J. (2005). *Evolution in Four Dimensions. Genetic, Epigenetic, Behavioral and Symbolic Variation in the History of Life.* Cambridge, MA, London: The MIT Press.

Johnson, M. (2021). Revisiting *Rethinking Innateness*: 20 Years on, In: Thomas, M.C., Mareschal, D. & Knowland, V.C.P. *Taking development seriously: A festschrift for Annette-Karmiloff-Smith.* (2021) London: Routledge.

Johnson, M., Karmiloff-Smith, A., Parisi, D., Plunkett, K., Elman, J.L. (1996). *Rethinking Innateness: A Connectionist Perspective on Development*. Bradford, PA: Bradford Books.

Jung, C.G. (1919). The Instinct and the Unconscious. In: *The Collected Works of C.G. Jung*. Vol. 8. London: Routledge.

Jung, C.G. (1928). On Psychic Energy. In: *The Collected Works of C.G. Jung*. Vol. 8. London, New York: Routledge.

Jung, C.G. (1935/1972). The Tavistock Lectures. In: *The Collected Works of C.G. Jung*. Vol. 15. London: Routledge.

Jung, C.G. (1937). Psychological Factors Determining Human Behavior. In: *The Collected Works of C.G. Jung*. Vol. 8. London: Routledge.

Jung, C.G. (1947/1954). On the Nature of the Psyche. In: *The Collected Works of C.G. Jung*. Vol. 8. London: Routledge.

Kropotkin, P.A. (1890). *Mutual Aid Amongst Animals. the Eclectic Magazine of Foreign Literature, Science, and Art. Old Series Complete in LXII*. Vols. January 1844 to December 1864. New Series, Vol. LII. July–December 1890. New York: E.R. Pelton Publisher.

Laland, K.N., Odling-Smee, F.J., Feldman, M.W. (2000). Niche Construction, Biological Evolution, and Cultural Change. *Behavioral and Brain Sciences*, 23, 1, 131–175.

Levin, M. (2021, April 15). Bioelectric Signaling: Reprogrammable Circuits Underlying Embryogenesis, Regeneration, and Cancer. *Cell*, 184, 1971–1989.

Levin, M., Pietak, A.M., Bischof, J. (2019, March). Planarian Regeneration as a Model of Anatomical Homeostasis: Recent Progress in Biophysical and Computational Approaches. *Seminars in Cell & Developmental Biology*, 87, 125–144.

Lévi-Strauss, C. (1949). *Le Strutture Elementari della Parentela*. Milano: Feltrinelli.

Lewontin, R. (2000). *The Triple Helix. Gene, Organism and Environment*. Cambridge, London: Harvard University Press.

Lewontin, R., Rose, S., Kamin, L.J. (2017). *Not in Our Genes: Biology, Ideology, and Human Nature*. Chicago: Haymarket Books.

Llinas, R. (2002). *I of the Vortex: From Neurons to Self*. Cambridge, MA: MIT Press.

Lutz, C. (1988). *Unnatural Emotions: Everyday Sentiments on a Micronesian Atoll and Their Challenge to Western Theory*. Chicago: University of Chicago Press.

Maclean, P.D. (1985). Brain Evolution Relating to Family, Play, and the Separation Call. *Archives of General Psychiatry*, 42, 4, 405–417.

Maclean, P.D. (1990). *The Triune Brain in Evolution: Role in Paleocerebral Functions*. New York: Plenum Press.

Mcginnis, W., Levine, M.S., Hafen, E., Kuroiwa, A., Gehring, W.J. (1984). A Conserved DNA Sequence in Homoeotic Genes of the Drosophila Antennapedia and Bithorax Complexes. *Nature*, 308, 5958.

Merchant, J. (2021). Archetypes and the 'Impoverished Environment' Argument: A Response to Goodwyn. *Journal of Analytical Psychology*, 66, I, 132–152.

Minelli, A. (2007). *Forme del Divenire Evo-Devo: La Biologia Evoluzionistica dello Sviluppo*. Torino: Einaudi.

Monod, J., Changeux, J.P., Jacob, F. (1963). Allosteric Proteins and Cellular Control Systems. *Journal of Molecular Biology*, 6, 4, 306–329.

Müller, G.B. (2013). Le Origini della Novità Morfologica. In: *Estetica e Scienze della Vita Morfologia, Biologia Teoretica, Evo-devo*. A. Pinotti, S. Tedesco (Eds.). Milano: Cortina.

Müller, G.B., Newman, S.A. (2003). *(a cura di), Origination of Organismal Form. Beyond the Gene in Developmental and Evolutionary Biology*. Cambridge, MA, London: The MIT Press.

Noble, D. (2008). *The Music of Life: Biology Beyond Genes*. Oxford: Oxford University Press.

Odling-Smee, F.J., Laland, K.N., Feldman, M.W. (2003). *Niche Construction: The Neglected Process in Evolution*. Princeton: Princeton University Press.

Pigliucci, M., Müller, G.B. (Eds.). (2010). *Evolution. The Extended Synthesis*. Cambridge, MA, London: The MIT Press.

Rasskin-Gutman, D. (2005). *Modularity: Understanding the Development and Evolution of Natural Complex Systems*. W. Callebaut, D. Rasskin-Gutman (Eds.). Cambridge, MA: The MIT Press.

Roesler, C. (2022). *Development of a Reconceptualization of Archetype Theory. Report to the IAAP*. https://iaap.org/wp-content/uploads/2022/04/report-archetype-theory-roesler-1.pdf.

Ross, S. (2004). *The Heretic in Darwin's Court: The Life of Alfred Russel Wallace*. New York: Columbia University Press.

Ruesch, J., Bateson, G., Pinsker, E.C., Combs, G. (1957). *Communication: The Social Matrix of Psychiatry*. New York: Norton.

Scott, G.F. (2003). The Morphogenesis of Evolutionary Developmental Biology. *International Journal of Developmental Biology*, 47, 7–8, 467–477.

Siegel, D.J. (1999). *The Developing Mind: Towards a Neurobiology of Interpersonal Experience*. New York: Guilford Press.

Sloman, A. (2021). Biological Evolution's Use of Representational Redescriptions. In: *Taking Development Seriously: A Festschrift For Annette-Karmiloff-Smith*. M.C. Thomas, D. Mareschal, V.C.P. Knowland (Eds.). London: Routledge.

Sloman, A., Chappell, J. (2005). The Altricial-Precocial Spectrum for Robots. In: *Proceedings IJCAI'05*, pp. 1187–1192. Edinburgh: IJCAI. http://www.cs.bham.ac.uk/research/cogaff/05.html#.

Sloman, A., Chappell, J. (2007). Computational Cognitive Epigenetics (Commentary On (Jablonka & Lamb 2005)). *Behavioral and Brain Sciences*, 30, 4, 375–376.

Solms, M., Panksepp, J. (2012). The "Id" Knows More Than the "Ego" Admits: Neuropsychoanalytic and Primal Consciousness Perspectives on the Interface Between Affective and Cognitive Neuroscience. *Brain Sciences*, 2, 147–175.

Suddendorf, T., Corballis, M.C. (1997). Mental Time Travel and the Evolution of the Human Mind. *Genetic, Social, and General Psychology Monographs*, 123, 133–167.

Sulloway, F.J. (1979). *Freud Biologist of the Mind*. New York: Basic Books.

Swadesh, M. (1955). Towards Greater Accuracy in Lexicostatistic Dating. *International Journal of American Linguistics*, 21, 121–137.

Tulving, E. (1972). Episodic and Semantic Memory. In: *Organization of Memory*, pp. 382–402. New York: Academic Press.

Tulving, E. (2002). Episodic Memory: From Mind To Brain. *Annual Review of Psychology*, 53, 1–25.

Vallortigara, G. (2021). *Il Pulcino di Kant*. Milano: Adelphi.

Vallortigara, G., Andrew, R.J. (1991). Lateralization of Response by Chicks to Change in Model Partner. *Animal Behaviour*, 41, 187–194.

Vallortigara, G., Andrew, R.J. (1994). Differential Involvement of Right and Left Hemispheres in Individual Recognition in the Domestic Chick. *Behavioural Processes*, 33, 41–58.

Von Uexküll, J. (1907/1913). *Die Umrisse Einer Kommanden Weltanschauung*. In: "Die neue Rundschau" 18: 641–661.

Von Uexküll, J. (1934). A Stroll Through the Worlds of Animals and Men. A Picture Book of Invisible Worlds. In: *Instinctive Behavior. The Development of a Modern Concept*. C.H. Schiller (Transl. and Ed.). C.S. Lashley (Intro.). New York: International Universities Press.

von Uexküll, J. (2013). Come vediamo la natura e come la natura vede se stessa? In: *Estetica e Scienze della Vita Morfologia, Biologia Teoretica, Evo-devo*. A. Pinotti, S. Tedesco (Eds.). Milano: Cortina.

Von Weitzsäcker, V. (1940). Der Gestaltkreis. Theorie der Einheit von Wahrnehmen und Bewegen. In: *Gesammelte Schriften*. Frankfurt: Suhrkamp.

Warburg, A. (2021). *Fra Antropologia e Storia dell'arte. Saggi, Conferenze, Frammenti*. Torino: Einaudi.

Weir, A.A., Chapell, J., Kacelnik, A. (2002, August 9). Shaping of Hooks in New Caledonian Crow. *Science*, 297, 981.

Wierzbicka, A. (1992). *Semantics, Culture and Cognition. Universal Human Concepts in Culture-Specific Configurations*. New York, Oxford: Oxford University Press.

Winnicott, D.W. (1960, January 1). The Theory of the Parent-Infant Relationship. *The International Journal of Psycho-Analysis*, 41.

Winnicott, D.W. (1965). *Family and Individual Development*. London, New York: Routledge.

Yong, E. (2022). *An Immense World*. Dublin: Random House.

Chapter 8

The Psychosomatic Complex

Earlier, I wrote that for Jung, the most elementary brick of the psyche is not the mere atomized stimulus that Freud called "drive", which is aimed at a non-specific object. For Jung, the most fundamental, pre-conscious structural element of the psyche is always a complex "constellation" of representations organized by, or "revolving" around, an affect.

Let's quote Jung's definition of the psychosomatic complex again, as he formulated in 1928:

> In my studies of the phenomena of association I have shown that there are certain constellations of psychic elements grouped around feeling-toned contents, which I have called "complexes". The feeling-toned content, the complex, consists of a nuclear element and a large number of secondarily constellated associations. The nuclear element consists of two components: first, a factor determined by experience and causally related to the environment; second, a factor innate in the individual's character and determined by his disposition.
>
> (Jung, 1928, §18)

Therefore, a complex is an organized set of memories, associations, fantasies, expectations and behavior patterns or tendencies around a core element which is accompanied by strong emotions. I would maintain that this "core element" *is* the emotion, the affect.

If we wanted to represent the complex by its sensory organization, its core would be musical/acoustic and would represent an emotional meaning/value, while its representations would be mostly visual/imagistic. While the complex undergoes a process of abstraction/spiritualization, its core turns into a sophisticated conscious feeling, as its representations become imbued with ethical values. Love and knowledge unite.

A complex may be as follows:

a) Conscious/Unconscious
b) Repressed/Unrepressed

DOI: 10.4324/9781003586258-8

c) Personal/Collective
d) Acute/Chronic.

A complex of representations is constellated and organized by an affect, the psychological manifestation of the libido, which acts as a motivational innate constraint and to which empirical experiences derived from the interaction with the environment are referred.[1]

When the process through which a complex takes shape – in which representations become organized by an affect – encounters some difficulty, this is felt through that unspecific type of affect that we call anxiety or, if it carries strong somatic correlates, anguish.

A special form of such an anxiety, related to the activation of a collective/impersonal and still completely or largely unconscious complex, is what Jung, after Rudolf Otto (1968), called *numinosum*. Hence, the feeling of the numinous points to the most fundamental activity of the psyche – the attempt to transform a non-repressed, unconscious, collective complex (an archetype) into a conscious, personal one. When the numinosum is constellated, it indicates that some archaic affects are still looking for integrated and personalized conscious representations. This process indicates the difficulty to contain something felt as infinite and compelling into a personal meaning that – thanks to the very nature of consciousness itself, which includes the consciousness of our objects – may be shared with others and become a relational, if not wholly *cultural*, meaning.

Here, I wish to highlight the following:

1) The two structural elements of the complex:

   a) The strong affective charge; and
   b) Its image representational – imaginal – character.

2) The seemingly constellating role of the affect, which, therefore, assumes the role of a *function* for the images, as it defines their intrinsic relationship (therefore, their "meaning").
3) The relationship of affects and the principles of integrity, subjectivity and consciousness.
4) The autonomy and integrity of the complex, which seems to function in a teleologically oriented way. The complex's autonomy and integrity (its wholeness) is clearly linked to the fundamental, basic element that forms our memories (the *episode*). In fact, an episode is a *unitary* aggregate of events stored in, and retrieved from, different memory storages, like the memory of faces, places, time, space, sounds, etc. Memory creatively re-collects elements from many storages and constructs an episode as a coherent, whole, unitary experience in time and space. Classical examples are the birthday party, or the first day of school. Unsurprisingly, the episode and episodic memory (Tulving, 1972, 1983) are also found to be heavily dependent on affects and feelings.

Given its nature, this organizing function of affects and feelings seems central for the emergence of self-reflective consciousness. In fact, subjective self-reflective consciousness has the peculiar qualities of always being:

a) Mine;
b) Cohesive; and
c) Unitary (Edelman & Tononi, 2000; Alcaro et al., 2017).

Whereas the unconscious contents are as follows:

a) Other;
b) Autonomous; and
c) Multiple.

Under this light, Jung's idea of the Ego as a complex at the center of self-reflective consciousness makes very much sense, as the Ego-complex would represent the structural organization that expresses these three features of consciousness – its being "mine", cohesive and unitary. Therefore, psychic organization, integrity, subjectivity and consciousness (we will see this later) manifest themselves through images and is constellated by an affect.

In Jung's motivational theory, the quantitative nature of the libido – of psychic energy – makes it easier to understand why too little or too much affectivity may be dangerous. Too little activation makes impossible the process of mind-building: it is the case of the pauci-symptomatic syndromes of schizophrenia, characterized by the presence of negative symptoms, or with a major depression.

Too much activation, on the other end, seems related to the productive forms of schizophrenia, or to the spectrum of manic disorders.

I think that the well-balanced, regulated activity of affectivity (the relative capacity of the mind to organize affects into images) is responsible also for the constellation – i.e., the coming into existence[2] – of what Jung called the Self. I will go back to this aspect when I discuss the neurobiological basis of affects, feelings and subjectivity.

From what I have been writing so far about Jung's motivational theory, the five innate motivational systems play the extra-psychic role of stimuli (albeit they seem to be very peculiar stimuli) for the initiation of all subsequent psychic activities. The function of these stimuli is the typical function of what we may call *attractors and constraints*.

8.1   Constraints, Attractors

In the bottom-up perspective that I am using, the issue that I am discussing involves the role of biological, psychological and, later I will add, *social* constraints and attractors. Such constraints and attractors and, further, what Sperber calls "susceptibilities" (see vol. II, § 5.1) play a key role in relation to the possibility that something like Jung's archetypes exists. The level of their influence may determine how much our psychology is constrained and pre-defined or, on the contrary, how much it is de-specialized and fully open to learning from experience. This issue is perhaps one of the most critical ones within Jungian psychology but is also still very much debated in the fields of evolutionary biology, general psychology and developmental psychology. For all these sciences, there is no question about the fact that constraints and attractors exist.

As we will see when I will discuss cognitive development, no one believes anymore that intelligence is wholly unconstrained, i.e., that it has the nature of a general intelligence, as Piaget believed. Therefore, the question is how much and how pervasively such constraints pre-determine our psychology – how much we are motivated by de-specialized drives and how much our psychology flows and develops within such constraints – as Jung's archetypal hypothesis maintains.

At this point, I wish to introduce the issue of constraints in general terms because this matter is deeply implicated in the discussion on "instincts" vs. "drives" that I have sketched out in the previous pages.

A constraint is defined as follows:

> refers to a reduction of the degrees of freedom of the elements of a system exerted by some collection of elements, or a limitation or bias on the variability or possibilities of change in the kind of such elements.
>
> Although the term has several meanings in diverse scientific fields, the idea of a constraint is usually employed in relation to conceptualizations in terms of levels or hierarchies.
>
> (Umerez & Mossio, 2013, p. 1)

Some general features of constraints are the following:

> Constraints do not interact with the elements they influence and their dynamics.
> They arise from dynamics at different levels of organization.
> Constraint relations are always a-symmetric and may give rise to new phenomena.
> Constraint refers to a reduction of the degrees of freedom of the elements of a system exerted by some collection of elements, or a limitation or bias on the variability or possibilities of change in the kind of such elements.
>
> (Umerez & Mossio, 2013, p. 1)

There is a general agreement on the presence of such constraints and attractors. In a way, we could define such constraints as archetypal conditions for organization and development. Starting from the "bottom" of the conceptual scale, in physics, a fundamental constraint is Heisemberg's indetermination principle; another one, among the many, are the Planck's constants. In biology, I have already mentioned the baffling case of the centipedes' number of legs and segments.

The perspective of this book is the transformation from biology to psychology. Maël Montévil and Matteo Mossio (2015) have understood that the fundamental physical-chemical autocatalytic processes that bind together different polymers – peptides – to reach a closure and form organized wholes that have the Kantian property for which their "parts exist for and by means of the whole" (for an overview: Kauffman, 2019) are also able to reproduce the very constraints out of which these polymers organize themselves. By such "constraint closure" (Montévil & Mossio, 2015), a system may construct itself through a nonequilibrium process; the next step will be the ignition of protocellular metabolic life.

Montévil and Mossio's groundbreaking contribution is situated at the threshold through which the physical-chemical domain trespasses into life, i.e., into biology. Thus, already from the very origin of life, the architecture of natural forms and functions evolve by and through constraints closure. This dynamic formal architecture, in my view, will also model the threshold from biology to psychology.

Under a psycho-biological perspective, biological constraints may shape the structural morphology of the body and of the sensory apparatus, which determine certain functional outcomes while inhibiting others. The classical example is that of the eye (Marr, 1982). The idea implicit in the notion of constraint – related to the conceptualization of levels and hierarchies – is clear with regard to the function of the eye and vision. In fact, it is important to remember that the eye is probably the organ that proves in the best way to be a product of evolutionary adaptation and that connect its "biological" feature with the *psychological functions* of vision for the production of image-schemas (see vol. I, § 9), which will eventually lead to proto-concepts and thoughts. Needless to recall the Greek etymology of the word "idea" from *eidos* (vision).[3]

I have already discussed what in *Homo sapiens* is de-specialized, therefore, excluding universal or recurrent psychological elements, like Jung's archetypes, and what is a specialized – i.e., what is a constrained product of natural selection.

Like the structure and the function of eye:

one could think of the eye as a tube that traverses metaphysical realms, one end of which obtrudes into the physical realm, the other into the mental. For modern monists, however, these two realms are simply alternative descriptions of the same thing, convenient for different analytic purposes. The "mental" consists of ordered relationships in physical systems that embody properties typically running under labels such as "information", "meaning", or regulation. From this point of view, there is no Cartesian tube: both ends of the visual system are physical and both are mental.

(Barkow et al., 1992, p. 58)

Another anatomical/biological constraint, which shows immediate hierarchical implications, is the existence of two biological sexes (not to be confused with psychosocial genders). From these biological constraints, psychological and anthropological outcomes arise, such as the reference to *binarism*,[4] or to the limited (constrained) possibilities of the combination of kin's relationships.

A central feature of the constraints and attractors we are discussing deals with the emergence from perception of image-schemas. For Lakoff and Johnson, it is from such schemas that the most important meaning-creating device emerges: the metaphor. For these authors:

> Concrete bodily experience not only constrains the "input" to the metaphorical projections but also the nature of the projections themselves, that is, the kinds of mappings that can occur across domains.
>
> (Johnson, 1990, 152)

For my discussion, the role of affects as constraints, and even more as attractors, is paramount. In fact, the triggering of an emotion will activate, channel and direct the organism's (in our case, the person's) whole representational and behavioral response towards a teleological goal, which may be described at the simplest, most general level as the *ongoing restoration of the organism's homeostatic metastability*.

In fact, we recall that homeostasis must be referred not to a process of stabilization (i.e., a process towards stasis and completion) but as a process guided by metastability – an ongoing process through which individual forms emerge through time as transient coagulations. The key feature of a metastable state, in physics, chemistry, biology but also in psychology, is that it is not the most stable state, but it can persist for a considerable amount of time, potentially transitioning to a more as yet potential stable state when triggered.

The role of constraints on (human) psychology – from behavior to learning – is inextricably linked with the discussion on how much of our psychological endowment is phylogenetically innate and inherited and how much is learned through ontogenetic development. I will discuss some relevant theories on cognitive development, such as those by A. Karmiloff-Smith and J. Mandler or M. Johnson later, especially because they are at the base of a much-quoted perspective against Jung's theory of innate archetypes by some Jungian scholars – first of all, Jean Knox. Now I would like to refer to the psycho-anthropological-biological branch of studies that we may refer to as "evolutionary psychology".

It is through the development of evolutionary psychology that, in recent years, evolutionary theory has had an important impact on cognitive psychology (Barkow et al., 1992).

Unlike sociobiology, evolutionary psychology focuses on what Cosmides and Tooby (1987) have described as the "missing link" (missing, that is, from sociobiological accounts) between genes and behavior, namely, the mind.

As Dan Sperber and Lawrence Hirschfeld write:

> Evolutionary psychologists view the mind as an organized set of mental devices, each having evolved as an adaptation to some specific challenge presented by the ancestral environment. There is, however, some confusion of labels, with some sociobiologists now claiming evolutionary psychology as a subdiscipline or even describing themselves as evolutionary psychologists.

. . . This perspective may help discover discrete mental mechanisms, the existence of which is predicted by evolutionary considerations and may help explain the structure and function of known mental mechanisms. As an example of the first type of contribution, the evolutionary psychology of sexual attraction has produced strong evidence of the existence of a special purpose adaptation for assessing the attractiveness of potential mates that uses subtle cues such as facial symmetry and waist-to-hips ratio (Symons, 1979; Buss, 1994).

(1999, p. cxiv)

Evolutionary psychologists seek to define universal psychological adaptations that have evolved by natural selection and to determine how such adaptations function in the contemporary environment. Therefore, they are interested in universals in human cognition, rather than in individual differences.

Natural selection is not a teleological process capable of foreseeing the future and planning ahead for it. Our evolved mechanisms were constructed and adjusted in response to the statistical composite of situations actually encountered by our species during its evolutionary history (Symons, 1992). These mechanisms were not designed to deal with modern circumstances that are evolutionarily unprecedented.

. . .

For these reasons, there is no warrant for thinking that selection would have favored cognitive mechanisms that are well-engineered for solving classes of problems beyond those encountered by Pleistocene hunter-gatherers. The widespread prejudice among cognitive psychologists for theories positing evolved architectures that consist of nothing but general-purpose problem solvers is therefore unjustified. The fact that a mechanism can sometimes solve novel modern problems can play no role in explaining how that mechanism came to have the design it does, because natural selection had no crystal ball. The fact that our evolved mechanisms sometimes operate successfully in changed modern circumstances is a purely secondary consequence of their Pleistocene-forged design. Moreover, well-engineered performance should be evident only under conditions that mimic relevant aspects of the ancestral environments in which these mechanisms were designed to operate.

In short, the statistically recurrent conditions encountered during hominid evolutionary history constituted a series of adaptive problems. These conditions selected for a set of cognitive mechanisms that were capable of solving the associated adaptive problems.

(Cosmides & Tooby, 1994, p. 87)

Therefore, if many developmental psychologists, some anthropologists and all "Durkheimiam" sociologists look at psychological competences as deriving from relatively unconstrained ontogenetic learning, i.e., from a supposedly *general* form of intelligence which would produce specific forms of adaptation (and imagination) based on local conditions, evolutionary psychologists refer to phylogenetic inherited modules, which are then activated during ontogenesis.

As we shall see, evolutionary psychology research offers an important convergence with Jung's theory of the archetypes, while at the same time recognizing and offering an explicatory model for anthropological and cultural variations.

I will use some references from evolutionary psychology, although I will do it in a cautious way for two reasons. First, neither sociobiology nor evolutionary psychology *sufficiently recognize the fundamental role of affects for phylogenetic evolution and ontogenetic development.* Second, sociobiology, but also evolutionary psychology, have a reductionist nature. Evolutionary psychology and especially sociobiology (Wilson, 1975) aim at explaining behavior, and in particular, social behavior, on the assumption that natural selection favors behaviors of an organism that tends to maximize the reproductive success of its genes. Also, evolutionary psychology tends to directly refer to a Darwinian concept of biological adaptation.

This reductionism is hinged on the interpretation of psychology as a form of Darwinian biological adaptation and, therefore, of the pivotal issue of biological selection through reproduction. Such an interpretation is based on the unilateral reference to Darwin's random processes of *natural* election over *sexual* selection. Already in Darwin (1871), the individual animal has a certain degree of individual freedom as to how use its lower biological constraints determined by its genome. In fact, as we will see, the higher-level formations that are built from the lower-level constraints, and which now make their environment, behave as teleological attractors that will use those constraints for their final goals. Every level of complexity, from the DNA to the social environment, has its own peculiar functions and problems to resolve within its specific space and provides top-down feedback all the way through this evolutionary and ontological ladder. In humans, this extends with a much more relevant scope to the degree of cultural and social variability and freedom vs. the lower psychological and biological constraints.

The most serious criticisms against such reductionism have come from anthropology, but we have already seen that today we have accumulating evidence that at a molecular-biological level, more complex systems – like the cell in relation to its DNA, or an individual in relation to its biological endowment – have already gained, together with their complexity, a degree of freedom by which they top-down interact and "harness" their lower constraints.

From this perspective, what for biology is "reproduction", for anthropology is "kinship". If the sociobiological paradigm held, kinship would be based exclusively on blood ties. In sociobiological terms and in terms of evolutionary psychology, kinship would be directly regulated by the Darwinian selective mechanism and by the preservation and passage of genes from one generation to another. This state of affairs has permeated anthropology since Lewis Henry Morgan founded the subject on that premise in *Systems of Consanguinity and Affinity in the Human Family* (1871). Therefore, kinship would be caused by such crypto-biological Darwinian conditions.

Contemporary anthropologists have very different opinions, to which I subscribe. Marshall Sahlins, for example, writes:

> Few concessions have been made to later ethnographic reports, none on the essential matter of the biological basis. One, however, is that the biological basis is "folk biology". The relations of procreation and birth turn out to be culturally relative, differently understood in different societies according to the local "theory of reproduction".
>
> (Sahlins, 2013, p. 64)

According to Sahlins, the keystone of sociobiology – i.e., that the Darwinian concept of biological fitness for selection and reproduction applies *directly* also to social and cultural structures – is folk biology. In fact, he provides a vast array of ethnographic data that clearly show that kinship is often based *not* on consanguinity but on symbolic, culturally determined forms of social organization.

> kinship is a thoroughly symbolic-cum-cultural phenomenon – as Lévi-Strauss said, for all his lingering nostalgia for the "biological family": Of course, the biological family is ubiquitous in human society. But what confers upon kinship its socio-cultural character is not what it retains from nature, but, rather, the essential way in which it diverges from nature. A kinship system does not consist in the objective ties of descent or consanguinity between individuals. It exists only in human consciousness; it is an arbitrary system of representations, not the spontaneous development of a real situation.
>
> . . . Besides the common means of establishing kinship in life rather than in utero – such as co-residence, commensality, living off the same land, friendship, etc. – such practices of participation in one another's existence are indefinitely many, inasmuch as they are culturally relative. One may be kin to another by being born on the same day (Inuit), by following the same tabus (Araweté), by surviving a trial at sea (Truk) or on the ice (Inuit), even by mutually suffering from ringworm (Kaluli). Somewhat more widely distributed is kinship through name-sharing between living persons, whereby the name-receiver takes on the personage and relationships of the name-giver, whether or not they were kin before. . . . This homonymous kinship is worth some discussion here, at once for notions of shared being that are completely independent of bodily connections and that are much more prevalent than relations of birth. In the exceptional case that proves this rule, kinship is virtually exclusively based on name-sharing.
>
> (Sahlins, 2013, pp. 64–69)

Sahlins rightly argues that in a cultural environment, it is not the Darwinian biological need for sexual reproduction (which implies consanguinity since what must be transmitted is the genome) that determines symbolic, social kinship, but it is the other way around. This position sets a precise limit to the reductionist nature of sociobiology and evolutionary psychology and needs a cautious and differentiated position in regard to these disciplines. So does the differentiation between biological constraints and psychological susceptibilities, which, as we shall see, are able to lift the biological realm towards the psycho-cultural one.

What I suggest is that at the social and cultural level, the protagonist is not anymore the biological subject that pursues its selective competition for reproduction; instead, it is the sum of those social structures, groups and institutions (i.e., symbolic entities) that now compete *to reproduce themselves* socially (here, the role of power is overwhelming: Bourdieu [1976, 1993a, 1993b]). Acting top-down, these higher formations – the social and cultural institutions – *use* sexuality and reproduction with a certain degree of freedom for cultural aims. Lévi-Strauss' theory of the prohibition of incest and the exchange of women (1947) as the cornerstone of social organization and social reproduction is a clear example of this.

Nevertheless, even if at this level we are not referring to a biological species[5] but to social groups, institutions and cultures, we are still referring to an *epidemiological, statistical* domain (Jung would have said the "collective") – not to *individual* destinies. In such a statistical domain, it is quite probable that a structural selective struggle for the fittest – which would act as a constraint, a general, not necessarily biological, rule to be followed – will anyway guarantee not only the survival of such social groups, structures and institutions based on cooperation but also, *through these social institutions*, that of their individual members. Therefore, Darwin's paradigm seems to be saved, yet at a non-reductive, non-biological, second-degree level – the level of the social, symbolic world.

Sahlins' position is important not only for his outstanding authority in the field of anthropology but also, and more specifically, for the direct connections of his theory of kinship to psychologists like Michael Tomasello's or Colin Trevarthen (1979; Trevarthen & Aitken, 2001), whose work I will refer in the next pages (see vol. I, § 10.1) and to the relationship and differentiation between biological constraints and psycho-cultural "susceptibilities" as described by Dan Sperber (see vol. II, § 5.1).

Despite the radical stance taken by important authors like Fodor, for whom real learning is not possible, as the mind's modules are rigidly encapsulated (Fodor, 1975),[6] in which the mind is, therefore, strictly constrained within its evolutionary modular nature, the modular and the developmental paradigms can and, I think, will eventually converge. We will see that the hypothesis of the existence of a non-specific, general intelligence is today obsolete, which for my discussion encourages the possibility that Jung's archetypal hypothesis was fundamentally correct.

For what concerns us here, I must underscore the fact that the constellation of a complex represents the emergence of a set of representations constrained by an affect. In fact, as I have already said, for Jung, the fundamental constraining agency, which limits and organizes psychic life, is the affect. The same constraining principle is described within different models and theories as *episodes* of episodic memory, as internal working models or "image-schemas" in cognitive science or as *modules' encapsulation* in evolutionary psychology.[7] Therefore, we may say that the complex is a sort of modularized psychosomatic structure/experience, whose representations are constrained by the affect.

From the beginning of biological life, affects are molded with motor activity and expressed by perceptions which produce modularized experiences (i.e., organized somehow like algorithms) and actions in which what Stern calls "developmental *fields*" describe "co-evolutionary niches", and therefore, they may be equated to Uexküll's *Umwelt*. Such modularized experiences will be infinitely metaphorized throughout individual and socio-cultural life. Without constraints and attractors, a combinatorial explosion would occur which would block any organism in a computational stalemate.

Referring to the need for constraints (which, as I said, form complexes/modules), Barkow, Cosmides and Tooby quote a beautiful line by Willam Blake, a quote that cannot but remind us of Bion's limit experience of O:[8]

> If the doors of perception were cleansed everything would appear to man as it is, infinite.
>
> (Barkow et al., 1992, p. 102)

In fact, to the question whether the human species is endowed with any, or a few, constraining biological predispositions (instincts) – i.e., in the principle of a supposedly wholly de-specialized nature of the human psyche – Jung's position is perfectly coincident with today's biologists, one of which is Giorgio Vallortigara.

> William James is of the opinion that man is swarming with instincts, while others restrict them to a very few processes barely distinguishable from reflexes, namely to certain movements executed by the infant, to particular reactions of its arms and legs, of the larynx, the use of the right hand, and the formation of syllabized sounds. In my opinion, this restriction goes too far, though it is very characteristic of human psychology in general.
>
> . . .
>
> The criterion of the all-or-none reaction proposed by Rivers has helped us to discover the operation of instinct everywhere in human psychology, and it may be that the concept of the primordial image will perform a similar service with regard to acts of intuitive apprehension.
>
> (Jung, 1919, § 271–278)

Vallortigara (1995), and then Lea et al. (1996), found out that human infants are able to perceptually complete a partially occluded image, only at 4–7 months of life, when chicks are able to do so right after the complete object (a red triangle) had been imprinted (a few days after birth).

The interesting point of the story is that in experiments with infants the perceptual completion of partially occluded objects emerges relatively late in development, between four and seven months of age, depending on whether moving or stationary stimuli are used. This seems to corroborate a rather widespread belief even among non-specialists, namely the idea that instincts would belong primarily to non-human animals (and particularly to supposedly lower animals) and learning to human beings. Thus, chicks would possess innate mechanisms for perceptual completion pre-set in their brains, while humans would need experience of the visual world to learn to display the same ability. I think this is wrong. The organisms living on the planet today are all equally evolved, reflecting the present but momentary outcome of an evolutionary radiation that began from common ancestors. Complex brains have evolved independently many times in the history of life. There are no inferior and superior animals, because evolution does not mean progress, but change.

(Vallortigara, 2021, p. 88)

In fact, Valenza et al. (2006) found out the following:

Human infants and infants up to a certain age have limited abilities to perceive continuous motion with their eyes and are instead more sensitive to stroboscopic motion, which can be generated by presenting static images in temporally and spatially discontinuous positions. For example, if an object is shown for a short time in one position and then, after a few fractions of a second, a second object is shown in a different position, instead of the successive presence of two objects, the movement of a single object moving through space is perceived. By repeating the perceptual completion experiment with stroboscopic instead of continuous movement, it was observed that human infants at very few hours of life show perceptual completion like chicks. The mechanism for completion is there from the beginning, but in species with inept offspring, such as humans, it does not manifest itself immediately (apart from under very special conditions such as stroboscopic motion) because it requires other parts of the visual system, such as those dedicated to the popular pursuit of continuous motion, to mature first.

(Vallortigara, 2021, p. 89)

So that Vallortigara, along with Jung, may argue the following:

In fact, in species deeply dependent on learning, as humans are rumoured to be, I would therefore expect more (not less) instincts (read: biological pre-dispositions), precisely because biological predispositions tend to make learning possible.

(Vallortigara, 2021, p. 88)

In my opinion, one way to interpret what Bion calls *nameless dread* (in conjunction with his bottom-up perspective of the irruption of O, untransformed by the alpha function), or what phenomenological psychiatry describes as *Wahnstimmung*, is the product of the absence or of a defective activity of those constraints that channel and limit all possible, imaginable responses and possibilities.

If one considers that the bodily perceptual apparatus – especially the visual one but the acoustic one as well – are basically a transmitter and a transformer of electrical impulses, or impulses that are conveyed by a relatively small number of biochemical molecules through the synapsis (i.e., below the Avogadro's number [see: Eccles, 1994]), we may say that some of the constraints to which I am referring may have to do with the transformation from the quantistic realm to the matter-extended (Newtonian) world.

Jung hypothesized that, after all, *the whole brain* might be a transformer of infinite not-extended energy (Bion's O, Jung's libido) into finite extended matter.

> On the other hand, one might ask the question whether we can, as hitherto go on thinking in terms of space and time, while modern physics begins to relinquish these terms in favor of a time space continuum. in which space is no more space and time is no more time. The question is, in short: shouldn't we give up the time-space categories altogether when we are dealing with psychic existence? It might be that the psyche should be understood as *unextended intensity* and not as a body moving with time. One might assume the psyche gradually rising from minute extensity to infinite intensity, transcending, for instance the velocity of light and thus irrealizing the body.
>
> (Jung, 1953, vol. 2, pp. 44–45)

For the definition of constraint that I have proposed, "the idea of a constraint is usually employed in relation to conceptualizations in terms of levels or hierarchies".

I have mentioned biological and psychological constraints and attractors, and I will develop further the theme later. As I said, the debates arise on *how constraining* are such constraints for humans, whose body and (conscious?) minds are highly flexible and de-specialized. As we saw speaking of precocial/altricial structures and competences, this discussion focuses on the neotenic nature of *Homo sapiens*, which implies a long process of psychological growth after birth (at least until the end of adolescence but quite probably until death), during which its biological and psychological endowment develops, through relationships, into cultural symbols.

Notes

1 This aspect sheds light on the co-evolutionary nature of Jung's paradigm, in which organism and environment are always structurally reciprocally correlated.

2 In Jung's – or Winnicott's, or my own – dispositional paradigm, this means the coming "out", the Aristotelian actualization of a potential.

3 For the relationship between the organ of the eye, its perceptual function and the role of image-formation for the development of categorial thoughts: Bucci, W. (1997).

4 With "binarism", I refer to the psychological and ontogenic principle of the oppositional structure of reality. Obviously, as no one may say what reality really is, a more parsimonious hypothesis is that such a binary structure is the way the human mind, not the world, is structured. Jung – or Hegel – imagined that reality emerges as a result of the interplay of *opposites*. Lévi-Strauss' anthropology revolves around this hypothesis (Lévi-Strauss, 1967), just as some post-structuralist anthropologists, like, for example, Rodney Needham (1980).

5 In fact, we must always remember that Darwin's natural selection regards not the individual but the overall species.
6 Encapsulation describes a particular form of encoding and organizing data. In the context of modules, it is about bundling the implementation details within the module and exposing only what is necessary for other parts of the program to interact with it. This helps in achieving information hiding and modularity.
7 These are some key aspects of module encapsulation:

1. Independence from general knowledge:
   Cognitive modules, if encapsulated, operate autonomously and independently of general knowledge or reasoning outside their specific domain. This means that the processes within a module are not easily influenced by information from other cognitive modules or general cognitive processes.
2. Limited access:
   Encapsulation implies that the information and processes within a module are not readily accessible to other cognitive modules. This limited access is thought to contribute to the specialized and efficient functioning of modules for their specific tasks.
3. Automatic processing:
   Encapsulated modules are often associated with automatic and rapid processing. This means that the operations within a module occur quickly and without conscious effort. For example, facial recognition might be considered an automatic and encapsulated process.
4. Task specificity:
   Module encapsulation is linked to the idea of task specificity. Each module is proposed to be specialized for a particular cognitive task, such as language processing, spatial navigation or face recognition. The encapsulation of these modules allows them to perform their tasks efficiently without interference from unrelated cognitive processes.

8 What Bion describes as K(nowledge) into O.

References

Alcaro, A., Carta, S., Panksepp, J. (2017). The Affective Core of the Self: A Neuro-Archetypical Perspective on the Foundations of Human (and Animal) Subjectivity. *Frontiers in Psychology*, 8, Article 1424.

Barkow, J., Cosmides, L., Tooby, J. (Eds.). (1992). *The Adapted Mind: Evolutionary Psychology and the Generation of Culture*. Oxford, New York, Toronto: Oxford University Press.

Bourdieu, P. (1976). Les Modes De Domination. *Actes De La Recherche En Sciences Sociale*, 2, 2–3.

Bourdieu, P. (1993a). Stratégies De Reproduction Et Modes De Domination. *Bulletin d'information de la Mission Historique Française en Allemagne*, 26–27, 125–141.

Bourdieu, P. (1993b). Esprits d'État. *Actes de la Recherche en Sciences Sociales*, 19, 96–97.

Bucci, W. (1997). *Psychoanalysis and Cognitive Science: A Multiple Code Theory*. New York: The Guiford Press.

Buss, D. (1994). *The Evolution of Desire: Strategies of Human Mating*. New York: Basic Books.

Cosmides, L., Tooby, J. (1987). From Evolution to Behavior: Evolutionary Psychology as the Missing Link. In: *The Latest on the Best: Essays on Evolution and Optimality*, pp. 277–306. J. Dupré (Ed.). Cambridge, MA: MIT Press.

Cosmides, L., Tooby, J. (1994). Origins of Domain Specificity: The Evolution of Functional Organization. In: M*apping the Mind: Domain Specificity in Cognition and Culture*. L. Hirschfeld, S. Gelman (Eds.). New York: Cambridge University Press.

Darwin, C. (1871/2000). *The Descent of Man, and Selection in Relation to Sex.* Project Gutenberg.

Eccles, J.C. (1994). *How the Self Controls Its Brain.* Verlin, Heidelberg, New York: Springer-Verlag.

Edelman, G., Tononi, G. (2000). *A Universe of Consciousness: How Matter Becomes Imagination.* New York: Basic Books.

Fodor, J. (1975). *The Language of Thought.* Harvard University Press.

Johnson, M. (1990). *The Body in the Mind.* Chicago: Chicago University Press.

Jung, C.G. (1919). The Instinct and the Unconscious. In: *The Collected Works of C.G. Jung.* Vol. 8. London: Routledge.

Jung, C.G. (1928). A Review of the Complex Theory. In: *The Collected Works of C.G. Jung.* Vol. 8. London: Routledge.

Jung, C.G. (1953). *Letters. Selected and Edited by Gerhard Adler in Collaboration with Aniela Jaffé.* 2 Vols. Princeton: Princeton University Press.

Kauffman, S.A. (2019). *A World Beyond Physics: The Emergence and Evolution of Life.* Oxford, UK: Oxford University Press.

Lea, S.E.G., Slater, A.M., Ryan, C.M.E. (1996). Perception of Object Unity by Young Chicks: A Comparison with the Human Infant. *Infant Behaviour and Development,* 19, 501–504.

Lévi-Strauss, C. (1967). *The Savage Mind.* Chicago: Chicago University Press.

Lévi-Strauss, C. (1969). *The Elementary Structures of Kinship (1947).* Boston: Beacon Press.

Marr, D. (1982). *Vision: A Computational Investigation into the Human Representation and Processing of Visual Information.* San Francisco: Freeman.

Montévil, M., Mossio, M. (2015). Biological Organisation as Closure of Constraints. *Journal of Theoretical Biology,* 372, 179–191.

Needham, R. (1980). *Reconnaissances.* Toronto: University of Toronto Press.

Otto, R. (1968). *The Idea of the Holy.* Oxford: Oxford University Press.

Sahlins, M. (2013). *What Kinship is and is Not.* Chicago: University of Chicago Press.

Sperber, D., Hirschfeld, L. (1999). *Culture, Cognition, and Evolution,* pp. cxi–cxxxii. Cambridge, MA: MIT Encyclopedia of the Cognitive Sciences (MIT Press).

Symons, D. (1979). *The Evolution of Human Sexuality.* New York: Oxford University Press.

Symons, D. (1992). *On the use and misuse of Darwinism in the study of human behavior.* In J. Barkow, L. Cosmides, & J. Tooby (Eds.), *The adapted mind: Evolutionary psychology and the generation of culture.* New York: Oxford University Press.

Trevarthen, C. (1979). Communication and Cin early Infancy. A Description of Primary Intersubjectivity. In: *Before Speech: The Beginning of Human Communication,* pp. 321–347. M. Bullowa (Ed.). London: Cambridge University Press.

Trevarthen, C., Aitken, K.J. (2001). Infant Intersubjectivity: Research, Theory, and Clinical applications. *Journal of Child Psychology and Psychiatry,* 42, 1, 3–48.

Tulving, E. (1972). Episodic and Semantic Memory. In: *Organization of Memory,* pp. 382–402. E. Tulving, W. Donaldson (Eds.). New York: Academic Press.

Tulving, E. (1983). *Elements of Episodic Memory.* Oxford: Clarendon Press.

Umerez, J., Mossio, M. (2013). Constraints. In: *Encyclopedia of Systems Biology.* W. Dubitzky, O. Wolkenhauer, K.H. Cho, H. Yokota (Eds.). New York, NY: Springer.

Valenza, E., Leo, I., Simion, F. (2006). Perceptual Completion in Human Newborn Infants. *Child Development,* 77, 1810–1821.

Vallortigara, G. (1995). Perception of Partly Occluded Objects by Young Chicks. *Perception & Psychophysics,* 57, 971–976.

Vallortigara, G. (2021). *Il Pulcino di Kant.* Milano: Adelphi.

Wilson, E.O. (1975). *Sociobiology: The New Synthesis.* Cambridge: Belknap Press.

Chapter 9

Cognitive Development

The previous discussion on perceptual/affective constraints and attractors was necessary to frame and introduce this chapter, dedicated to cognition.

To further my discussion on affects, feelings and emotions, I would like to refer to Jean Knox's influential approach to the formation of complexes, including the collective ones (the archetypes) and, later, to a model proposed by John Merchant (2016), which I find at the same time interesting and debatable.

In several of her contributions (2001, 2003, 2004a, 2004b, 2009, 2010) on the formation of complexes, Knox refers to the research by Jean Mandler, Mark Johnson and George Lakoff, who theorize what they call "perceptual analysis". This is a mechanism by which infants actively derive meaning from perceptual activity. Infants use this mechanism to redescribe perceptual information into an abstract, image-schematic format.

Referring to this model, Knox writes (and I agree):

> genes and the self-organization of the human brain] do not encode complex mental imagery and processes, but instead act as initial catalysts for developmental processes out of which early psychic structures [like image schemas] reliably emerge. . . . [Archetypes are] emergent structures resulting from a developmental interaction between genes and environment that is unique for each person. Archetypes are not 'hard-wired' collections of universal imagery waiting to be released by the right environmental trigger.
>
> (Knox, 2004a, p. 4)

Adopting a bottom-up analysis, Knox focusses her discussion on the early mind/brain development of the human infant's perceptual processes and utilizes Johnson's (2013) model of the image-schema as the early psychic structure which she believes constitutes the basis of later concept formation and related imagery. Knox says:

> Whilst image schemas are without symbolic content, they provide a reliable scaffolding on which meaningful imagery and thought is organized and constructed, thus meeting the need for a model that provides for the archetype-as-such and

DOI: 10.4324/9781003586258-9

the archetypal image. If we adopt this model for archetypes, we have to discard the view that they are genetically inherited and consider them to be reliably repeated early developmental achievements.

(Knox, 2004a, p. 9)

Johnson's image-schemas create a conceptual structure from the spatial structure of objects and their movements, resulting in notions such as *animacy, inanimacy, agency and containment.*

Mandler explains:

Image schemas are simplified redescriptions of various relations that are involved when objects take part in events. . . . Most of the image schemas that have been analyzed have a kinetic or dynamic character, representing movement and, in some accounts, forces acting in space.

(Mandler, 2012, p. 19)

In contrast with most perceptual processing, which is not analyzed in this fashion, redescription into the image-schematic format simplifies perceptual information and makes it potentially accessible for purposes of concept formation and thought.

In addition to enabling preverbal thought, image-schemas provide a foundation for language acquisition by creating an interface between the continuous processes of perception and the discrete nature of language (I will come back to this in § vol. II, 9.3). They are like elementary ideas that cannot be further defined or analyzed within a particular conceptual system. Instead, they serve as the starting point for constructing more complex thoughts and expressions. They are *non-propositional* (which means that they cannot be proven to be true or false), *analogical* representations grounded in the perceptual world of the infant (where "perceptual" refers especially to percepts-in-movement).

From these formats, the earliest meanings – called *conceptual primitives* – are formed. Conceptual primitives, therefore, refer to the basic building blocks, or fundamental concepts, that form the foundation of human cognition and language.

If perceptual analysis results in concept formation, there must be some vocabulary, or set of elementary meanings, from which the concepts are composed. Whatever meanings infants derive from perceptual analysis, they seem likely to be rather global in character. Even for adults, conscious conceptualizations about objects and events tend to be crude and contain vastly less information than the perceptual knowledge used for recognition. Infants' concepts are apt to be cruder still and may not even be couched in prepositional form as many adult concepts appear to be.

(Mandler, 1992, p. 590)

Such primitives are the base for the emergence of what are called "ontological categories". They are the most general categories whose instances have the same

Table 9.1   *Perceptual analysis and conceptual primitives.*

J. MANDLER'S PERCEPTUAL ANALYSIS AND CONCEPTUAL PRIMITIVES

PATH	±MOVE START
PATH	ANIMATE MOVE
END PATH	BLOCKED MOVE
PATH TO	INTO
LINK	OUT OF
THING	BEHIND
±CONTACT	APPEAR
CONTAINER	DISAPPEAR
OPEN	EYES
LOCATION	

Suggested list of primitives used in building the first image-schemas (J. M. Mandler & C. Pagán Cánovas, 2014)

criterion of identity. Indeed, a large number of classificatory concepts are formed by reference to prototypes that condense, in a network of associated representations, sets of particular cases that have a "family air". A classic example is the concept of a house, which is not constructed from a list of specific traits but is the result of a synthetic classificatory process produced from an intuitive schematic representation of what a typical house should conform to (Rosch, 1973, 1978).

For what I am trying to argue, ontological categories have a very important role. An example of an ontological category is that of ANIMAL; others may be the following: TOOL, NUMBER, PERSON, etc.

Not only are such categories very general (for instance, the ontological category PLANT may describe all objects that grow without moving away, that need water and soil, etc.) but they are also very stable, so much so that they are hypothesized as being universally present. Their function is inferred by the fact that when a child (but also an adult) learns a new concept, this concept will be immediately inserted into an ontological category and will allow the subject to produce *default inferences*.

Even though every piece of information that enters in one's mind is constantly distorted and reshuffled and interpreted, the mind is not a free-for-all of random associations. One major reason is the presence of mental dispositions for arranging conceptual material in certain ways rather than others. Crucial to this explanation is the distinction between concepts and ontological categories, or, as Boyer calls them, "templates".

some generalizations are produced automatically when you learn a new concept. The move from "this one has live cubs" (a particular fact) to "they all have live cubs" (a generalization) is made automatically because the animal template does not allow several different values in the "reproduces" box. So the child does not have to learn how an animal reproduces more than once for each animal kind. The child is told: "This is a walrus. See how big her belly is! She'll probably give birth to cubs very soon". A few days later this child may well tell a friend that walruses do not lay eggs; they get pregnant and deliver live babies. This is not a replication of information she received but an inference from that information. Even very young children can produce such inferences because they connect the information received about a particular animal to an abstract template ANIMAL. This template works like a recipe and could be called "recipe for producing new animal-concepts". There are, obviously, fewer templates than concepts. Templates are more abstract than concepts and organize them. You need only one ANIMAL template for the many, many different animal concepts you will acquire. You need one TOOL template although you may have concepts for many different tools. Concepts depend on your experience, your environment, but templates are much more stable.

(Boyer, 2001, pp. 54–55)

The hypothesis of the existence of such ontological categories will explain that the infinite individual and cultural variations at the conceptual level are constrained from the beginning. The existence of these categories is connected with the concept of susceptibility, which I will discuss in vol. II, § 5.1.

These elegant theories are purely cognitive. They are so persuasive that it is very easy to lose sight of the fact that normal psychological functioning has to do with organizing one's experience, not with theorizing intellectually about concepts, perhaps of no personal interest. All the categorization and inferential processes are not a product of something like a Kantian "Pure Reason" but of the whole personality (in fact, Kant did not limit his work to pure reason but extended it in his "Critique of Practical Reason" and in the "Critique of Judgement").

This means that cognitive categories have a meaning because they are triggered by an emotional interest, which may also disturb the very process of their formation. After all, Jung's career started precisely by studying the role and the interference of (unconscious) highly active affects (also) on cognition through language and on the formation of *affective-cognitive* categories. Therefore, I will keep emphasizing the need to put back affects and emotions at the center, even if what has been mostly researched is the cognitive – imaginal and, further, conceptual – part of the psyche's workings.

When I will directly deal with images as organizations that emerge from affects, I will come back to such conceptual primitives and ontological categories as organizations that emerge from the constraints of the human mind (and its perceptual systems), which, in turn, constrain and scaffold the organizations that will emerge from them – mental abstract representations, all the way to the semantics of words.

The main idea is that from the basic constraints at the level of the ectopsychic latent, dispositional structure of the BrainMind (let's call it level 1), new formations reflectively emerge (here, I have in mind Jung's transgressive "instinct" of reflection) at level 2. This is the level that contains conceptual primitives. From these constrained, scaffolded formations, new constrained ones will emerge at level 3 – at the level of metaphorized representations and abstract concepts. The contents of level 3 will be much more numerous (potentially infinite) and will present an increasing variability as transformations and variations-on-a-theme, up until language appears at the declarative cultural, symbolic, semantic level.

This ontogenetic perspective is far from being new and original. It is at the base of Hjemslev's linguistic structuralism (Hjelmslev, 1961), in which the original raw matter of language is the meaningless acoustic inputs (such as a gust of wind, a cracking noise), which are transformed into phonetic spaces (still virtual), such as /a/, /b/, /p/.[1] By virtue of these articulations, linguistic substances (now concrete) can be produced. The form of expression articulates the matter according to phonological patterns, and vowels and consonants can be produced and recognized, transforming natural sounds into phonemes and morphemes.

The issue that interests us here is that this primary "acoustic stuff" is constrained by the human earing apparatus, as the transformation of natural sounds into phonemes is constrained by the human phonatory apparatus, which can utter just a few dozen sounds, which, at the next levels, will produce an infinite number of sentences.

This would be level 1 From this level, the process of transformation and abstraction from level 1 will produce morphemes (level 2), which at this point already represent a meaning expressed by a sound.

The combination of morphemes will produce an indeterminate number of words (level 3), and the combination of words will produce a virtually infinite number of syntagms, metaphors, narratives, etc. (as Borges reports from his *Library of Babel*).

I will go back to this ontogenetic scheme in vol. II, § 9.3, when I will discuss the possibility that from something like these conceptual primitives (very few), a larger – but still limited – number of meanings expressed in words in *all the natural languages* (lexical universals) may emerge. From their combination and further abstraction, the stunning, colossal diversity of the cultural realm would be produced, yet still constrained within the same limits that were set at level 1.

This ontogenetic development unfolds as a transition from procedural unconscious knowledge to declarative conscious knowledge. The question is this: Why is it so important? It is important to understand the relation between the hardwired, implicit, inaccessible, procedural knowledge rooted in *neurosensory motor mechanisms* on the one hand (level 1) and the explicit, verbal, symbolic, accessible, public, conceptual, declarative knowledge rooted in *socio-cultural mechanisms* on the other levels (from the ectopsychic level 1 to all the further levels, which have a psychic nature).

In the current literature, sensory-motor intelligence is mostly assimilated into what is generally known as procedural knowledge, against declarative knowledge (Mandler, 2004). During cognitive development, a child undergoes the transition from a domain-specific[2] modular, unconscious, nonverbal stage to non-modular, or non-domain-specific, conscious, conceptual and verbal declarative knowledge.

Therefore, since we do not begin with a display of verbal declarative knowledge at birth, we must account for this transition.

This issue implies other important questions, which I will discuss later in this book: How much and how is conscious knowledge determined by the unconscious one? How much such an unconscious "knowledge" is inherited? Can such an inherited module change during ontogenesis, or does it remain exactly what it is? And if it changes, how and in which ways does it change?[3]

Piaget's model of cognitive development aptly identifies the problem of such a transition as the focus on the transition from the first stage to the second. He mentions that sensory-motor operations provide the early schemes for developing the corresponding concepts (schemas) (Piaget, 1970). In his model, cognitive agents act on objects, and this action is essential for learning. In this sense, each subject constructs by acting on experience.

Piaget made a strict connection between motor competence and conceptual competence. Although he underestimated infants' cognitive abilities and considered the sensory-motor stage to be preconceptual, his studies continue to be relevant to date, for his identification of the problem is arguably correct. Subsequent studies on infants showed that such a stage may not be more than a few months after birth, while nativists argued that conceptual knowledge and consciousness are innate (Carey & Gelman, 1991).

In a contribution, based on the work of several other researchers, Jean Mandler provides an account of Piaget's limits, in assuming that infants during the first stage do not have declarative knowledge. Mandler argues that both sensory-motor competence and conceptual competence develop almost at the same time and that this happens very early, as early as six months after birth (Mandler, 2004).

I would like to emphasize the fundamental role of perceptual analysis, i.e., the bodily movement (motor patterns) and the movements of objects which the infant perceives not by their common features but around some (possibly quite primitive) notion of *kind* (this brings us back to Jung's definition of psychic energy as "motion relation"). In fact, goal-oriented (i.e., meaningful, teleological) movement coordination and movement perception seem to be the decisive factors for image-schemas formation, which will lead to conceptual primitives. We may recall Jung's idea of psychoid "energy", libido, as an abstract concept of motion relations. Jung is clearly making explicit that what he called "energy" is not a real "thing" but an explicatory principle – something like what in physics is called "quantity of motion" of a body. Once applied to the empirical world, such a concept of energy/motion fits quite well with the role of motion for the formation of structured mental (unconscious) schematic images (motion relations), which will provide the "cognitive" format for the meaning that affects activate.

Associated to this theory, in *Beyond Modularity* (1996), Annette Karmiloff-Smith describes her theory of *representational redescription* to explain how children learn how to conceptualize, understand and follow proper formal cognitive rules in various domains, like language, mathematics, physics, etc. Such redescription of procedural information is a more complex version of Mandler's perceptual analysis.

During the process of representational redescription, implicit *procedural* knowledge transforms into explicit declarative conceptual knowledge by a process of re-encoding (Karmiloff-Smith, 1996).

According to the theory, cognitive development involves a sequence of stages, and at each stage, there is a reorganization or redescription of cognitive representations.

Karmiloff-Smith argued that cognitive development is not a linear process, and different cognitive domains may develop at different rates. She also emphasized the importance of considering both typical and atypical development to gain a comprehensive understanding of cognitive development.

Karmiloff-Smith proposed that *implicit* learning plays a crucial role in the early stages of cognitive development. She argued that children engage in implicit learning processes that contribute to the formation and reorganization of mental representations through a sequence of stages (see Figure 9.1). These mental representations, or cognitive structures, undergo redescriptions over time as the child interacts with the environment and develop from an initial phase in which the format of representations is implicit, to a next phase in which the format is *explicit*, to a third phase in which the child accesses data in a conscious way, to a final phase in which such data are available for a verbal report. I assimilate such an inborn ability to redescribe these representations and transform their format to Jung's reflective "instinct" and to its transgressive nature.

ANNETTE KARMILOFF-SMITH REPRESENTATIONAL REDESCRIPTION

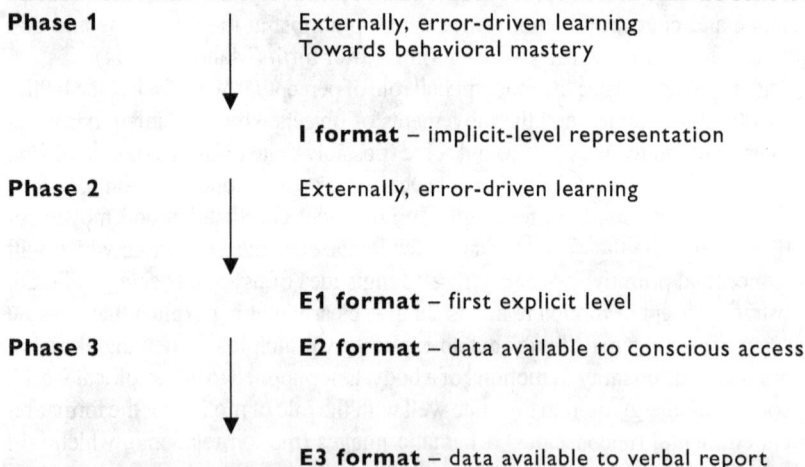

Phase 1   Externally, error-driven learning
                       Towards behavioral mastery

                       I format – implicit-level representation

Phase 2   Externally, error-driven learning

                       E1 format – first explicit level

Phase 3   **E2 format** – data available to conscious access

                       E3 format – data available to verbal report

---

Figure 9.1 The redescription from **I** to **E1** involves perceptual analysis and primitive categorization. Here, the role of affectivity should be taken in more careful consideration by researchers. What produces the subsequent reflexive redescriptions from **E1** to **E2** seems to be something like Jung's "instinct" of reflexivity. This will be at work also for the development of emotions from primary emotions to secondary and tertiary emotions.

Karmiloff-Smith's redescriptions result from the interaction between genetic factors and the child's experiences with the environment. For instance, she refers to "*innately specified attention biases*" from which learning, further constructivist modularization and redescriptive representation begin. Therefore, she tries to integrate innatism and learning.

Karmiloff-Smith writes:

> but perhaps you have by now have acquired . . . some of my epistemological schizophrenia – accepting the need for some innate predispositions for the initial architecture of the infant mind while maintaining a constructivist view of subsequent development. Clearly the nativist perspective is important for our present purposes. The static nativist view cannot explain why children go beyond successful learning.
>
> (1996, p. 77)

I agree with Annette Karmiloff-Smith. Yet we must once again underline that she is referring specifically to *cognitive* development, and she is using "*learning*" in a specific, restricted sense, the sense that I decided to call secondary, "epistemic". Its epistemic character derives directly from its sensory-motor origins. This feature is at the same time a strength and a weakness. It is a strength for the obvious very relevant scientific results of this cognitive line of research. It is a weakness because it does not take in consideration the fundamental role of affects and emotions, which confer a primary meaning to human cognition.

An important implication of these theories on the emergence of conceptual primitives and on the way cognitive development unfolds from the biological body is the idea that all cognitive processes, from the simplest to the most abstract ones such as mathematics (Lakoff & Nuñez, 2001), all are fundamentally based on the production of metaphors.

Within this so-called "embodied cognition" perspective, Lakoff and Johnson (1999, 2003) argue that human cognition, up to the most abstract reasoning, depends on the production of metaphors. Metaphors make use of the concrete, "low-level" structures of the sensory-motor system, like the ones Mandler described. While Mandler speaks of conceptual primitives, emerging from the abstraction of the perceptual-motor system (primarily the visual one) made possible by "perceptual analysis", for Lakoff and Johnson, "primary metaphors" also emerge from the same perceptual-motor system.

Such primary metaphors, therefore, are *embodied* forms of cognition, which generalize and abstract sensory-motor experiences, such as, for example, the up-down orientation of the human body, the perceptual experience of inside-outside or the sensory experience of a sweet food. From bodily experiences, primary metaphors may emerge, like "*Rising* [up] to success", "Chairs are *contained* in the class of sitting objects" or "*Sweet* are the uses of adversity" (as in Shakespeare's *As You Like It*). One fundamental implication of all this is that the endless creativity of the human spirit and the diversity of human languages and cultures emerges as explicit abstractions, generalizations and cross-domains synthesis, from constrained, embodied, innate sensory-motor maps activated, imbued with meaning and held together by affectivity.

> To say that image schemata "constrain" our meaning and understanding and that metaphorical systems "constrain" our reasoning is to say that they establish a range of possible patterns of understanding and reasoning. They are like channels in which something can move with a certain limited, relative freedom.
>
> Some movements (inferences) are not possible at all. They are ruled out by the image schemata and metaphors. But within these limits, there is a measure of freedom or variability that is heavily context dependent. Which inferences are sanctioned will depend, as we have seen, on the metaphorically organized background against which phenomena appear, questions are posed, investigations are performed, and hypotheses are formulated.
>
> (Johnson, 2013, p. 137)

According to Lakoff and Johnson, metaphors are propositional concepts that emerge when two domain-specific representations or concepts derived from their original constraining non-propositional[4] image-schemata are related and juxtaposed in a cross-domain way.

If, for instance, we take the metaphor "time is money", we may see what is really involved:

> is our understanding of a situation by means of connections across domains of our experience (here, the domains of temporality and of monetary transactions). The metaphorical "proposition" TIME IS MONEY only represents certain discrete and abstractable structures of a complex cross-categorical experience (=our understanding) of temporal relations, and this experience involves bodily orientations, perceptions, and actions that have linguistic and cultural dimensions.
>
> (*Ibidem*, p. 103, See also: Lakoff, 1987; Lakoff & Johnson, 2003)

As Goodwyn summarizes, for Lakoff and Johnson:

> Metaphors are "mappings" that translate data from one domain, say the emotional domain, and "map" it into another domain, say "traveling" to create things like the LOVE IS A JOURNEY metaphor, and this mapping is used by the brain to make nebulous concepts more concrete and understandable.
>
> (Goodwyn, 2012, p. 47)

In a way, this focus on cognition is amply justified by the discoveries and the extremely refined and powerful models that these paradigms developed. So for these authors, the patterns that organize our bodily experiences preconceptually have their own specific sensory-motor logic. Structural preconceptual correlations in experience made by movements and perceptions produce metaphors, which generate a map of this biologically-based sensory-motor logic (out of which Mandler's conceptual primitives emerge) onto a more abstract, semiotic domain. Hence, cognition is originally constantly moved by affects, organized by the "logic" of the sensory-motor patterns and "filled" with perceptual material (like the visual one, which produces images), which, via further abstraction, will turn into abstract concepts and words.

Lakoff and Johnson's theory of metaphors as cross-domain syntheses rests upon the evidence that humans – and surely, animals in general – are able to solve the issue of perceptual unity thanks to the presence of innate competences. Daniel Stern's masterful account of the child's development (1985) rests on the basis of our innate ability to recognize that the object that we see is the same input that we feel, or hear, or smell. Starting from Meltzoff's observations and experiments in 1979, there is no doubt that infants are predesigned to be able to perform a cross-modal transfer of information that permits them to recognize a correspondence across their sensory-motor apparatus. Meltzoff refers to the findings of several experiments carried out in the late 1970, which raised profound doubts about how infants learn about the world, that is, how they connect experiences.

> What was at stake was the longstanding philosophical and psychological problem of perceptual unity – how we come to know that something seen, heard, and touched may in fact be the same thing. How do we coordinate information that comes from several different perceptual modalities but emanates from a single external source? These experiments drew widespread attention to the infant's capacity to transfer perceptual experience from one sensory modality to another.
>   . . . Meltzoff and Borton's . . . blindfolded three-week-old infants and gave them one of two different pacifiers to suck on. One pacifier had a spherical-shaped nipple and the other was a nipple with nubs protruding from various points around its surface. After the baby had had some experience feeling (touching) the nipple with only the mouth, the nipple was removed and placed side by side with the other kind of nipple. The blindfold was taken off. After a quick visual comparison, infants looked more at the nipple they had just sucked.
>   . . . On theoretical grounds, infants should not have been able to do this task. A Piagetian account would have required that they first form a schema of what the nipple felt like (a haptic schema) and a schema of what the nipple looked like (a visual schema); then these two schemas would have to have some traffic or interaction (reciprocal assimilation), so that a coordinated visual-haptic schema would result (Piaget, 1952). Only then could the infants accomplish the task. Clearly, the infants did not in fact have to go through these steps of construction. They immediately "knew" that the one they now saw was the one they had just felt. Infants are predesigned to be able to perform a cross-modal transfer of information that permits them to recognize a correspondence across touch and vision.
>
> (Stern, 1985, pp. 810–832)

Such innate cross-modal competence needs no learning and coordinates all senses to construct a coherent perceptual world (Meltzoff & Moore, 1977; Meltzoff & Borton, 1979; Lewcowicz & Turkewitz, 1980, 1981; Allen et al., 1977; Wagner & Sakowitz, 1983; Miller & Byrne, 1984; McGurk & MacDonald, 1976).

What is relevant for us is that such mechanism, at a biological level, seems to be the exact reflection (hence, Jung's reflective "instinct" at play) of the one that occurs at a cognitive and semiotic level; it is a precursor of the process of metaphorization that coordinates different domains into one. I will soon go back to this reflective aspect. For the moment, it is necessary to distinguish between the nature of perceptual coherence that makes it possible to perceive an object – an apple, for instance – as something unitary (and, therefore, that produces a feeling of certainty and orientation regarding the nature of our perceptions; something impaired in some forms of schizophrenia) from true metaphors, which, by integrating different domains into one, actually do not denote anything precise as a perception but connote an open, creative, symbolic space that organizes an ongoing process of reflection and learning. In a way, we might say that with perceptual unity, exploration may *end* because I feel sure that the object – and my own self – is what it is. With a true semiotic metaphor, exploration *begins*. While cross-modal coherence belongs to the altricial level of the mind, semiotic metaphors and symbols, which emerge from them, belong to the infinitely open, precocial level.

This process involves not only the emotionally laden meanings expressed by sensory data (mostly visual) in dreams but also those thought in waking life. Images in dreams would also be condensed sources of meaning – symbols. They are the image-like, non-discursive configurations which emerge from the body's sensory-motor activity patterns and are triggered and regulated by affects. These symbols may be further unraveled into discursive metaphors and thoughts.[5] Their symbolic nature and destiny is to be fully meaningful only if not completely explainable.

As we are now dealing with the reflective transformation from the biological sensory-motor logic to the psycho-logic of thinking and meaning, I would like to point to an analogy between Jurij Lotman's concept of the "semiosphere" (2001) and the archetype as a connecting function (in this case, see also Brooke, 1991). In fact, I think that the archetype may be also interpreted as the fundamental function of Lotman's semiosphere.

In Lotman's holistic perspective, the semiosphere designates the semiotic individual and global environment from which the meanings of the parts – the *signs* – that compose it emerge. In my view, the archetype as a function-in-between is consistent with these characteristics in two distinct and related senses.

First, the archetype may be seen as a relational function between the parts that compose any whole, "individual" space and to which it provides meaning, therefore, acting as the meaning-giver connection-between.

Second, the archetype may be seen also as a *transformative* device. This transformative device is described by Jung when he is discussing the relationship and differentiation between the "biological" instinct and the "psychological" meaning with these words:

> Just as we have been compelled to postulate the concept of an instinct determining or regulating our conscious actions, so, in order to account for the uniformity and regularity of our perceptions, we must have recourse to the correlated concept of a factor determining the mode of apprehension. It is this factor which I call the archetype or primordial image. *The primordial image might suitably be described as the instinct's perception of itself, or as the self-portrait of the instinct,* in exactly the same way as consciousness is an inward perception of the objective life-process.
>
> (Jung, 1919, pp. 136–137. My italics)

In a semiotic sense, it seems to me that Jung is telling us that at a certain level of reflective redescription, the archetype is a [semiotic] reflection of the [biological] instinct upon itself. This second characteristic is consistent with the description of the processes of metaphorization emerging from sensorimotor structures described by Johnson and Lakoff.

Indeed, in this second sense – taking into account the close relationship between what the Russian biologist Ivan V. Vernadsky (2013) called the "biosphere" (as the global biological environment constituted by the relationships between living organisms on the planet's surface), to which Lotman explicitly refers, and the semiosphere – the archetype can also be thought of as a metaphorical function between the biological level of the biosphere and the semiotic (i.e., psychological and symbolic) level of the semiosphere itself. In other words, it may be seen as a meaning-giving function that transcends the biological and psychological individual, connecting it to its position in the biosphere as a living creature.

In my opinion, two other features link archetype and semiosphere.

The first: According to Lotman, the emergence of meaning does not proceed from the "atomic" components of the verbal utterance studied by Pierce or de Saussure, a discursive meaning which proceeds diachronically (one word after another) to being fully signified (and in which syntax, i.e., the arrangement of what comes first and what follows, is crucial, according to Chomsky's theory). Meaning, for Lotman, emerges from its inextricable global relational context – the semiosphere. Similarly, in a Jungian psychological view, it is not the discursive linguistic *sign* that produces symbolic meaning but the *image*, which is itself, like the semiosphere, made up of parts synchronically represented all together.

Secondly, both (for Lotman) the semiosphere and (for Jung) the archetype possess the characteristic of "individuality" (i.e., of organic wholeness). In fact, outside their boundary, there is neither meaning nor true alternative representability. While for Lotman's semiosphere, this boundary is defined by the "sum of the linguistic filters of translation" (Lotman, 1985). For the archetype, the boundary is manifested by the fact that, when an archetype bursts into consciousness, the personality is invaded "across the board" since, for the subject "invaded" by an archetype, what is outside this archetype becomes utterly meaningless, whereas, within its "semiotic space", the activated archetype seems to constitute the total emotional-cognitive environment by and within which everything is explained. Referring to an acute activation of an autonomous complex, Jung wrote:

> a traumatic complex brings about dissociation of the psyche. The complex is not under the control of the will and for this reason it possesses the quality of psychic autonomy.
>
> Its autonomy consists in its power to manifest itself independently of the will and even in direct opposition to conscious tendencies: it forces itself tyrannically upon the conscious mind. The explosion of *affect is a complete invasion of the individual*, it pounces upon him like an enemy or a wild animal.
>
> (Jung, 1921b/1928, §266. My italics)

On a psychopathological scale, a very simple example is that of delusional thinking, while on a cultural (collective) scale, one contemporary example may be the loss of any positive meaning connected to the Senex in our Puerile capitalistic world. Slowness, age, spirit, past, preservation, meditation, etc., have become so meaningless that everyone seems obsessed with youth, excitement, consumption, materialism, novelty, velocity, action and future. If we take into account Panksepp's description of the basic features of primary emotional systems, we may recall that one of them seems to describe such a feature of "individuality".

As Montag and Davis summarize (2018), for Panksepp:

> the emotional arousal elicited by these primary emotional systems influences sensory gating processes of the brain. This means that activation of emotional neural networks can modify what information ultimately will be processed from the brain (and also in what manner). In addition, the salience of a stimulus is modified by the activity of neural networks underlying primary emotional systems: When strong FEAR is triggered a person could have difficulty shifting attention to other stimuli aside from the FEAR eliciting source.
>
> (pp. 1–2)

If we take into account another one of Lotman's definitions of the semiotic boundary, for which "the boundary is a bilingual mechanism that translates external communications into the internal language of the semiosphere and vice versa", we can say that the archetype performs and actually *is* this translative and transformative boundary.

One of the most challenging issues of analytical psychology is the relationship between the hypothesis of inherited archetypes and the possibilities and scopes of human learning. Even though a nativist like Fodor did not believe in the developmental view of cognition, he, too, correctly recognized that the harder problem is to understand the relation between the modular and the non-modular components of the mind (Fodor, 1983, 2000), an issue connected to altricial and precocial features or, in analytical terms, with the collective unconscious and the Ego.

Fodor proposed that the mind is constituted by peripheral (perceptual), domain-specific, informationally encapsulated, dissociable, functional subsystems that are mandatory, swift and involuntary processing units, wholly determined by evolutionarily selected genetic endowment. However, the high-level central cognitive systems that are involved in belief, creativity, reasoning, etc., are also, according to Fodor, a-modular and non-encapsulated (Fodor, 1983, 2000).

In this model, the mind consists of several input subsystems producing swift *thoughtless* outputs. Interestingly, Fodor included language also as an output of a module.

While Fodor argued that the outputs are processed by non-modular central processing, which works relatively slowly and *thoughtfully*, Tooby, Pinker, Sperber and Carruthers argued that every faculty of the mind is modular, aka *massively* modular (Cosmides & Tooby, 1994; Pinker, 1997; Sperber, 1994; Carruthers, 2006).

As the reader has seen, in this book, along with authors like Karmiloff-Smith, Mandler, Johnson or Lakoff and others, I am quoting the work of authors like Fodor, Cosmides or Tooby. In a critical comment on Goodwyn's *The Neurobiology of the Gods* (2012), Hogenson writes:

> [Goodwyn's] survey is by no means complete and many of his suggestions for understanding archetypes are precariously balanced on his particular selection of sources. This problem is well captured by the contrast between Cosmides and Tooby on the one hand and Karmiloff-Smith on the other. In both instances, a form of computational modeling underlies their respective theoretical conclusions. But in the case of Cosmides and Tooby, the computational model is based on the evolution of complex innate algorithmic formulas similar to those used in classical artificial intelligence modeling, while Karmiloff-Smith's computational model derives from parallel distributed processing models, also known as neural networks, which do not employ preset algorithms and militate strongly against complex innate structures. The conclusions that derive from these two very different approaches to computational modeling are dramatically different, and to lump these quite distinct approaches together in the same text without carefully examining the distinction is, to my mind, highly misleading.
>
> (Hogenson, 2013, p. 101)

Hogenson is obviously right in defining the nature of these two approaches – computational and algorithmic. Regardless of whether Goodwyn did it or not, he is also obviously right in warning against lumping theories together. Yet I also think that his criticism is too severe, and this is not only in regard to Goodwyn's work – which I find informative, stimulating and scientifically very reasonable – but, most of all, with regard to the idea that the two visions are absolutely incompatible. I will go back to this point in the following pages, especially in reference to recent research on the possible modular plasticity within an evolutionary connectionist perspective (hence, a non-absolute modular "encapsulation"), which could contribute to har-monize the issue of innate encapsulated constraining modules and learning (Cala-bretta, 2002; Calabretta et al., 2003; Nagarjuna, 2006).

Since in this book I refer to both sets of theories, the modular and the developmen-tal, I wish to clarify my position. I base my proposal on the possibility that modu-lar plasticity is possible. In Jungian terms, learning may actually be triggered and developed from archetypes and within their constraining horizon. In my opinion, what is modular, algorithmic and encapsulated belongs to the affective altricial neu-robiological layer – the a-noetic affects that Panksepp and, in a slightly different way, Damasio (2005) have described. I am not surprised that in his book, Goodwyn exten-sively refers to Panksepp. From their "modular" altricial *affective* blueprints, these affects trigger, motivate, orient and organize altricial "cortical" cognition and *cogni-tive* development. This means that upon these primary emotional altricial activations, which seem to have a pre-formed, fixed nature, the precocial structures – eminently cognitive – come into play. While moved bottom-up by affects, these developing cognitive competences, in turn, modify them top-down, transforming them into sec-ondary and tertiary emotions. This development looks like a Moebius string.

From an embodied biological basis, through the inter-domain transformations described by Lakoff and Johnson, the development described by the connectionist theories – like Karmiloff-Smith's, Johnson's or Mandler's – produces what might be considered the engine of linguistic meaning-making: metaphorization. The trigger and the meaning of such symbolic formations is the affect. Nevertheless, as I already said, the altricial development, which rests on more recent neurobiological and ana-tomical evolutionary structures, contributes in differentiating the affects and in trans-forming them, especially through reflectivity, into secondary and tertiary emotions.

While Hogenson rightly underscores that modular/algorithmic theories and developmental/connectionist theories refer to very different perspectives, we can-not help but realize that they do have at least one thing in common: their exclusively cognitive nature, i.e., the fact that their authors refer exclusively to cognition. As I have already said, in my opinion, it is paramount to understand that besides cogni-tive categorization processes derived from the sensory-motor activity, which have a precocial nature and develop throughout ontogenesis, there are innate affective categorizations processes, i.e., processes triggered and assembled by innate affects that integrate and infer meaning to those somatic (sensory-motor) afferences (con-scious and unconscious sensations) out of which cognition develops.

Jung's association experiments are the foundation for this essential affective ele-ment, which cognitive research often overlooks. In fact, the proper integrating role and the value-giving function to sensory experiences carried out by the affects is the key-factor for the organization of *all* psychic complex formations. This is why I think that the word "complex" is still a good name for such formations, as "schema" underscores just the cognitive aspect of this affective-sensorimotor-imaginal-cognitive compound.

Therefore, in my opinion, the purely cognitive meaning of "learning", as studied by most infant research, is insufficient, as any true learning by any complex living creature (not [yet?] by artificial intelligence) must be primarily referred to affects, emotions and feelings, which, integrated with their abstract cognitive forma, express what I called primary *gnostic* learning and knowledge, which is made possible by what Jung called the "transcendent function".

Besides affective/cognitive categorization, learning involves memory. After all, the continuity and integrity of our life – the sense of having an "identity" – has to do with remembering who we are. Once again, the key-factor for this is not cognitive but affective. Festinger's "cognitive dissonance" (Festinger, 1957) psychologically means something only if it involves categorial conflicts about emotionally relevant thoughts. An excess of emotional charge (i.e., of libido) traumatically disrupts psychosomatic and Ego-continuity, as a lack of it does. No psychotherapy has any meaning if it does not refer to this affective level of psychosomatic integration (for example: Bucci, 2021). Here, "integration" refers to the possibility to construe a personalized biography, which organizes and remembers who we are.

In Annette Karmiloff-Smith's words:

Although the innate predispositions and early learned principles set the boundaries within which development takes place, I have repeatedly stressed that they do not rule out the need for subsequent representational change.

(1996, p. 84)

Once again, while I agree on both parts of this sentence, I also think that this specific epistemic meaning for the word *learning* does not encompass other dimensions of learning – the gnostic ones – that cannot really be described just as representational abstractions. Yet for the purposes of this book, one of the most important authors of reference is still Annette Karmiloff-Smith, as her model of cognitive development and learning, based on the notion of representational redescription, seems to me coherent with Jung's "instincts" of reflection and creativity.

Seen through the perspective of Jung's reflection and creativity, Karmiloff-Smith's representational redescription seems to be one *cognitive* model of the more encompassing transcendent function that Jung described. In Jung, the scope of reflection and creativity is much broader, and as I mentioned earlier, Jung's reflection and creativity seem to be activities that stand at a higher level of comprehensiveness, as they are moved by affects and, psychologically speaking, do not refer to just cognitive competences but to the development of the whole personality.

Reflection and creativity coincide with psychic life itself, insofar as the psyche creatively plays with itself through a process of "mind-wandering" and within a certain *abaissement du niveau mental*. Mythopoetically producing images, the psyche imagines itself and, in so doing, spiritualizes and re-creates itself. For Jung, it is not we who produce reflection: we ourselves are the product of it as a complex of emotional images in which, identifying ourselves, we recognize ourselves as an Ego. It is not the Ego that thinks the psyche; the Ego is thought by the psyche. Reflection, therefore, belongs to the natural mind and constitutes the essence of the human psyche.

The integration between unconscious reflective activity and consciousness, involving a process of differentiation, also entails the well-known risk of intellectualization, whereby the original mythopoetic reflection, which the soul produces in imagining the Ego, is transformed into a fundamental defense against the unconscious. As Winnicott pointed out, the intellect – with its useful (because of its freedom, given by its dissociation from affects) and dangerous (exactly for the same reason) characteristics – is the way the False Self works.

9.1   Categorization and Images

As I said, Karmiloff-Smith's cognitive representational redescription operates on image-schemata, which function as cognitive constraints – formal Gestalten that provide a cognitive form, derived from sensory-motor experience, to cognition. Such schemata are then metaphorized and conceptualized. Discussing the motor-perceptual image-schema "balance", Johnson writes:

> the metaphorical projections move from the bodily sense (with its emergent schema) to the mental, epistemic, or logical domains. On this hypothesis, we should be able to see how it is that our experience of bodily balance, and of the perception of balance, is connected to our understanding of balanced personalities, balanced views, balanced systems, balanced equations, the balance of power, the balance of justice, and so on.
>
> (Johnson, 2013, p. 87)

In the previous chapter, I have briefly mentioned the classic example of the constraining role of vision.

According to Johnson:

> Sweetser examines several Indo-European roots that originally referred to vision, but which eventually developed meanings appropriate to mental operations. What emerges is a recurring pattern of metaphorical development from visual seeing to intellectual seeing. Sweetser suggests three bases for this parallelism between vision and intellection: (i) Vision is our primary source of data about the world. It typically gives us far more information than any of the other senses, and it appears that children rely most heavily on visual features in their early categorization. In other words, vision plays a crucial role in our acquisition of knowledge, (ii) Vision involves the remarkable ability to focus at will on various features of our perceptual array, to pick out one object from a background, or to differentiate fine features. All of these operations have parallels in intellectual acts, (iii) Furthermore, vision is more or less identical for different people who can take up the same viewpoint. It thus seems to provide a basis

for shared, public knowledge. Perceptual phenomena of this sort make vision a primary candidate as a metaphorical basis for intellectual acts in which one must discriminate features, examine details, and perform mental operations that are held in common with other people. There are, of course, other experiential bases for knowledge metaphors (such as touching, hearing, and tasting), but none of these is as dominant as vision.

(ibidem, pp. 108–109)

The founding role of vision is apparent in the description of his paranoid delusions described by A., a schizophrenic, in his beautiful, introspective and faithful diary. His illness exploded after one of his eyes was permanently partially wounded in an accident:

> In my illness, the sense of persecution is also closely related to the impressions [delusions] of reference, and these in turn also relate to the visual disturbance. That is, these "things", which disturb, are there in front, foreign and yet "referred" to me.
> Somehow there is a bodily root of the referred impressions as well. I think that from this disturbance of vision comes an impairment in eye contact and about attention in the verbal-emotional relationship, certainly in itself not serious, but noticeable under certain negative general psychological conditions. The fact is that the person in front of me does not know, does not see, that part of my attention is disturbed, and so it is as if I have a gnat bothering me and my interlocutor does not see it. The impression of reference comes from the fact that the speck, the dot and the marks move almost irregularly in the field of vision. That is, I see them, they move away from the center of the field but then almost suddenly they pop up again "in reference to me.

The metaphor is perhaps the central means by which we project structures across categories to establish new connections and organizations of meaning and to extend and develop image-schemata.

Jung's position regarding the relationship between image (schemata) and meaning is quite clear:

> Image and meaning are identical and as the first takes shape, so the latter becomes clear. Actually, the pattern needs no interpretation: it portrays its own meaning. There are cases where I can let interpretation go as a therapeutic requirement. Scientific knowledge, of course, is another matter. Here we have to elicit from the sum total of our experience certain concepts of the greatest possible general validity, which are not given *a priori*. This particular work entails the translation of the timeless, ever present operative archetype into the scientific language of the present.
> (Jung, 1947/1954, p. 204)

Jung is describing the relationship between image and meaning, where "image" precisely indicates a schema out of which an infinite attempt for interpretation might emerge in a declarative form; while images provide a form to affects, we think and speak *from* images. This is the clear case of the dream, or of metaphors.

As I have already said, the process that under a cognitive/epistemic domain we call *redescription* is part of that more general and pervasive feature of the psyche that Jung called *transcendent function*. In fact, the transcendent function describes in a wholly coherent way the cognitive mechanisms that are so well studied by authors such as Mandler or Karmiloff-Smith yet embedding them in the more pervasive gnostic process of learning that describes not just the "experimental child" (Stern's observed child") but also the real one (Stern's "clinical child") (Stern, 1985).

The product of the transcendent function – the generation of symbolic equivalents at a more encompassing level of meaning and complexity, together with a potentially higher level of spiritualization/abstraction – paves the way for the formation of metaphors and the production of abstract concepts (like scientific ones) that make it possible for a person to meaningfully come into his/her own (emotional/cognitive) existence.

Not only in accordance with Jung but also with Bion, more abstract and general knowledge – scientific knowledge – may emerge from these original formations in a way that seems coherent with the process of transformation from perception to proto-concepts and then to concepts as described by Mandler et al. The only – yet fundamental! – difference being that in the cognitive/epistemic literature of infant research, the object of study is the *intellect*, while affects, feelings and emotions are not included. Therefore, infant research abstracts the child's mind from her whole human – fundamentally affective – nature. If we want to really approach the totally of the human being, we must not just refer to cognitive studies and to infant research but we must also integrate them as part of a larger whole in which affects and feelings have the role of primary organizers. Therefore, as I argued since the first pages of this book, we must be careful when we try to base our understanding of the human psyche on such beautiful, elegant and essential – yet *alas!* – reductive studies.

Earlier, I referred to one example among many – something analytical psychologists should think about: the relationship between complex modular sensory-motor schemas, neural patterns and mathematical thinking (Lakoff & Nuñez, 2001; Feldman & Narayanan, 2004). When a subject is busy with an arithmetical problem, the same patterns and neural networks that organize sensory-motor responses are activated. Yet within this paradigm of the embodied mind, very little space is given to affects, feelings and emotions.

The same lack of interest about the role of affects and feelings can be said about a second paradigm: "evolutionary psychology".[6] As I have already recalled, leaning on the innatist end of the spectrum, evolutionary psychology is partly incompatible with the developmental cognitive paradigm. In fact, differently from the pervasive role of learning attributed to psychological development by authors such as Annette Karmiloff-Smith or Jean Mandler, evolutionary psychologists (and anthropologists) refer to innate, encapsulated modules biologically inherited through the

Darwinian selection process that must have taken place during the 2.5 million years man evolved during the Pleistocene. Their view of the mind is deeply modular.

> Modularity, as a general feature, is commonly seen in biological organization at all levels of complexity. There is greater consensus that an organism is gradually and hierarchically constructed out of several subsystems (Simon, 1962). This therefore is taken as an argument in favor of massive modularity.
>
> (Nagarjuna, 2006)

While the paradigm of evolutionary psychology, which is strikingly like Jung's reference to archetypes as inherited "patterns of behavior",[7] differs from Jung, it still interprets affects and feelings under a purely cognitive perspective. Therefore, we should refer to this paradigm with the necessary care.

To explain why I think that this cognitive notion of learning may conflate other dimensions, it is necessary to understand the nature of such an "epistemic drive" and the context in which it is embedded. This clarification of what learning might mean involves one of the bases for an understanding of the relationships between what we may call the four *functional* levels of the psychosomatic organism (in our case, the person):

1) Affects.
2) Sensations (and later perceptions).
3) Action.
4) Cognition (and language).

The description of human learning – i.e., the nature of human experience – cannot be reduced to the epistemic child studied by infant research like the ones carried out by Karmiloff-Smith and to which authors like Jean Knox tend to refer. In fact, the production of images and further cognitive development – abstraction, critical thinking and thinking possibilities and impossibilities – takes a very long time. The 4th phase of the representational redescription process [see Table 9.1] happens around the 10th year of age, and thinking possibilities and impossibilities matures only during adolescence. On the contrary, the maturation of secondary and tertiary emotions happens much, much earlier, around the 3rd–4th year of life.

Primary emotions refer to innate affects. Paul Ekman, for example, initially identified six primary emotions: happiness, sadness, fear, anger, surprise and disgust. Secondary emotions are more complex and often arise as a result of the interplay between primary emotions or in response to cognitive processes. Examples of secondary emotions include feelings like jealousy, guilt, shame, embarrassment or pride (Ekman, 1992). These emotions may involve a higher level of cognitive processing and self-reflection.

Among the many models of emotions, Robert Plutchik developed a model that is known as the "wheel of emotions" (Plutchik, 1980, 1991, 2001). Plutchik theorized 24 "primary", "secondary" and "tertiary" dyads (feelings composed of two emotions). The wheel emotions can be paired in four groups:

Primary dyad = one petal apart = *Love* = *Joy* + *Trust*
Secondary dyad = two petals apart = *Envy* = *Sadness* + *Anger*.
Tertiary dyad = three petals apart = *Shame* = *Fear* + *Disgust*.
Opposite emotions = four petals apart = *Anticipation* ∉ *Surprise*.

There are also triads, emotions formed from three primary emotions, though Plutchik never described them in any detail.

Similar emotions in the wheel are adjacent to each other. Each emotion is categorized by its positive or negative valence. Anger, anticipation, joy and trust are positive in valence, while fear, surprise, sadness and disgust are negative in valence. Anger is classified as a "positive" emotion because it involves "moving toward" a goal, while surprise is negative because it is a violation of someone's space. What is important for our discussion is the possibility of a differentiation into complex emotions from basic innate affects in which evolutionary considerations have a primary role (Plutchik, 1980).

Complex or secondary/tertiary emotions do not seem to be reducible to affects or basic emotions. Basic emotion theorists, faced with the problem of accounting for secondary emotional phenomena, have mostly adopted two alternative strategies: 1. Show that complex emotions are nothing more than a mixture of basic ones; 2. consider complex emotions as the combination of an affect program with an appropriate cognitive state.

The first strategy is well exemplified by David Buss' hypothesis on sexual jealousy. As an evolutionary psychologist, Buss theorized a modular system underlying sexual jealousy, which can be activated by simple perceptual stimuli, such as unusual scents, change in sexual conduct, excessive eye contact and violation of the rules governing interpersonal space. Since it is a module, this system employs domain-specific algorithms and, like an emotional program, operates as an emergency system.

> Nevertheless, when considered from an input perspective, however, an emotion such as jealousy is sensitive to a much wider range of information than is available. At the form of a basic emotion: "If Othello's jealousy had been an affect program, or a cognitive affect downstream of that program, he should have surprised Desdemona in bed with Cassio, or at least have seen the handkerchief before it could have started".
>
> (Griffiths, 1997, p. 117)

Moreover, from an output perspective, jealousy is a longer-lasting response than basic emotion responses. It does not exhibit the stereotyped repertoire of physiological affects that characterizes the latter and appears far more integrated into cognitive tasks, such as long-term action planning.

The latter aspect is instead prominent in Robert H. Frank's sociological theory of moral emotions (Frank, 2011). Here, complex emotions are short-term, irrational responses designed to ensure the agent's long-term rationality; for example, loyalty would often lead to long-term cooperation rather than short-term defection in social interactions that have the structure of an iterative prisoner's dilemma.

There is, therefore, good reason to believe that, contrary to what Buss proposed, a complex emotional phenomenon such as jealousy rests on psychological mechanisms other than those underlying basic emotions.

To account for complex emotions, the second strategy consisting of considering such emotions as the combination of an affect program with an appropriate cognitive state appears more promising. This approach was adopted by Antonio Damasio, according to whom secondary emotions result from the integration of the activity of phylogenetically ancient brain structures with the activity of the neocortex (Damasio, 1995).

For Damasio, what distinguishes a primary emotion from a secondary one is not the pattern of body changes, which is similar in the two cases, but rather, the mode of activation of the body pattern. In the case of primary emotions, this pattern is automatically activated by a specialized circuit in the limbic system. In the case of secondary emotions, initiating the process is the uprise system which it activates, due to the mediation of certain prefrontal circuits that operate unconsciously (the specialized circuit of the limbic system), which in turn triggers the bodily response. Since these prefrontal circuits are knowledgeable of the relationship between the types of situations that occur to an individual and the emotional states elicited, the emotional response that is produced has a less stereotypical and more idiosyncratic character. After that, in a manner entirely analogous to the case of primary emotions, the bodily reaction is represented in the brain, giving rise to the emotional sensation. Secondary emotions, therefore, exploit the apparatus of primary emotions, which is thus a prerequisite for secondary emotions, both on the logical level and on the evolutionary one.

It is impossible to discuss in sufficient detail the scientific debate on emotions; nevertheless, what must be pointed out is the criticism that anthropologists address against the biological basis of emotions and against its reductionist implications, for which every human in every historical moment within every social group would *feel* the same emotions. As a matter of fact, some emotional feelings cannot be translated in all languages. This may be the case of the Portuguese *saudade* or the German *schadenfreude*, which have no corresponding name in English. This, once again, calls into play the need for a theory in which innate affective predispositions, like Panksepp's seven primary affects, act as *vectors* for the progressively more refined and differentiated interpretation of one's experience based on their mixing and on cognitive development. We should remember that complexes have both an affective/emotional component and a cognitive, epistemic component. For this point of view, while the affects would be innate and modularized, they would act as vectorial forces to promote a further differentiation into culturally specific forms of existential apprehension, to which different social groups give a specific name.

As an Italian, I think that to be able to consciously differentiate between *nostalgia* (in English: *nostàlgia*) and *saudade* so much so as to have the need to give to these two existential states different names would mean a wholly real, deep, moving moment of higher knowledge. The same would go for the German *gemütlich*, the Japanese *jjirashi*, or *amae*, the Baining *awumbuk* or the Inuit *iktsuarpok*.

I will go back to this issue in my second volume (see my discussion of Wierzbicka's "lexical universals", in Vol. II § 9.3). For the moment, I wish to underscore that this knowledge is precisely the kind of knowledge that an analyst must struggle to attain. It may be learned only from our patients – from the "Other". As any emotion that I feel, even when I feel it through empathy, and even if, therefore, it belongs to the other, this emotion is still an emotion that *I* feel. I may think a concept as something that does not belong to me, something to which I do not subscribe – for instance, the concept that us humans are fundamentally different from other animals because only we are an image of God. I may well understand it and yet not feel it as part of me. Nevertheless, I cannot feel something that is not immediately and factually *mine*. If I empathetically feel a certain feeling that may be a patient's, still, the one who is feeling it is me, and if I am really learning, I may feel exactly what he is feeling. This is an example of gnostic knowledge.

The day that, together with a patient, I feel a sudden, strange sense of atmospheric emptiness and heaviness that would make it difficult for me to work, and I feel it would get better if I could just be able to imagine a particular object that could represent it and absorb it (a picture, or even a glass of water . . .), my Baining patient might tell me: "You are feeling what I feel. It's called *awumbuk*" (but this is obviously not restricted to the analytical situation). In this case, mourning a loss with him would be the indispensable prerequisite to help him, and at the same time, it would be the sign that I am adding his otherness to my own self. This form of learning is always an experience that intrinsically changes who is learning from it. It is what I will call a *gnostic* form of knowledge, what Bion describes as the integration of L(ove) and K(nowledge). Real learning is actually a becoming.

As we will see in vol. I, § 10, secondary emotions have a *reflective* nature on the self (shame, pride, embarrassment), on the other's inner world (jealousy) or on normative values (guilt). This reflective nature of secondary emotions includes the fact that they may be emotions on emotions (one may be happy to finally feel the pain and sadness of his mourning) and, therefore, also on somebody else's emotion. Hence, secondary emotions include the Other. Resentment, on the other hand, is an example of a tertiary emotion. It is linked to the concept of relative deprivation. Resentment contains three secondary-level emotions: contempt (anger and disgust), shock (surprise and disgust) and outrage (surprise and anger) (TenHouten, 2018).

In vol. I, § 10, I will refer to the literature on the *observed child* (Stern, 1985), in which affects and feelings are seen as primary motivational and co-structuring elements (together with perception/movement) of the more general epistemic activity of cognition. As we have seen, through time, the relevance of the structural relationships between the sensory-motor networks[8] for cognition has been the polar star since Piaget, but there has been no serious recognition of the role of core affects, feelings, emotions and their subsequent development into secondary emotions.[9]

This discussion on cognition is meant to describe the literature to which most articles on analytical psychology refer, as well as to serve as a starting point for the necessary reevaluation of the role of affects as the fundamental motivational factors for the subsequent formation of images and, further on, via redescription and abstraction, cognitive activity.

Further in the book, when the primacy of affects and feelings will be clear, I will go back to the nature and role of images.

9.2   Modularity, Learning and Evolutionary Issues

The issues about affects, feelings and emotions, the dynamic glue of the integrating process of psychic life, that I have discussed so far also involve the *imaginal* side of psychological development and the structure of the complex.

Now that I have emphasized the primacy of affectivity, it is possible to turn our sight towards mental images and cognition, something that I will also do in the third part of this book when dealing with cultural images.

The Jungian issues I have dealt with so far – or better to say, the *legitimacy* of some of such issues, like that of the universal nature of some complexes – are open to debate and are, indeed, much discussed within the scientific community. Within the Jungian theory, the dispositional nature of the BrainMind is strictly connected to the crucial and challenging problem of the collective unconscious as Jung meant it, i.e., of a genetic endowment that precedes and, therefore, organizes phenotypical expressions. The issue of a collective unconscious (at this point, I am referring to a formal idea of a collective unconscious, not necessarily to the *Jungian* collective unconscious) includes the relationship between the two fields of evolutionary biology and developmental biology, the so-called Evo-Devo biology that I mentioned in vol. I, § 6.

What and how much is inherited? And how much of what is inherited[10] determines the phenotype, starting from biology all the way up to behavior (perceptions and movement), cognition and the anthropological, symbolic environment in which we humans live – what Heidegger rightly called our "*world*"?

In Jungian terms, we could translate this as follows: How much does the archetype-as-such determine and constrain the personal complexes?[11]

For a long time, in biology, evolutionary and developmental considerations did not integrate in a unitary theory. This is the case also of psychology, where, as we have already seen, the issues of dispositionality and heritability *vs.* the perspective of development through learning refer to the clash, within the cognitive paradigm, between the modular evolutionary psychology, anthropology"[12] and the "connectionist" (Rumelhart & McCelland, 1986) and developmental paradigms, in which Mark Johnson's, Jeanne Mandler's and Annette Karmiloff-Smith's positions, which I have previously discussed, are very relevant.

As we have seen, in *Beyond Modularity* (1996), Karmiloff-Smith describes her theory of *representational redescription*, where she tries to somehow reconcile Fodor's nativist model (Fodor, 1983) with Piaget's developmental model.

In *Beyond modularity*, Karmiloff-Smith writes:

> The view that I adopt throughout the book is that nature specifies initial biases or *predispositions* that channel attention to relevant environmental inputs, which in turn affect subsequent brain development.
>
> (1996, p. 5, my italics)

In criticizing Fodor's theory of the innate modular nature of the BrainMind (not to speak of the *massive* theory of the modular BrainMind that I have referred to), Karmiloff-Smith writes:

> Fodor's detailed account of the encapsulation of modules, focuses predominantly on their role in online processing. There is little discussion of antagonistic change except to allow for the creation of new models (such as a reading module). Fodor takes it as demonstrated that modules for spoken language and visual perceptions are innately specified. By contrast, I wish to draw a distinction between the notion of pre-specified modules and that of a process of *modularization*, which I speculate occurs repeatedly as the *product* of development.
>
> (Karmiloff-Smith, 1996, p. 4)

The difference between innate encapsulated modularity and ongoing modularization throughout ontogenetic life is crucial and very clear: modules exist but are formed through experience, most of all during infancy.

Annette Karmiloff-Smith rightly criticizes the aspect of Fodor's theory for which development and learning seem to be excluded. She does so based on the encapsulated nature of Fodor's modules. However, also according to Fodor, the high-level central cognitive systems that are involved in belief, creativity, reasoning etc., are, a-modular and non-encapsulated (Fodor, 1983, 2000). *Furthermore, such encapsulation might not be a necessary component even of innate Fodorian modules*, and this may pave the way for the possibility of "modulating the modules" (Nagarjuna, 2006), i.e., learning through intersubjective, interpersonal, social experience and epigenetic influences.

This is a truly crucial issue, for several reasons. First, because today, there is a general agreement on the fact that our mind is not a general explanatory machine but consists of many different specialized "explanatory engines" (as Pascal Boyer calls them) which work as differentiated, automatic (unconscious) inferential systems, each of which is adapted to particular kinds of events. As I already argued in vol. I, § 6, these inferential systems may be interpreted as features of the human *Umwelt*, provided that this is not limited to its biological sensory-motor apparatus but is "abstracted" into sets of specific representations and emotional evaluations.

Specific modes of apprehension (hence, of interpretation) based on implicit inferences, common all over the world and, therefore, structurally innate, are activated in an indefinite number of situations (meaning that they will interpret them), such as when the bidimensional visual images that are projected in the brain are automatically seen (interpreted) three-dimensionally; or when one automatically understands his natural language when one hears someone speaking it; or when one automatically understands where a tennis ball will end up in its trajectory; or when a (quite limited) number of highly peculiar inferences are produced by a religious disposition (Boyer, 2001).[13] Such modularized inferential systems are activated when an affect triggers them, precisely like complexes.

For instance:

> If something activates physics, goal-detection, as well as some biological expectations . . . then it is what we usually call an "animal". If it activates all that plus intuitive psychology, it is what we usually call a "person". If it activates physics and structure-function, it may be either a "man-made object" or an "animal part". If in addition it activates intentional use, it is what we usually call a "tool". Instead of having a complex mental encyclopedia with theoretical declarations about what animals and artifacts and persons are, all we have are flags that switch on particular systems and turn other systems off.
>
> (Boyer, 2001, p. 119)

There exist several inference systems and subsystems that may be activated in a certain situation.

For instance:

1) *Understanding the physics of solid objects*, which, activated automatically and unconsciously, produces a form of knowledge that we may call *intuitive physics*. Intuitive physics uses observable phenomena (like the motion of objects) to infer what is intrinsically invisible (see the "causal illusions" studied by Michotte, 1963). If a glass vase falls on the floor and bounces back like a ball, this system will detect a violation of the expectation that it should have broken in pieces. In fact, the automatic, unconscious inferential activity interprets the nature of objects and experiences, classifying them into specific ontological categories; in this case, the glass would be interpreted as a SOLID OBJECT and, therefore, produces specific expectations and intuitive "folk" theories.

Other inferential systems are as follows:

2) *Understanding physical causation*, by which we automatically infer causation and why something happened. The workings of this system are very apparent already in children, who automatically infer that a negative parent is, for example, angry at her *because* she has been bad and not because her parent is emotionally dissociated. This automatic inference has evolutionary advantages since

it tries to save the parental imago's idealization (Kohut, 1971), *although it is harmful at the individual level.*[14]

    a) Another causal inferential subsystem, experimentally tested already in 6-month-old infants, intuitively differentiates between "physical causation" (push, pull, hit) and "social causation" (chase, avoid) (Rochat et al., 1997).

3) *Detecting goal-directed motion*, which organizes our construction of how the physical world works and, together with other inferential systems, contributes to differentiate the ontological category of ANIMAL from ARTIFACT (Gelman et al., 1983), insofar as the first moves intentionally, while the second moves because a force has acted upon it (this derives directly from the process of perceptual analysis and refers to conceptual primitives).

4) *Linking structure to function*, which determines the intuitive inference for which one interprets a book as an object that contains written texts, instead as something that may be used as a stool.

5) *Keeping track of who's who*, which allows us to recognize who a certain person is or *what* a certain object or a certain animal are. As trivial as this seems, this is a complex construed process, which has an interesting effect on our unconscious heuristic and inferential strategies, as we tend to group and recall together objects or persons that look similar, even if the appearance has nothing to do with the specific category in which we are including them. A delicate look does not necessary correspond to belonging to a category of a shy person.

    Another important aspect of this inferential system is that, resorting to the activation of other systems, we recognize who a person is because we refer her image to herself, whereas we automatically tend to recognize an animal or an object in reference to the kind it belongs to.

    a) For a subsystem of this specific system, children intuitively infer that they know what is inside an animal must be the same as another animal that belongs to the same species (for instance, what is inside two mice must be the same). This does not apply to TOOL or ARTIFACT (like a computer or a telephone). Apparently, a specific subsystem produces inferences based on an essentialist bias, which is triggered by stimuli that are perceived (by the activation of other concurring systems) as living species (Gelman & Wellman, 1991).

6) *Understanding mental representations* by which we automatically infer the complex connecting threads that form a reasonable plot of the situation we are facing.

    Furthermore, Boyer argues:

> some inference systems are activated by several different kinds of objects. Goal-detection is applied to dogs and to persons. Structure-function is applied both to artifacts and to some body parts. Also, the way I talked of "ontological categories" as if these were real kinds of things in the world

was misleading because many objects migrate from one of these so-called categories to another, depending on the way we consider them. For instance, once you take a fish out of the sea and serve it poached, it has ceased to be only an animal and has become, to some extent, an artifact. If you use it to slap someone's face, it has become a tool. It is of course not the object itself that has changed but the kinds of inferences the mind produces about it. At some point it seemed to be an "animal", which means that our goal-detection system was activated when we looked at it moving about and spontaneously wondered what it was looking for. When we say that the fish has become an "artifact", what we mean is that questions such as "who made it?" or "what for?" are now produced spontaneously. When the fish has become a "tool", this only means that we produce inferences such as "if it is heavy it will strike hard", "the tail is narrow and therefore affords a good grip"–that is, our structure-function system is active.

(Boyer, 2001, pp. 120–121)

For the purposes of this book, this limited account of how innate inferential systems work may be sufficient. What should be noted is that, according to contemporary cognitive and evolutionary psychology, these inference systems have been selected throughout evolution because they provided solutions to problems that were recurrent in normal human environments during the Pleistocene for hundreds of thousands of years. *I would like to underscore that this converges with Jung's idea that what he called "archetypes" are the product of such a selective process.* Although evolutionary psychologists, sociobiologists and cognitive anthropologists refer to "classical" random evolutionary selective mechanisms, today, there is an important accumulation of evidence about the fact that randomness is actually "harnessed" by top-down *teleological* regulative functions already at cellular level, something like what Lamark was trying to explain (for a discussion: Noble, 2008). Jung was on the same wavelength, and it seems that he might have been right.

These inferential systems and the ontological categories that they aggregate may be interpreted as components of Jung's archetypes, provided that they are integrated with other essential elements, first of all, the activating feeling of *numinosum* and the transgressive, psychoid nature of archetypes.

These theories of inferential systems refer to the concept of "domain" and do not exclude the reference to modules. To emphasize and "take seriously" learning, Karmiloff-Smith chooses not to refer to modules but to "domains". In my opinion, if we interpret psycho-biological modularity as procedures that function as inferential systems do, the idea of a modular mind does not contradict the possibility of a true, flexible learning but always within the confines of the human *Umwelt*. This would agree with Karmiloff-Smith's domains, provided that there are many more of them than the few, somewhat unspecific ones she has studied – like the domain of "physical knowledge" or "mathematical knowledge".

The possibility that at certain levels – like reasoning and creativity – even a radical modular scientist like Fodor admits the possibility of learning and non-encapsulation supports the hypothesis of the double nature of human minds as both precocial (the collective unconscious) and altricial (consciousness). Furthermore, if *inherited* modules are not incapsulated, this opens the way for a *subsequent* process of encapsulation, such as the one described by Annette Karmiloff-Smith, which might take place throughout the individuation process by metastable dynamics (Simondon, 2020).[15] I think that while modularity is difficult to deny, encapsulation represents the real problem, even at low levels, such as visual perception, which is constantly altered by beliefs, attitudes, expectations, etc. (for a discussion against encapsulation in the visual domain: Masrour, 2015). Therefore, the question is how existing innate modular patterns – like the inferential systems – are used as themes for a certain number of possible variations.

If we compare the structure of a module, with its innate, automatic, unconscious inferential system without the rigid constraints of encapsulation, it may look like those of the archetypes about which Jung says that each one of them connects, influences and even contaminates the others. A second feature of this non-rigid encapsulation of modules (which would define them quite differently from those of evolutionary psychology) is the possibility that a "module" – in our case, an archetypal pattern/image-schema – may be composed of several subcomponents (sub-modules), each one of which may partially influence or overlap with other "modules".

> The engaging problem therefore is either to understand the functional *relation* between modular and non-modular aspects of mind, as a nativist would like us to say, or the *transition* from procedural knowledge to declarative knowledge, as developmentalists would want us to say. I tend more towards the developmentalists, though I hope to see a reconciliation, as Karmiloff-Smith did, and to grapple with the transition problem. Either way, it is clear that this is a non-trivial problem in cognitive science, and a solution to this problem will have serious implications in understanding human cognition.
>
> (Nagarjuna, 2006, p. 25)

I think that the debate is still open, although the two positions – rigidly encapsulated modularity vs. cognitive development through learning – might, should and perhaps are already being integrated (Calabretta, 2002; Calabretta et al., 2003; Nagarjuna, 2006). One evidence is the top-down action on visual perception, in which beliefs and attitudes modify what a person perceives.[16]

If in the Jungian world, one heated and relevant discussion is about what exactly an archetype may be, in the larger scientific community, it is the question of how to define what a module is that is still going on.[17] For what concerns us now, we may *roughly* connect the notion of a module to that of the complex as Jung saw it and then, possibly, to the archetype in itself, in which the intra-domain and inter-domain processes of representational redescription proposed by Annette Karmiloff-Smith *could* be used as one of the possible scaffolding mechanisms for self-reflection and abstraction of the procedural affective impulse into an image and, eventually, a thought and, finally, a word.

Another important development is the integration between the "cognitive" and the "connectionist" paradigm by the so-called "evolutionary connectionism" (Calabretta et al., 2003), based on artificial life (AI) simulations of neural networks. This integration is very relevant for the crucial issue of the heritability/learning issue.

> In fact, differently from classic connectionist simulations, Artificial Life simulations do not simulate just a single neural network, which learns certain skills from its own experience, but simulates whole populations of neural networks that passes through a series of generations of individuals, since each individual is born with a genotype inherited from its parents. The use of such a "genetic algorithm" shows how the codified information in the inherited genotypes changes through the generations, as its reproduction is selective, and how new genotypic variants are constantly added to the genetic pool of the population by genetic mutations and sexual recombination. *At the end of the simulation, it is possible to see how the inherited genotypes codify the properties desired by the neural network and that have the function of innate constraints to development and behavior.*
>
> (Calabretta, 2002, p. 2. My translation. Italics by the authors.
> See also: Calabretta & Nirotti, 2014)

Another interesting feature of the original findings of Calabretta (2002) is that throughout their activation within AI models, there is a production of *new* modules. This is another feature that contributes to the integration between modularity and creative learning, in which the bottom-up and top-down interaction is circular.

These models justify the possibility that, throughout ontogenetic life, new modules emerge (what Jung called personal complexes, to which I would add the cultural complexes). Therefore, there would be no need to presuppose anything like a pre-formed template in the mind to hypothesize the existence of archetypes. Given certain conditions, the dispositional world of the organism – in our case, the person's inner world – will produce new "modules" (complexes), although still constrained by the organism's potential dispositional endowment.

Part of my clinical experience had to do with supporting the personnel of a pediatric oncology ward. More than once, I witnessed the deeply moving situation in which a young adolescent would show an unforeseen, unexpected wisdom (this is the best word possible) before his death. One may obviously distort his own direct *experience* with twisted explanations, yet the most parsimonious explanation that I feel able to formulate is that in these cases, a potential innate emotional process was triggered, which led the young-old patient to a serene farewell to parents, friends and – very moved, indeed – doctors and nurses.

In a non-modularized mind with a non-archetypally organized collective uncon-scious learning would be related to the existence of a non-modular form of intel-ligence, similar to what Spearman referred to as the *g factor* (Spearman, 1904). It is upon the unproven and untenable assumption of human intelligence as based on such a general competence, an assumption given for granted, that Durkheim based the autonomy of his sociological paradigm as a level of reality that would *contain and explain cognition and individual psychological features in wholly sociologi-cal, relativistic terms.* In fact, the developmental paradigm, if not sufficiently har-monized with the role of the constraints and attractors and with "modularization" (i.e., Jung's theory of complexes), cannot resolve some fundamental problems, a few of which I have already recalled. These problems are, therefore, like Kuhn's *anomalies*, which can be solved within Jung's archetypal paradigm (once "proven", of course).

These problems are as follows:

1) The issue of the so-called "frame problem",[18] i.e., the ambiguity and poverty of stimuli which might not make it possible to organize them in coherent aggre-gates or categories without some pre-specified module.
2) The issue of combinatorial explosion.[19]
3) The issue of the "Unreasonable effectiveness of mathematics in the natural sci-ences" (Wigner, 1960) – i.e., the nature of the natural number as a qualitative organizer at the same time found and discovered – raises the question of why mathematics actually *works* (Von Franz, 1986).
4) The possibility to think impossibilities, which for Kant is a fundamental aspect of mathematics (Sloman, 2021). Within a non-modular development, a devel-opment guided by a general, non-domain-specific module like as Spearman's *g factor*, which interacts with empirical experience, it would be impossible to identify necessities and impossibilities but just statistical probabilities.
5) The existence of synchronistic phenomena.
6) Finally, the empirical presence – a founding Jungian tenet – of what appear to be universals, or better to say *near-universals*[20] (see vol. II, § 8), between individu-als and cultures (Brown, 1991). This is the basic feature of Jung's "discovery" of archetypal images. Obviously, all these anomalies may be found irrelevant or non-existent. The most evident case is the existence of quasi-universals between cultures. I will discuss this issue in the second volume.

The whole point of this chapter is that, to understand the nature of images and human cognition and, possibly, consciousness, it is important to understand, on the one hand, the relationship between the hardwired, implicit, inaccessible, pro-cedural knowledge – probably rooted in neurosensory motor mechanisms (the "patterns of behavior" of Jung's "instincts", modified for what concerns encapsula-tion) – which are *triggered*[21] *in a modular fashion by the binding and teleological*[22] *dynamic action of impulses-affects* and, on the other, the explicit, symbolic, acces-sible, public, conceptual, declarative, *conscious* knowledge rooted in socio-cultural milieus and institutions (one would be the "tuning" of the baby with the caregiver or the indicators of attachment behaviors, e.g., crying, reaching, crawling, etc.). (I will come back to this point in vol. II, § 10.1 and vol. II, § 9.)

If, as I already written, the challenge is to understand the relation between the modular and the non-modular components of the mind (Fodor, 1983, 2000), we might reformulate this problem as the relationship between a dispositional *vs.* a situational development, or the relationship between the archetypes in themselves, ontogenetic learning and the emergence of a self-reflective consciousness informed by a great amount of plasticity and free will. In neurobiological terms, the focus would be on the transition from biologically rooted procedural and affective a-noetic experiences to a socially rooted declarative meta-noetic knowledge organized by the qualitative diversity of secondary and tertiary emotions – hence, from the collective mind to self-reflective Ego.

Notes

1 The organization of the acoustic continuum into specific and discrete sounds that will be interpreted not as "natural sounds" but as linguistic sounds happen around the 7th month of life. The infant's babbling is a sign of such a process of transformation (from natural sounds to linguistic acoustic signals) and organization (so that a Japanese may have difficulty not only in uttering an Italian r sound but also in hearing the difference between r and l if a machine reproduces this shift very slowly and continuously). An interesting neurological finding indicates a possible correlation between autism and the lesion of the superior temporal sulcus, which indicates an impairment of the infant's ability of social perception (Zilbovicius et al., 2006) but also to actively recognize and select human, linguistic sounds from natural ones (Gervais et al., 2004; Raschle et al., 2014).

2 Annette Karmiloff-Smith moves away from the structural notion of "module" towards the functional one of "domain". A domain is, for example, mathematical thinking, another is physics' thinking, a third one is language, etc. It is not clear to me what the structural bases are of such domains. It seems Annette Karmiloff-Smith did not explain this and treated such domains – which are fundamental for her paradigm – in a descriptive fashion.

3 To frame these questions properly, it must be clear that if there exist innate potential modular constraints, they need not appear at birth, during infancy or in early life, but they may always be *awakened* by both maturational processes and/or situational needs throughout life.

4 Image-schemata are non-propositional, as they do not refer to any true-false possible proposition. They are embodied forms of action-patterns.

5 See Pauli's idea of some dream images (but they may also be like visions or hallucinations) that, when unraveled, thought out, express scientific metaphors – theories in Pauli, 2012.)

6 Buss, 1989; Cosmides, 1985; Cosmides & Tooby, 1987, 1989, 1992; Daly & Wilson, 1986.

7 See: Walter, S., 1994.

8 As for the fundamental role of what Jung calls "sensation" and of its relationship with affects for the development of the psyche, see: Jung (Definitions), 1921a.

9 Therefore, this fundamental line of research and interpretation on the development of the mind seems to agree with Jung regarding the sensory-motor part yet proves to be

partial and insufficient, as it is not able to integrate the real deep core of the mind's motivational nature – the affects.

10 Inheritance might not necessarily restrict itself to genotypic transmission (or mutations). As we will briefly see, it is possible that the relationship between the phenotype and its environment (in this case, the human environment), *being both the product of co-evolution*, produces inherited/inheritable patterns – perhaps archetypal ones.

11 Clumsily because we still should learn *how precisely* the specific form of an inherited set of potential preconditions for the development of a phenotype, such as the Jungian collective unconscious – a highly specific construct – is equivalent to the genotypic mechanism studied by evolutionary developmental biology. At this point, an equivalent such as this is just an analogy. Yet it may be heuristic as a hypothesis to be studied.

12 Such as Jerry Fodor, but much more strictly, Cosmides, Tooby, Pinker and Marr, who advocate a principle of *massive modularity*, while Fodor limits modules to the systems dedicated to perceptual analysis.

13 It should be noted that each species, together with its innate sensory-motor structure, is equipped with its own repertory of inferential systems. This implies that each species experiences natural laws differently from us humans. The truly wonderful thing is that (besides humans, who tend to destroy the natural balance) all species still live in the same ecospace.

14 We must always differentiate the statistical, collective level at which evolutionary selective processes work with the individual specific cases.

15 For instance, by connecting in a stricter sense modules and domains, which Annette Karmiloff-Smith distinguishes, and taking into consideration not only epigenetic effects on the inherited – genotypic – modules but also creating new complexes derived from shared *meanings*.

16 Probably, the beginning of this discussion on the top-down influence of complex psychological states on more fundamental mental processes like perception was Bruner's groundbreaking article *Value and Need as Organizing Factors in Perception*, 1947.

17 If the definition and nature of modularity is still under discussion, it seems to me that neither does Karmiloff-Smith make really clear what the relationship is between her "domains" – such as the domains mathematical or verbal competence – and their biological and evolutionary substrates.

18 *Unconstrained* general intelligence runs into the problem that any artificial intelligence is unable to solve even a simple problem that humans find easy, such as seeing, moving objects or even tying shoelaces, unless we provide a "*frame*" for the task (e.g., Boden, 1977; F. M. Brown, 1987; Fodor, 1983).

19 I would like to point to the possibility that a general, unconstrained intelligence might work without incurring the frame problem or combinatorial explosion, if the human BrainMind (differently from any known AI) worked quantistically. As far-fetched as this hypothesis may seem, it is not at all impossible, given that quantistic processes at a biological temperature level is already certain for phenomena such as photosynthesis, oxygen absorption in the lungs, catalytic enzymatic processes and perception of magnetic fields in migratory birds (Al-Khalili & McFadden, 2015).

We cannot at all rule out that brain neurodynamic activity works at this level. This would eliminate both the frame problem and combinatorial explosion.

20 No one seems yet to have thought about where to place the cutoff that distinguishes near-universals from merely widespread traits and complexes. Perhaps a cutoff at a 95% distribution, by analogy with the 5% rule for statistical significance, might make sense in some cases.

21 Therefore, the modularization process would take place by the action of an initial "instinctive" (as in Darwin's, Romanes' or Lorenz's way), affective, teleological impulse together with the descriptive representational process.

22 The teleological feature of this process lies in the nature of the mind as a complex, integrated, dynamic system, in which systemic laws of equifinality, morphogenesis and morphostasis dominate against pure linear causality. The fundamental ontogenetic paradigm for this is Winnicott's object presenting, which works appropriately only if the object presented fits with the intrinsic purposiveness (dynamic organization) of the psyche.

References

Al-Khalili, J., Mcfadden, J. (2015). *Life on the Edge: The Coming of Age of Quantum Biology*. St. Louis: Black Swan.

Allen, T.W., Walker, K., Symonds, L., Marcell, M. (1977). Intrasensory and Intersensory Perception of Temporal Sequences During Infancy. *Developmental Psychology*, 13, 225–229.

Boden, M.A. (1977). *Artificial Intelligence and Natural Man*. Hassocks, Sussex: Harvester.

Boyer, P. (2001). *Religion Explained: The Evolutionary Origins of Religious Thought*. New York: Basic Books.

Brooke, R. (1991). *Jung and Phenomenology*. London, New York: Routledge.

Brown, D.E. (1991). *Human Universals*. Philadelphia: Temple University Press (English and Kindle edn).

Brown, F.M. (Ed.). (1987). *The Frame Problem in Artificial Intelligence*. Los Altos, CA: Morgan Kaufmann.

Bucci, W. (2021). *Emotional Communication and Therapeutic Change: Understanding Psychotherapy Through Multiple Code Theory*. London: Routledge.

Buss, D.M. (1989). Sex Differences in Human Mate Preferences: Evolutionary Hypotheses Tested in 37 Cultures. *Behavioral and Brain Sciences*, 12, 149.

Calabretta, R. (2002). Connessionismo Evolutivo e Origine della Modularità. In: *Scienze Della Mente*, pp. 47–63. A. Borghi, E.T. Iachini (Eds.). Bologna: Il Mulino.

Calabretta, R., Di Ferdinando, A., Wagner, G.P., Parisi, D. (2003). What Does It Take to Evolve Behaviorally Complex Organisms? *Biosystems*, 69, 245–262.

Calabretta, R., Nirotti, J. (2014). *Adaptive Agents in Changing Environments, the Role of Modularity: Neural Processing Letters*. New York: Springer Science+Business Media.

Carey, S., Gelman, R. (Eds.). (1991). *The Epigenesis of Mind: Essays on Biology and Cognition*. Hillsdale, NJ: Erlbaum.

Carruthers, P. (2006). The Case for Massively Modular Models of Mind. In: *Contemporary Debates in Cognitive Science*. R. Stainton (Ed.). Hoboken, NJ: Wiley-Blackwell.

Cosmides, L. (1985). Deduction of Darwinian Algorithms? An Explanation of the 'Elusive' Content Effect on the Watson Selection Task. *PhD Dissertation*. Harvard University.

Cosmides, L., Tooby, J. (1987). From Evolution to Behavior: Evolutionary Psychology As the Missing Link. In: *The Latest on the Best: Essays on Evolution and Optimality*, pp. 277–306. J. Dupré (Ed.). Cambridge, MA: MIT Press.

Cosmides, L., Tooby, J. (1989). Evolutionary Psychology and the Generation of Culture, Part I: Case Study: A Computational Theory of Social Exchange. *Ethology and Sociobiology*, 10, 51–97.

Cosmides, L., Tooby, J. (1992). Cognitive Adaptations for Social Exchange. In: *The Adapted Mind: Evolutionary Psychology and the Generation of Culture*. J. Barkow, L. Cosmides, J. Tooby (Eds.). Oxford, New York, Toronto: Oxford University Press.

Cosmides, L., Tooby, J. (1994). Origins of Domain Specificity: The Evolution of Functional Organization. In: *Mapping the Mind: Domain Specificity in Cognition and Culture*. L. Hirschfeld, S. Gelman (Eds.). New York: Cambridge University Press.

Daly, M., Wilson, M. (1986). Theoretical Challenge to a Caricature of Darwinism. *Behavioral and Brain Sciences*, 9, 189–190.

Damasio, A. (1995). *Descartes' Error: Emotion, Reason and the Human Brain.* London: Penguin Books.

Damasio, A. (2005). *Descartes' Error: Emotion, Reason, and the Human Brain.* London: Penguin Books.

Ekman, P. (1992). Facial Expressions of Emotion: New Findings, New Questions. *Psychological Science*, 3, 1, 34–38.

Feldman, J., Narayanan, S. (2004). Embodied Meaning in a Neural Theory of Language. *Brain and Language*, 89, 385–392.

Festinger, L. (1957). *A Theory of Cognitive Dissonance.* Stanford, CA: Stanford University Press.

Fodor, J.A. (1983). *Modularity of Mind.* MA: MIT Press.

Fodor, J.A. (2000). *The Mind Doesn't Work That Way: The Scope and Limits of Computational Psychology.* MA: MIT Press.

Frank, R.H. (2011). The Strategic Role of Emotions. *Emotions Review*, 3, 3, 252–254.

Gelman, R., Spelke, E., Meck, E. (1983). What Preschoolers Know About Animate and Inanimate Objects. In: *The Acquisition of Symbolic Skills*, pp. 121–143. D.S. Rogers, J.A. Sloboda (Eds.). London: Plenum.

Gelman, S.A., Wellman, H.M. (1991). Insides and Essence: Early Understandings of the Non-Obvious. *Cognition*, 38, 3, 213–244.

Gervais, H., Belin, P., Boddaert, N., Leboyer, M., Coez, A., Sfaello, I., Barthélémy, C., Brunelle, F., Samson, Y., Zilbovicius, M. (2004). Abnormal Cortical Voice Processing in Autism. *Nature Neuroscience*, 7, 8, 801–802.

Goodwyn, E. (2012). *The Neurobiology of the Gods. How Brain Physiology Shapes the Recurrent Imagery of Myths and Dreams.* London, New York: Routledge.

Griffiths, P.E. (1997). *What Emotions Really Are: The Problem of Psychological Categories.* University of Chicago Press.

Hjelmslev, L. (1961). *Prolegomena to a Theory of Language.* Madison: University of Wisconsin Press.

Hogenson, G.B. (2013). The Neurobiology of the Gods: How Brain Physiology Shapes the Recurrent Imagery of Myth and Dream. *International Journal of Jungian Studies*, 5, 1, 100–103.

Johnson, M. (2013). *The Body in the Mind: The Bodily Basis of Meaning, Imagination, and Reason*, pp. 108–109. Chicago: University of Chicago Press.

Jung, C.G. (1919). The Instinct and the Unconscious. In: *The Collected Works of C.G. Jung.* Vol. 8. London, New York: Routledge.

Jung, C.G. (1921a). Psychological Types. In: *The Collected Works of C.G. Jung.* Vol. 6. London: Routledge.

Jung, C.G. (1921b/1928). *The Therapeutic Value of Abreaction.* Vol. 16. London, New York: Routledge.

Jung, C.G. (1947/1954). On the Nature of the Psyche. In: *The Collected Works of C.G. Jung.* Vol. 8. London: Routledge.

Karmiloff-Smith, A. (1996). *Beyond Modularity – a Developmental Perspective on Cognitive Science.* Cambridge: Bradford Books, MIT Press.

Knox, J. (2003). *Archetype, Attachment, Analysis. Jungian Psychology and the Emergent Mind.* London: Brunner-Routledge.

Knox, J.M. (2001). Memories, Fantasies, Archetypes: An Exploration of Some Connections Between Cognitive Science and Analytical Psychology. *Journal of Analytical Psychology*, 46, 613–635.

Knox, J.M. (2004a). From Archetypes to Reflective Function. *Journal of Analytical Psychology*, 49, 1, 1–19.

Knox, J.M. (2004b). Developmental Aspects of Analytical Psychology: New Perspectives from Cognitive Neuroscience and Attachment Theory. In: *Analytical Psychology: Contemporary Perspectives in Jungian Analysis.* J. Cambray, L.C. Hove (Eds.). New York: Brunner-Routledge.

Knox, J.M. (2009). The Analytic Relationship: Integrating Jungian, Attachment Theory and Developmental Perspectives. *British Journal of Psychotherapy*, 25, 1.

Knox, J.M. (2010). Response to Erik Goodwyn's "Approaching Archetypes: Reconsidering Innateness". *Journal of Analytical Psychology*, 55, 4, 522–533.

Kohut, H. (1971). *The Analysis of the Self: A Systematic Approach to the Psychoanalytic Treatment of Narcissistic Personality Disorders.* Chicago: University of Chicago Press.

Lakoff, G. (1987). *Women, Fire, and Dangerous Things: What Our Categories Reveal About the Mind.* Chicago: University of Chicago Press.

Lakoff, G., Johnson, M. (1999). *Philosophy in the Flesh: The Embodied Mind and Its Challenge to Western Thought.* New York: Basic Books.

Lakoff, G., Johnson, M. (2003). *Metaphors We Live By.* Chicago: University of Chicago Press.

Lakoff, G., Nuñez, R. (2001). *Where Mathematics Comes From: How the Embodied Mind Brings Mathematics into Being.* New York: Basic Books.

Lewcowicz, D.J., Turkewitz, G. (1980). Cross-Modal Equivalence in Early Infancy: Audio-Visual Intensity Matching. *Developmental Psychology*, 16, 597–607.

Lewcowicz, D.J., Turkewitz, G. (1981). Intersensory Interaction in Newborns: Modification of Visual Preference Following Exposure to Sound. *Child Development*, 52, 327–332.

Lotman, Y.M. (1985). *La Semiosfera: l'Asimmetria e il Dialogo nelle Strutture Pensanti.* Milano: La Nave di Teseo.

Lotman, Y.M. (2001). *Universe of the Mind. A Semiotic Theory of Culture.* A. Shukman (Transl.). Bloomington, IN: Indiana University Press.

Mandler, J.M. (1992). How to Build a Baby: II. Conceptual Primitives. *Psychological Review*, 99, 4, 587–604.

Mandler, J.M. (2004). *The Foundations of Mind: Origins of Conceptual Thought.* Oxford: Oxford University Press.

Mandler, J.M. (2012). Perceptual and Conceptual Processes in Infancy. *Journal of Cognition and Development*, 1, 1, 3–36.

Mandler, J.M., Cánovas, C.P. (2014). On Defining Image Schemas. *Language and Cognition*, 6, 4, 510–532.

Masrour, F. (2015). The Geometry of Visual Space and the Nature of Visual Experience. *Philosophical Studies*, 172, 7, 1813–1832.

Masrour, F., Nirshberg, G., Schon, M., Leardi, J., Barrett, E. (2015, November 4). Revisiting the Empirical Case Against Perceptual Modularity. *Frontiers in Psychology*, 6, 2015.

Mcgurk, H., Macdonald, J. (1976). Hearing Lips and Seeing Voices. *Nature*, 264, 5588, 746–748.

Meltzoff, A.N., Borton, W. (1979). Intermodal Matching by Human Neonates. *Nature*, 282, 403–404.

Meltzoff, A.N., Moore, M.K. (1977). Imitation of Facial and Manual Gestures by Human Neonates. *Science*, 198, 75–78.

Merchant, J. (2016). The Image Schema and Innate Archetypes: Theoretical and Clinical Implications. *Journal of Analytical Psychology*, 61, 1, 63–78.

Michotte, A. (1963). *The Perception of Causality.* London: Methuen.

Miller, C.L., Byrne, J.M. (1984). The Role of Temporal Cues in the Development of Language and Communication. In: *The Origin and Growth of Communication.* L. Feagans, G. Garvey, R. Golinkoff (Eds.). Norwood, NJ: Ablex.

Montag, C., Davis, K. (2018). Affective Neuroscience Theory and Personality: An Update Personality. *Neuroscience*, 1, E12, 1–12.

Nagarjuna, G. (2006). Layers in the Fabric of Mind: A Critical Review of Cognitive Ontogeny. In: *Research Trends in Science, Technology and Mathematics Education.* J. Ramadas, S. Chunawala (Eds.). Mumbai: Homi Bhabha Centre for Science Education, TIFR.

Noble, D. (2008). *The Music of Life: Biology Beyond Genes.* Oxford: Oxford University Press.

Pauli, W. (2012). *The Interpretation of Nature and the Psyche.* Bronx, New York: Ishi Press.

Piaget, J. (1952). *The Origins of Intelligence in Children.* New York: International Universities Press.

Piaget, J. (1970). Piaget's Theory. In: *Carmichael's Manual of Child Psychology.* Vol. I, 3rd edn. P.H. Mussen (Ed.). New York: Wiley.

Pinker, S. (1997). *How the Mind Works.* New York: Norton.

Plutchik, R. (1980). *Emotion: A Psychoevolutionary Synthesis.* New York: Harper & Row Publishers.

Plutchik, R. (1991). *The Emotions,* p. 110. University Press of America. ISBN 9780819182869. Retrieved 16 September 2017 – Via Google Books.

Plutchik, R. (2001, July 16). The Nature of Emotions. *American Scientist,* 89, 344–350.

Raschle, N.M., Smith, S.A., Zuk, J., Dauvermann, M.R., Figuccio, M.J., Gaab, N. (2014). Investigating the Neural Correlates of Voice Versus Speech-Sound Directed Information in Pre-School Children. *PLoS ONE,* 9, 12, 1–23.

Rochat, P., Morgan, R., Carpenter, M. (1997). Young Infants' Sensitivity to Movement Information Specifying Social Causality. *Cognitive Development,* 12, 4, 441–465.

Rosch, E. (1973). Natural Categories. *Cognitive Psychology,* 4, 3, pp. 328–350.

Rosch, E. (1978). Principles of Categorization. In: *Cognition and Categorization.* E. Rosch, B.B. Lloyd (Eds.). Hillsdale: Lawrence Erlbaum.

Rumelhart, D.E., McClelland, J.L. (1986). *Parallel Distributed Processing, Explorations in the Microstructure of Cognition I and II.* Cambridge: MIT Press.

Simon, H. (1962). The Architecture of Complexity. *Proceedings of the American Philosophical Society,* 162, 467–482.

Simondon, G. (2020). *Individuation in Light of Notions of Form and Information.* Minneapolis, London: The University of Minnesota Press.

Sloman, A. (2021). Biological Evolution's Use of Representational Redescriptions. In: *Taking Development Seriously: A Festschrift for Annette-Karmiloff-Smith.* M.C. Thomas, D. Mareschal, V.C.P. Knowland. London: Routledge.

Spearman, C. (1904). "General Intelligence," Objectively Determined and Measured. *American Journal of Psychology,* 15, 2, 201–293.

Sperber, D. (1994). Modularity of Thought and the Epidemiology of Representations. In: *Mapping the Mind: Domain Specificity in Cognition and Culture.* L.A. Hirschfeld, S.A. Gelman (Eds.). New York: Cambridge University Press.

Stern, D.N. (1985). *The Interpersonal World of the Infant: A View from Psychoanalysis and Developmental Psychology.* Kindle edn. Karnac Books.

Tenhouten, W. (2018). From Ressentiment to Resentment as a Tertiary Emotion. *Review of European Studies,* 10, 49. https://doi.org/10.5539/Res.V10n4p49.

Vernadsky, V.L. (2013). *The Biosphere.* Göttingen: Copernicus Books.

Von Franz, M.L. (1986). *Number and Time: Reflections Leading Toward a Unification of Depth Psychology and Physics.* Evanston: Northwestern University Press.

Wagner, S., Sakowitz, L. (1983). *Intersensory and Intrasensory Recognition: A Quantitative and Developmental Evaluation.* Paper Presented at the Meeting of the Society for Research in Child Development, Detroit, Michigan in Stern, D. (1985).

Walter, S. (1994). Algorithm and Archetypes: Evolutionary Psychology and Carl Jung's Theory of the Collective Unconscious. *Journal of Social and Evolutionary Systems,* 17, 3, 287–306.

Wigner, E. (1960, February). Reprinted from Communications. *Pure and Applied Mathematics,* 13, I.

Zilbovicius, M., Meresse, I., Chabane, N., Brunelle, F., Samson, Y., Boddaert, N. (2006). Autism, the Superior Temporal Sulcus and Social Perception. *Trends in Neurosciences,* 29, 7, 359–366.

Chapter 10

Dispositionality, Teleology, Complexity and Object Presenting

Let's try to summarize the essence of the co-evolutionary relational entanglement between the organism, and especially a person, and its object world. I will discuss three main features: I. the organism hit by an *impulse*; II. the trigger of an interpretive *agency*; and III. motor activity, perceptions, affects and cognition interact and develop towards a unitary self.

I. The Organism Is Hit by an *Impulse*

We may conceptualize this impulse as a pre-psychic something, like an imbalance, something like Freud's economical description of the drive as an *Arbeitanfrage* ("work request"). Probably Bion had something like this in mind when he referred to the proto-mental realm and to the "beta elements" arising from O (Bion, 1965). As we saw, Jung, on the other end, refers to this as an *ectopsychic factor*.

It is essential not to reduce such a factor to an *external* stimulus, as the (highly relative, if not illusory) differentiation between what is external and what is internal at this point has yet to be established. This stimulus may well be an expression of a genetically timed ontogenetic development *within the co-evolutionary* (relational) *field*. This stimulus does not necessarily need to be activated at birth or, for that matter, at an early age but may be triggered by maturational factors or by situational conditions.

Such a factor is a limit-concept, a working hypothesis, as it cannot exist without a complex context in which it is dynamically embedded. In Jung's quotation, this context would be the "pre-existing pattern", the dispositional *potential* background that he called "collective unconscious".

This concept is essential; I am using it both in Winnicott's sense and in this description by Jung, in which he distinguished between archetype-as-such and archetypical images:

> By this I do not mean the existing form of the motif but its preconscious, invisible "ground plan". This might be compared to the crystal lattice that is pre-formed in the crystalline solution. It should not be confused with the variously structured axial system of the individual crystal.
>
> (Jung, 1948, footnote, §590)

DOI: 10.4324/9781003586258-10

A striking neurobiological convergence on Jung's hypothesis is the view that has been confirmed in the last 20 years of the nature of the brain's activity when the subject is sleeping (and not dreaming), or when he is sedated – i.e., when the brain is in a total state of inactivity. In such a situation, one would imagine that the brain is not consuming much energy, but this is not true. In fact, while not engrossed in any stimulation or dreaming, the brain is consuming 60% of its total consumption of energy (calculated through the BOLD – *blood oxygenation level dependent* – analysis) (Gusnard & Raichle; 2001; Biswal et al., 1995).[1] What has been discovered is that in such a situation, the brain produces a constant endogenous, spontaneous, stable activity at a very parsimonious frequency (0,1–1 Hertz), by which the same areas that *will* be soon triggered by a task are already active (Figure 10.1) (Gusnard & Raichle, 2001; Corbetta & Shulman, 2002).

Fig. 10.1 is perhaps the first neuroimage that shows the amazing identity between activated areas and those that are anticipating such activation by an endogenous low-frequency level of 0,1–1 Hertz. Region b of Figure 3b represents a central pixel in the left motor cortex. Areas of right and left motor cortex are labeled a, b. They are about the same in both Figures 3a and 3b. This apparent discrepancy is because 5 or 6 pixels in region a of Figure 3b lay outside the right motor cortex boundary as determined by FMRI (i.e., region a of Figure 3a), but were contiguous to it. Pixels posterior to region c, labeled d, belong to the paracentral lobule. Region d may be an extension of the primary sensorimotor cortex into the inner hemispheric fissure. The activated area in Figure 3b labeled e, which is also seen occasionally in motor-task FMRI data, although not in this case in Figure 3a, may represent the premotor area.

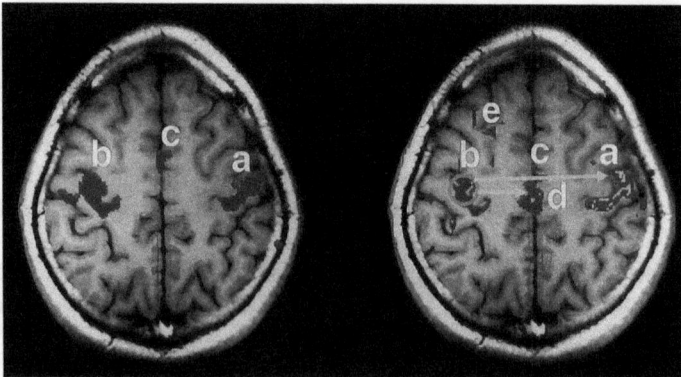

Figure 10.1 A comparison between the brain's activity while performing a motor task (left) and at rest (right). This is perhaps the first neuroimage that shows the amazing identity between activated areas and those that are anticipating such activation by an endogenous low-frequency level of 0,1–1 Hertz.

Source: Biswal et al. (1995)

This converging set of research is showing the following:

a) The brain's activity does not respond to stimuli but is *anticipatory and predictive*.
b) Its teleological activity is highly organized, both structurally and functionally.
    This is what Fox et al. (2005) write in the abstract of this work, which has
    been quoted over 9,000 times:

> During performance of attention-demanding cognitive tasks, certain regions of
> the brain routinely increase activity, whereas others routinely decrease activity.
> In this study, we investigate the extent to which this task-related dichotomy
> is represented intrinsically in the resting human brain through examination of
> spontaneous fluctuations in the functional MRI blood oxygen level-dependent
> signal. We identify two diametrically opposed, widely distributed brain net-
> works on the basis of both spontaneous correlations within each network and
> anticorrelations between networks. One network consists of regions routinely
> exhibiting task-related activations and the other of regions routinely exhibiting
> task-related deactivations. This intrinsic organization, featuring the presence of
> anticorrelated networks in the absence of overt task performance, provides a
> critical context in which to understand brain function. We suggest that both
> task-driven neuronal responses and behavior are reflections of this dynamic,
> ongoing, functional organization of the brain.
>
> (p. 9673)

c) This continuous, latent activity is highly patterned into fields that will assimilate
   the stimulus (for instance, a visual or a motor task) within their dispositional,
   constraining limits. Yet such constraints are not rigid but represent the activation
   of endogenous multi-layered, hidden, deep neural networks that will integrate
   the incoming stimulus. Therefore, the brain seems to work like the "instinct"
   does, as I have defined it so far – a triggering *flexible* action pattern.

Glasser et al. (2016) have produced an impressive mapping of these latent, dispositional fields of endogenous, spontaneous activation by which the brain produces
teleological anticipatory expectations (and, in so doing, construes the subjective ecological niche to which I referred when I discussed the co-evolutionary paradigm).

Using multimodal magnetic resonance images from the Human Connectome
Project (HCP) and an objective semi-automated neuroanatomical approach, the
authors delineated 180 areas per hemisphere bounded by sharp changes in cortical
architecture, function, connectivity and/or topography. These latent functional and
structural fluctuating networks are further organized in only five main basins (in
the human brain, they are related to visual, auditory, sensorimotor tasks oriented
towards the outer world and tasks oriented to the inner world). These fields function like archetypes, insofar as they are produced by hidden, deep-layered neural
networks that *anticipate and predict* the incoming stimuli. This means that these
networks are innate and not learned, while constraining and direct learning by
encapsulating it within their confines.

This is the example that Maurizio Corbetta, one of the researchers, makes: If you are visiting the Louvre, in your brain, a deep, latent, fluctuating and highly patterned activity is already activated, as you are foreseeing (almost all the time unconsciously) what will happen. The areas of the brain that one may see through visual imaging *before* anything happens will be the same that will light up much more brightly when the stimulus will arrive – for instance, when you will finally see the Mona Lisa. At that moment, the multi-layered neural network that was already active at a low level of oxygen consumption will increase its activity because its neurons will start spiking up. The point is that *before* seeing the Gioconda, at a deep level, the fundamental layers of the neural networks – for instance, at the level of the midbrain's superior colliculus, or at the level of the lateral geniculate nucleus (both ancient subcortical structures in which the visual inputs are already mapped) – of your brain are expecting to see a statistically probable image (Figure 10.2).

This point is very important because it shows the openness of the field of activation, which represents a sort of a probability field, and at the same time, its constraining nature. The schematic, average face that your brain is expecting is not the Mona Lisa's face, but when Leonardo's image hits your retina, it will be assimilated to this statistical set of probable images already pre-activated deep in your brain, and it will be understood as a relevant, meaningful and *specific* face.

Even if this description does not include affects, it is quite clear that it will take place precisely because the stimuli that we are talking about are salient stimuli, endowed by an affective charge, a charge that takes place at the same neuroanatomical level of the brain in which such proto-mapping activity takes place – the midbrain.

What I am describing is one aspect of the learning process through which a formal schema – in Jungian terms, an archetypal schema – becomes a personal complex. At the deep, archetypal level, this fluctuating, highly integrated basin of activation expresses a formal set of schematic rules of probable states (in which the Mona Lisa matches a very high probability to be recognized as a face, although, as we know, *something* in this uncanny image will keep us busy in the attempt to fully resolve it). These states will be filled with the necessary visual, empirical contents by the subject's experience. At that point, I argue, the probability cloud collapses into the specific, unique experience – a singularity (i.e., a *phenomenological conscious reality*). Such latent, predictive basins of activations look very much like Jung's image of the crystal lattice that I quoted (and to von Uexküll's *Bauplan*), as they are always spontaneously active yet non-perceptible until a stimulus transforms their formal nature by producing an empirical image.

This sort of *kenosis* (very similar to Bion's alpha function by which O becomes "realized" into a conception) happens because these fluctuating anticipatory fields are in a state of hypercriticality and need a minimal input to tilt into a sudden phase transition, a dramatically new state, precisely like Jung's example.

From these studies, which are already quite relevant for confirming the possibility of an archetypal foundation of experience triggered by "flexible action patterns", a last point must be made, which refers to the nature of this stimulus that

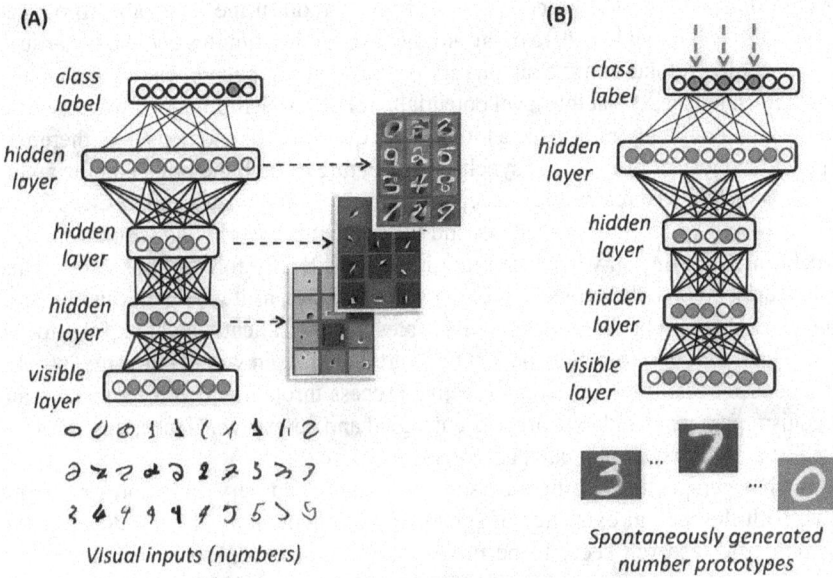

Figure 10.2 (A) Deep Boltzmann Machines (DBMs) are deep neural networks of symmetrically coupled stochastic neurons organized in a hierarchy of multiple layers. The DBM learns a hierarchical generative model of the input (e.g., sensory) data presented on the "visible layer". "Hidden layers" contain neurons that encode latent causes of the data: when trained on images (here, handwritten digits) they become tuned to visual features that are increasingly more complex in deeper layers (examples of receptive fields of individual neurons are shown in the right panels). Learning is unsupervised (i.e., it does not require external teaching or reward signal): its objective is to learn a probability distribution that approximates the true probability distribution of the training data. Recurrent connections convey the information sampled from the upper layers downstream to generate data on the visible layer in a top-down fashion. The divergence between real input and its top-down reconstruction drives the change of connection weights during learning, using Hebbian rules. After learning, recurrent interactions support stochastic inference that leads to denoising, completion or "filling in" of ambiguous (or missing) inputs, in the same sensory modality or in different modalities if the architecture is multimodal (e.g., learns visual and linguistic inputs). Discriminative tasks (here, digit classification) can be learned by adding a layer of neurons representing the class labels. During learning, the model acquires "generic priors": here, prototypical digit shapes that abstract away from many input details. (B) After learning, sampling can be conditioned by the class labels to generate prototypical digit shapes "spontaneously", i.e., in the absence of sensor inputs (Pezzulo et al., 2021).

is responsible for such phase transitions (i.e., for the process of transforming a potentiality into a reality).

In fact, it is not at all implausible that the magnitude of these stimuli needed to trigger such phase transitions within this hypercritical state is at an atomic or subatomic level, as happens within the biological realm for enzymatic activity, for the synthesis of chlorophyll or for the process by which the alveoli in the lungs absorb oxygen (Al-Khalili & McFadden, 2015). The atomic level of the stimulus and the collapse of the probability cloud into the singularity of the subject's phenomenological experience (consciousness) – at this level potentially related to Schrödinger's wave – opens the way to a radically new vista, as it involves quantistic phenomena and, therefore, a possible physical base for the synchronistic nature of both the brain and the archetypes. Within such a realm, the concept of a brain that anticipates and foresees future events would be literally pushed beyond the perceptible world and would refer to a synchronistic reality in which the brain is able to literally foresee those events that will deeply involve the subject's life *in his whole future*, as it would constantly guide him towards those background affective states that are salient – meaningful – for his individuation. Therefore, the concept of a foreseeing brain would converge into that of a constant reality-constructing, creative process through which the subject – any organism perhaps – and its world are entangled and co-evolve. Hence, this would be not just a *creatio continua* but a *co-creatio continua*.

Such a perspective – Jung's perspective – is indeed very audacious; nevertheless, both the factual existence of synchronistic phenomena and the development of scientific research seem to be progressively indicating them as if not real or probable, at least surely as *possible* (Freeman & Vitiello, 2005, 2006, 2008, 2016; Vitiello, 2023; Tagliagambe & Malinconico, 2018). From this perspective, the collective unconscious seems to be the realm from which one person's probable may become real, and this can happen, perhaps paradoxically, because there exist fundamental constraints that teleologically preselect what for each one of us is more probable and what is less probable. Without any constraint, it would be impossible to learn *anything* through one's empirical experience, and most importantly, it would be impossible to learn what one was meant to learn so as to become himself.

In some infinitely precious moments of one's relational life, one may feel with outmost certitude that what he is in that precise moment in time is the full realization, within that very instant, of what he was meant to be.

Another important issue has to do with the question whether these impulses are visceral sensation or affects. Up to the embryologically and anatomically oldest structures of the brain, at the level of the brainstem and the mesencephalon, they may be considered purely somatic impulses, "raw" sensations, but if they must be integrated in the nervous system, from reptiles on, they will assimilate and organize "meaningful" patterns. In fact, we may hypothesize the existence of purely sensation-like (i.e., non-affective) visceral impulses in lower organisms, without a centralized nervous system but not in more evolved animals.[2] In any case, even if the impulse is a reflex "fixed action pattern" arising from the organism's visceral body, we must remember that it is always entangled with the organism's specific co-evolutionary niche.

II.   Such an a-noetic affect represents the origin, the trigger of an interpretive *agency* and always implies the activation of the motivational system of SEEKING, which is the most pervasive primary affect, as it participates in most of the others when they are activated. What is crucial is that, while it ignites a process, such an affect also *constellates* a specific neuronal environment, which may be described as a neurological *module*.[3] This has important features:

a) This module works by the principles of *relative encapsulation* and *degeneracy* (Edelman & Tononi, 2000).
b) If the impulse is a complex, it will activate more modules and/or a complex module made up of sub-modules.
c) Following Webb's principle for which "neurons that fire together wire together", the stronger the a-noetic activation, the more encapsulated the module will be.
d) If the affect is a complex affect and the relative intensity of every primitive affect is moderate, the complex module, made by sub-modules, will be internally flexible and open to the integration of other modules.

All this means is that it is *impossible* to conceptualize something like a stimulus without a context. In such a landscape, an input is always assimilated by the latent potential organization *which, at the same time, it will concur to activate*. I cannot emphasize enough this ecological paradigm, in which the focal point of any analysis shifts from the objects to their interactions (Bateson, 1972, 2002). Therefore, within this complex systems' paradigm, the affect at the same time triggers a process and constellates an emotional environment which will confer value and orientation to the process itself.

A clinical application of this perspective is the systemic-relational paradigm, especially the version developed by the so-called "Milan group" (Selvini Palazzoli et al., 1994). For this model, within a dynamic complex system, such as a family, every "behavior" is interpreted as a pragmatic performative message whose meaning will *emerge* from the network of the system's (the family's) relations. The excessive intensity of the *emotional* constraints (what in the systemic model are called "systemic rules") that connect the members of the family (i.e., the strength of the emotional dependence of each member from the others) determines a situation that is described as an "overly intricated system", i.e., an excessively encapsulated system – a system rigidly inhibited towards learning and change (Boszormenyi-Nagy & Spark, 1973/1984).

A family organized in such a way – often a family in which psychotic symptoms are kept at bay precisely by such an organization – functions in a rigid homeostatic way. If one member expresses any sign of individuality – hence, separating herself from the group – the whole group will (unconsciously, i.e., automatically) react to block this individuating move, which is felt as a catastrophic loss.

Another more theoretical example of the pervasive epistemological influence of this paradigm is that of the relationship between a *meaning* conveyed by a *Parole*, as in the original theory by de Saussure (1916). Such a meaning will be fundamentally determined by its position within the context of its *Langue*. The *Parole* represents a "text", being the *Langue* its context, which indicates *how* the text must be interpreted.

On the other end of the continuum of the overly encapsulated (rigid, "morphostatic") system, it is relevant to notice that, if the constraints that represent the associations between mental objects is too loose, this may give rise to schizophrenic symptomatology. Such a deficit in forming stable patterns (modules) confirms Bleuer's (and Jung's) interpretation of schizophrenia as a disturbance of the association activity of the mind due to the dysfunctional activity of the affects, which do not properly constellate and organize images. Such a dysfunctional activity may be due to an excess or a deficit of affective activation.

III.   From this quick background introduction, I have recalled that motor activity, perceptions, affects and cognition interact and develop towards a unitary self, in which, as Bion would say, a thinker is able to think emotional thoughts while feeling them as his own, hence, experiencing an ongoing, unitary, integrated, flexible, conscious, subjective state.

The fundamental relevance of affects for the development of personality is connected to Daniel Stern's fruitful metaphor of the *clinical child vs. the observed child*, in which the observed child, studied by infant research, is mostly a cognitive child.

Along with Stern, I think that we cannot understand the clinical child just through the observed child but that we must unite these two perspectives. For this *whole child*, what seems to be foundational is the role that Stern recognizes in cross-modal perceptions – connected with mirror neurons – together with the "vitality affects" within what he calls the *emergent relational field* (Stern, 1985).

Both cross-modal perceptions and vitality affects are modularized experiences, i.e., experiences that that are structured and constrained in invariant forms. I have already mentioned the role of cross-modal perception when I discussed the process of metaphor-formation. Therefore, now I may limit myself to describe what vitality affects are:

> There is a third quality of experience that can arise directly from encounters with people, a quality that involves vitality affects. What do we mean by this, and why is it necessary to add a new term for certain forms of human experience? It is necessary because many qualities of feeling that occur do not fit into our existing lexicon or taxonomy of affects. These elusive qualities are better captured by dynamic, kinetic terms, such as "surging", "fading away", "fleeting", "explosive", "crescendo", "decrescendo", "bursting", "drawn out", and so on.
>
> These qualities of experience are most certainly sensible to infants and of great daily, even momentary, importance. It is these feelings that will be elicited by changes in motivational states, appetites, and tensions. The philosopher Suzanne Langer (1967) insisted that in any experience-near psychology, close attention must be paid to the many "forms of feeling" inextricably involved with all the vital processes of life, such as breathing, getting hungry, eliminating, falling asleep and emerging out of sleep, or feeling the coming and going of emotions and thoughts. The different forms of feeling elicited by these vital processes impinge on the organism most of the time. We are never without their presence, whether or not we are conscious of them, while "regular" affects come and go.

The infant experiences these qualities from within, as well as in the behavior of other persons.

(Stern, 1985, pp. 926–934)

Cross-modal innate competencies based on perceptual invariants are, therefore, rooted in the sensorium, while vitality affects, also expressing invariant patterns, couple sensory-motor behavior and affects. Once again, we have the three fundamental elements for the development of the mind: perception, movement and affects, where the vitality affects indicate the organization of the affects as the fundamental teleological, meaning-giving attractors that make possible psychological development and the individuation process. Therefore, it is from the beginning of life that affects, conveyed in modularized, invariant forms, molded with motor activity and perception, teleologically aim towards the progressive development of what Stern describes as four different "senses of the self", each one defining a different domain of self-experience and social relatedness.

Stern's senses of the self are the following: the sense of an *emergent self*, which forms from birth to age 2 months, the *sense of a core self*, which forms between 2 and 6 months of age, the sense of a *subjective self*, which forms between 7 and 15 months, and a sense of a *verbal self*, which forms after that.

These senses of the self develop within the relationship between the infant and his environment. This situation requires a very specific and coherent matching cooperation between infant and (m)other – i.e., the emergence of a "co-evolutionary niche".

This is the meaning of Jung's lines in the quotation that I have been analyzing throughout this discussion:

the immediate determining factor is not the ectopsychic instinct but *the structure resulting from the interaction of instinct and the psychic situation of the moment*. The determining factor would thus be a modified instinct.

(Jung, 1937, p. 115)

In my example, the mother-infant complex relationship is precisely such a "psychic situation of the moment", a situation that cannot be imagined completely free but that is organized by specific constraints and attractors, which is what Jung meant when he wrote these lines, that I have already quoted several times:

Instinct as an ectopsychic factor would play the role of a stimulus merely, while instinct as a psychic phenomenon would be *an assimilation of this stimulus to a pre-existent psychic pattern*. A name is needed for this process. I should term it psychization.

(Jung, 1937, p. 115)

Obviously, at this point, the meaning of psychization may be interpreted as the process of mentalization that takes place within the mother's container and her *rêverie*.

10.1   We-ness: Becoming Human and the Psychological Birth of Culture

At this point of my discussion, Michael Tomasello's studies are very relevant.[4] One of the many important features of Tomasello's work is that his findings, while having profound cognitive implications, are molded by emotional/value-laden contents. In effect, the description of the development of cognitive competences that Tomasello describes brings Stern's "clinical child" and "observed child" closer.

Seen from this angle, Tomasello's research is coherent with human reality and happens within the child's co-evolutionary space.

In fact:

> Ordinary cognitive activity does not take place in a fixed experimental setting where the information available is strictly limited and controlled, but in a complex, information rich, ever-changing environment. In social species, conspecifics occupy a salient place in this environment, and much of the individual-environment interaction is, in fact, interaction with other individuals. In the human case, moreover, the environment is densely furnished with cultural objects and events most of which have, at least in part, the function of producing cognitive effects.
>
> In most experimental psychology this ecological, social, and cultural dimension of human cognition is bracketed out. This practice has drawn strong criticisms, both from differently oriented psychologists and from social scientists. Clearly, there are good grounds for these criticisms. How damning they are remains contentious. After all, all research programs, even the most holistic ones, cannot but idealize their objects by abstracting away from many dimensions of reality. In each case, the issue is whether the idealization highlights a genuinely automous (*sic!*) level about which interesting generalizations can be discovered, or whether it merely creates an artificial pseudodomain the study of which does not effectively contribute to the knowledge of the real world.
>
> (Sperber & Hirschfeld, 1999, p. cxiii)

This quote comes from the work of Dan Sperber and Lawrence Hirschfeld, two cognitive anthropologists. The real world that they mention, rather than a scientific laboratory, is precisely what an analyst deals with, and the direct reference to the cognitive laboratory research by Jungian writers may run the risk to refer to findings – cognitive competences – that are the product of an idealized, abstracted "observed child".

Here, I am anticipating my discussion on the relationship between the human cognitive development embedded within an affective, social co-evolutionary field and cultural/anthropological issues which I will fully develop later.

Although he mostly refers to cognitive development, one aspect of Tomasello's overarching research implicitly describes the underpinning development of secondary emotions, i.e., social, cultural emotions that express not merely individual (egocentric) competitive reactions typical of our evolutionarily closest kin: the chimpanzees.

M. TOMASELLO
From "egocentric" primary emotions to social, cultural (universalized) emotional meanings

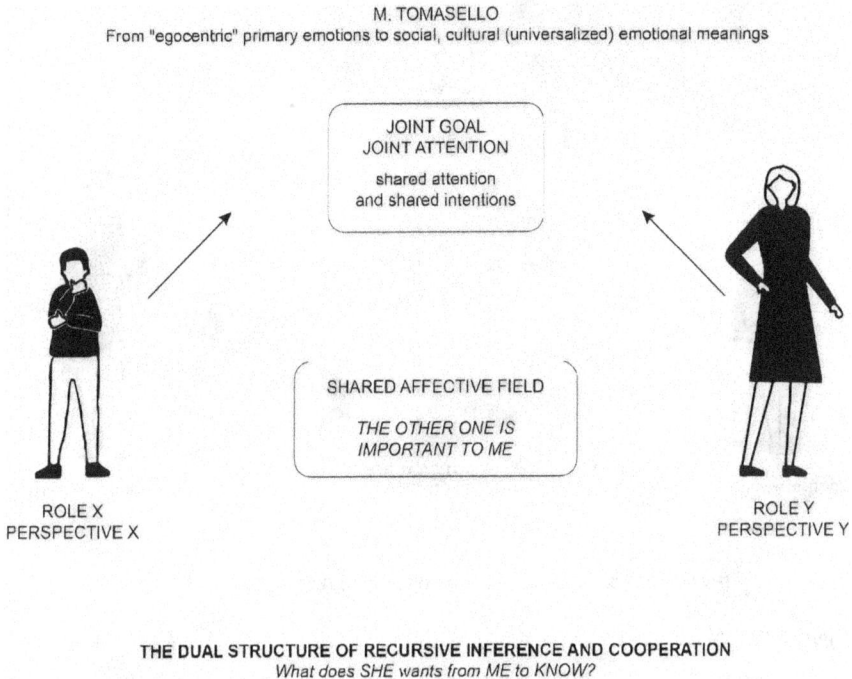

JOINT GOAL
JOINT ATTENTION

shared attention
and shared intentions

SHARED AFFECTIVE FIELD

*THE OTHER ONE IS
IMPORTANT TO ME*

ROLE X
PERSPECTIVE X

ROLE Y
PERSPECTIVE Y

THE DUAL STRUCTURE OF RECURSIVE INFERENCE AND COOPERATION
What does SHE wants from ME to KNOW?

Figure 10.3 Tomasello calls "recursive inference".

In fact, at 9 months and at 3 years of age, the child undergoes two revolutions.

At 9 months, differently from the competitive, egocentric primates, the human infant is capable of collaboration through shared, joint attention *towards a third object* (referencing through pointing and showing. This implies what Tomasello calls "*recursive inference*": What does *SHE* want for *ME* to *KNOW*?) (Figure 10.3).

This describes a shared intentionality schema, in which the following are observed:

• At a behavioral level: two individual roles become coordinated towards a shared goal.
• At the cognitive level: the attention of the two participants is now joint attention, and their perspectives become coordinated.

Tomasello calls this crucial maturational advancement *perspective-recursive cognition*.

These abilities that the child develops through his biological maturation *in a favorable environment* mean that the child has acquired what Tomasello calls "*perspectival cognition*", for which she now understands that, within a dyadic structure, an object may be interpreted from multiple points of view, which now should be negotiated.

To these paradigms (pointing, shared intentionality, shared attention, perspectival cognition), it is crucial to add the paradigm of shared *affectivity*, at first conveyed once again by movements expressing vitality affects. In fact, it is such shared

We-ness

Joint commitment
to role ideals

LEGITIMATELY
SELF-REGULATE

EMOTIONAL BOND
RESPONSIBILITY

2p agent w/cooperative ID

2p agent w/cooperative ID

THE TERNARY STRUCTURE OF THE PERSPECTIVAL NORMATIVE RELATEDNESS

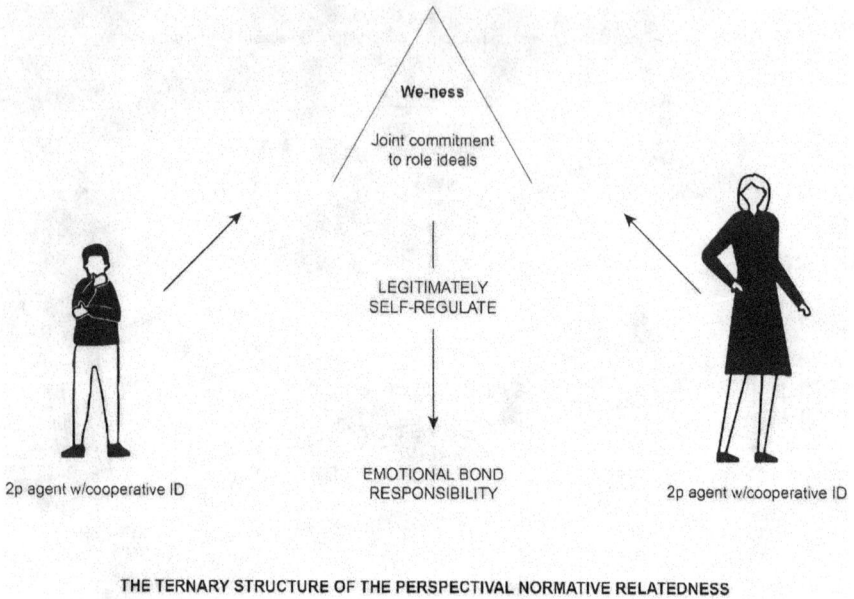

Figure 10.4 Normative cooperation.

affectivity which motivates and molds into a meaningful unit the child's experience. In a few words, the possibility to be-together within such a perspectival cognitive structure is something that the child feels to want and something that emotionally regulates his self in an adequate way.

At 3 years of age, we witness a second revolution, as normative cognition appears within a *triadic* structure (Figure 10.4).

At this point, if two children are involved in a joint commitment, a common goal is not reached if only one gets the reward. If after a joint action one of the two gets a better reward (let's say, three candies instead of one), she will almost always even up the prize.

In a study by Hamann et al. (2011), 2- and 3-year-old children always ended up in a situation in which there was a lucky child – who got more rewards – and an unlucky one. In such a situation, to distribute the rewards would require a sacrifice. In the first case, the two children simply walked in a room and found the rewards each at the end of a platform. In this case, there was no redistribution. In a second case, to get the rewards, they had to pull a rope, and the lucky child got more than the other. In the third condition, asymmetrical distribution resulted from a cooperative effort of the two children pulling together. In this case, the lucky child redistributed part of her prize with the unlucky one 80% of the time.

Presumably, they felt that if they both had worked equally to produce the rewards, they both deserved them equally. When the same experiment was run with chimpanzees, they hardly shared at all, even when all they had to do was not block the other from accessing the extra reward; whether there was collaboration made no difference.

The important finding is that three-years-olds (but not two-years-old or apes) will actually sacrifice resources in order to balance things with a collaborative partner.

(Tomasello, 2019, pp. 236–237)

At 3 years of age, the child complains if treated unfairly, hence showing that the expected behavior should be the fair and cooperative one and needs excuses (reasons) to break a joint commitment (not if the commitment is not a joint one).

Morality is based on fairness, and as we have seen, fairness appears through cooperation. This implies that at this point, the child must not think in an egocentric way but in a group-minded way. We may say that fair human culture and society begins at around four years of age although there are societies – like the Western capitalistic societies – whose principles are not based on cooperation and fair redistribution (to the point of ritual dissipation) but on competition and accumulation.

In fact, in normative cooperation, WE self-regulate each other through common norms we feel responsible for: NOT "I DON'T LIKE IT" BUT "YOU SHOULDN'T DO IT".

Fairness is a general principle that guides all the other social norms (i.e., norms that regulate mutual cooperative efforts) to which, from now on, the child may refer to.

This normative cooperation is a sign of what Tomasello calls "*perspectival-objective-recursive thinking*" (at this point, false beliefs and objective knowledge appear) and takes place through *coordination on perspectives on a shared object of interest*.

It might be interesting to notice that the age in which such conducts based on fairness and perspectival coordination – all ethical principles – corresponds plus or minus to the age in which Freud thought the Oedipus complex is resolved. Within this perspective, the predated, endogenously triggered, species-specific oedipal configurations observed by authors, such as Melanie Klein or Winnicott, should not be considered corrections of a Freudian mistake but may be considered as an ongoing structure on its way towards a maturation that reaches a phylogenetic and ontogenetic peak at the age indicated by Freud and Tomasello. This observation does not mean that I agree with Freud's idea of the birth of "morality" through the identification with the castrating father. In fact, I do not think that such an identification with the aggressor is the necessary mechanism for the birth of ethics, as I do not interpret the unconscious like a blind Id – a pure energy devoid of structure. The introduction of the concept of "Self" and the raise of ethology have radically transformed this paradigm.

One main point of this book is to root cognition into affects and feelings. In fact, when we refer to fairness, we are essentially talking about a feeling/value. Equally, when we talk of the development of a "theory of mind", we are not really talking about a theory of cognition but about the birth of secondary emotions, as the theory of mind does not imply just the cognitive development of objective knowledge but also the possibility to feel what another person is feeling. The case in which a person is able to cognitively understand what the other's point of view is but is not able to understand (feel) his feelings and the emotional meaning of the reasons of his being does not seem to describe a healthy human.

Thus, at around 4 years of age, human emotions are already developed as *secondary emotions*. They may express ethical normativity and social perspectivity, i.e., shared social and cultural values. On the contrary, as I said before, cognitive developmental structures will mature much later, at the end of adolescence.

If these developments are biologically determined and proceed at the same rate in all children, they cannot develop properly if they are not embedded in a specific environment. The fact that the direction of these developments is towards the realization of a normative morality and shared values is a proof of this. Furthermore, as Vygotsky argued, children are scaffolded by cultural artifacts and symbols which enable them to accomplish things before they are fully able to understand from an adult point of view what they are doing.

Let me give you just one example of this co-evolutive scenario from one of the most relevant scientists within this field: Louis Sander. Sander's observations and developmental theory are deeply rooted in the complex systems paradigm, and he often makes direct reference to the works by Peter Weiss, Jacob von Uexküll and Ludwing von Bertalanffy. Here, Sander et al. (2014) refers to the biologist Peter Weiss' fundamental notions of *specificity, integrity and rhythm* as organizers of all biological life.

For Sander, there are three possibilities within a relational, intersubjective moment of meeting between two persons:

1) If the encounter is characterized by the presence of Paul Weiss' specificity device – what we may also call *tuning* – we will have a positive moment, a vitalization or, in Tomkins' language, an amplification or affluence.
2) Instead, in case of discrepancy, the reorganization that follows in the flow of successive moments gives room for the negotiation of the mutual modification necessary to achieve a more durable coordination, to which the word adaptation has always implied.
3) A third possibility is that the moment of encounter is a moment of failure, with relative disorganization and diminished cohesion. You will remember Tronick's experiences on the still-face paradigm.

You will recall how many times, starting from the complex, I referred to the principle of integrity and to the integrative role of affects. Let me share with you this wonderful scene, quoted by Sander:

The scene is taken from three minutes of a film made by Sander's research group, which was filming one of the newborn subjects on the eighth day after birth on the lawn in front of the parents' house.

In that scene a baby girl is observed in her father's arms, while he is talking with some friends. Seen at normal speed of 30 frames per second, this is all that can be seen, but observing the same few minutes, frame by frame, one catches the father's gaze dropping for a moment toward the baby's face.

Surprisingly enough, in the same frames, one can see that the little girl looks up toward the father's face. Then the little girl's left arm, hanging down along her father's left arm, begins to move upward.

Miraculously, in the same frame, the father's right arm that hung down by his side begins to move upward. Frame by frame, the little girl's hand and the father's hand simultaneously move upward.

Finally, they meet over the little girl's belly. The little girl's left hand grasps the little finger of the father's right hand.

At that moment, the little girl's eyes closed, and she fell asleep, while the father continued to speak, seemingly completely unaware of the small miracle of specificity of time place and movement that occurred in his arms.

(Sander et al., 2014)

Sander's questions are the following:

How do we explain such specificity of coherence between father and child?

Was there a representation of the father's little finger in the child's brain?

Did she know where it was to grasp it? When the father's hand approached the little girl's body, the father extended his little finger separating it from the other fingers; otherwise, the little girl could not have grasped it.

How did he know that the little girl wanted to grasp it?

How could the baby's and the father's movements match so precisely in time and space, eight days after birth?

Are we observing a principle of integrity, that is, building on an underlying principle of specificity in time, space, and movement that unites directionality between component subsystems, a union that is necessary to compel a cohesive integrity in a system that can be said to be living?

(Sander et al., 2014)

The same happens for the child who does not *react* (in a False Self way) to the environment but dispositionally initiates an action within it. In fact, it is the subject who, initially moved by primary affects, selects and activates her own environment, therefore, realizing her own dispositional self *through and by* it.

Another crucial feature that distinguishes the emotional process from the cognitive one is that the object presented is not an objective problem that must be solved, but it is the very *subjective* object that *the person is looking for, a deeply and uniquely qualitative object*. Upon this aspect, all clinical developmental researchers agree.

Here, I wish to highlight what is for me an important point: the cognitive descriptions of the *representational* contents (the images) of complexes, which are developmentally on their way to become concepts, are ontologically incommensurable with their affective core. Feeling, imagining and thinking are three qualitatively incommensurable universes which may miraculously converge in an experience of one's subjective existence as necessary, inevitable and true.

10.2   Epistemic Knowledge, Gnostic Knowledge

Differently from cognitive tasks, the object I am talking about is an object emotionally searched for and actively selected by the Self. It expresses a dispositional action and not a reaction to the environment. This is described by the paradigm that Winnicott called "object presenting".

The cognitive "object", the "input" and the task that the subject must understand and solve by his/her intellect, like almost all the tasks in infant research, are psychologically incommensurable with the deeply emotional psychodynamic nature of the Winnicottian object. Therefore, both the process and the object of cognitive learning is very different from the learning that involves the relationship with a psychodynamic object. I propose to call the kind of knowledge that results from cognitive activity "*epistemic knowledge*", while I may call the kind of knowledge that involves a psychodynamic experience "*gnostic knowledge*". The epistemic knowledge is a secondary form of knowledge *about* something, which entails a process of schematization and further abstraction from the object, while the gnostic knowledge is a primary participative knowledge *of* something. One might also say that the first is a knowledge by Bion's K, while the second is a knowledge through L.

In fact, the specific cognitive meaning for the word "*learning*" does not encompass other dimensions of learning that cannot really be described as representational abstractions, nor this notion of "learning" seem to cover what happens in psychotherapy, in which, as Winnicott writes:

> The patient is not helped if the analyst says: "Your mother was not good enough" . . . "your father really seduced you" . . . "your aunt dropped you". Changes come in an analysis when the traumatic factors enter the psycho-analytic material in the patient's own way, and within the patient's omnipotence.
>
> (Winnicott, 1960, p. 585)

Here, the "object" is not only a "mental content"; it is part and parcel of the subject's Self. It is not a representation from the abstraction of a factual object – an intellectual problem that needs to be thought through or solved – but the attractor of the mother's emotional idiom (Bollas, 2018) into the performative, material, bodily realm: the mother's physical existence.

The object the mother "handles" (Winnicott) for, with and towards her child – whatever object – becomes an embodied metaphor of the emotional meaning of her relationship with her child. In fact, any object, insofar as it is the incarnation of an emotional meaning, becomes a re-collected part of the subject's experience – in my example, the child's. It *is* the subject herself.

The mother's gift for "guessing" the baby's inner states is based on an innate disposition (Trevarthen, 1979), whose structure Jung described in *Psychology of*

Transference and which Bion called *rêverie*. In the context of the mother-child relationship, the agent is always the child, and the mother, who responds correctly by presenting the "right" object to her, has the role of the environment[5] within a co-evolutionary milieu.

In a sense, in such a scenery, if there is an archetype at play, it would be located between baby and mother – i.e., between the organism and his co-evolving environment. The affective value of this process – the core emotional process of individuation – is the regulation of psychosomatic homeostasis through the constant emotional connection of not-yet integrated aspects of our ongoing experience.

It is this process of integration that is at the base of the formation of metaphors; it is connected to cognition and, therefore, symbolization, but it is, above all, connected to the formation of subjectivity as a gradual teleological process of the coming into existence of the potential Self as it was meant to be.

Let's now schematically look at the developmental lines of affects.

I think it useful to refer to Jung's idea of affect and feeling and to the developmental continuum of each affect from a bodily *sensation* (like, for example, a muscular tension) all the way up to a conscious emotion, or even to the function of self-reflective consciousness that we call *feeling function.*

> Sense-perceptions tell us that something is. But they do not tell us what it is. This is told us not by the process of perception but by the process of apperception, and this has a highly complex structure. Not that sense-perception is anything simple; only, its complex nature is not so much psychic as physiological. The complexity of apperception, on the other hand, is psychic.
>
> (Jung, 1927/1931, §288)

This is a process that goes from a liminal affect-sensation to a conscious emotion through a process of transformation. It is a process of further abstraction parallel to that described by Mandler and Karmiloff-Smith for images and cognitive apprehension and in which affects, feelings and emotions develop through what we call the individuation process. As for epistemic cognition, the gnostic development based on affects will transcend the concrete local conditions that *contain and express such conditions* and expand them into progressively more universalized "containers".

So, on one side, affects and feelings become more and more conscious and universalized throughout the process of social/interpersonal perspectival sharing that Tomasello called "we-ness" and, hence, transcend merely egocentric, concrete images, perceptions and inferences. On the other hand, universal concepts are extracted through Karmiloff-Smith's representational redescription.

As I said, this cognitive development, the one to which Jean Knox and other critics refer, seems to be fundamentally at the base of the functioning of the *intellect*, which produces and exchanges *signs*. On the contrary, emotional images and, later, emotional words may describe the form of *gnostic comprehension* that Jung called *symbol*. This form of comprehension overrides the mind's splitting/differentiating mechanisms and connects the content (the presented object) to the Self that is looking for it. Cinderella's shoe will be a further metaphorical completion of Cinderella's emotional and imaginal body, her *"Leib", which implies her prince.*

As I already hinted at before, this form of gnostic comprehension is a refined process of metaphor-creation in which the metaphors do not just express a more general *intellectual* meaning from the fusion of two different signs or domains (Caesar is a lion) but *also* create a transcendent emotional *and* conceptual meaning – a true piece of a new ontology created anew and expressed by the metaphor itself. This is what I try to do in analysis: the creation and sharing of cognitive-emotional metaphors towards the infinite transformation of somatic impulses into emotional thoughts or of purely epistemic – rationalized – knowledge into gnostic comprehension.

Epistemic knowledge makes it possible for the patient to get hold of an intellectual content, to "get it". On the other hand, through gnostic comprehension, the patient will comprehend that *he* is that knowledge. If the outcome from epistemic knowledge is "I have it!", the outcome of the gnostic one is the Hindu *tat tvam asi* ("Thou art that") of the *Chandogya Upanishad*, which describes the relationship between the individual and the Absolute.

Notes

1 The whole consumption of energy of the brain amounts to 20% of the total bodily consumption, which, for an organ that weighs 2% of the body's weight, is quite a lot.
2 Yet this is not at all sure. The case of bees has been widely discussed regarding the possibility of an intelligent life and an a-noetic, or even noetic, sense of subjectivity (See: Griffin, 1976).
3 An easy example of a module is the way the cerebellum stores procedural motor patterns. It does it in packages. If one needs to correct a piece he is playing on the piano, he has to slow down his movements in order to disassemble – de-encapsulate – the motor module, which, otherwise, would be performed as an integrated unit.
4 My discussion on Tomasello's contributions are taken from two thorough works: *Becoming, Human* (2019) and *A Natural History of Human Thinking* (2014).
5 So much so that Winnicott explicitly talks of a "mother-environment", who precedes the "mother-object". When the mother environment, made by precise atmospheric feelings, is personalized in a specific object, the environment will represent the connection between the two, what Ogden called the "analytical third" or, before him, Gaetano Benedetti (1992) called the "transitional subject".

References

Al-Khalili, J., Mcfadden, J. (2015). *Life on the Edge: Tthe Coming of Age of Quantum Biology*. St. Louis: Black Swan.

Bateson, G. (1972). *Steps To an Ecology of Mind: Collected Essays in Anthropology, Psychiatry, Evolution, and Epistemology*. University of Chicago Press.

Bateson, G. (2002). *Mind and Nature: A Necessary Unity*. New York: Hamton Press.

Benedetti, G. (1992). *Psychotherapie Als Existentielle Herausforderun*. Göttingen: Vandenhoeck & Ruprecht.

Bion, W.R. (1965). *Transformations*. London: William Heinemann. (Reprinted London: Karnac Books, 1984).

Biswal, B., Yetkin, F., Haughton, V., Hyde, J. (1995). Functional Connectivity in the Motor Cortex of Resting Human Brain Using Echo-Planar MRI. *Magnetic Resonance in Medicine*, 34, 537–541.

Bollas, C. (2018). *The Shadow of the Object. Psychoanalysis of the Unthought Known.* London: Routledge.

Boszormenyi-Nagy, I., Spark, G. (1973/1984). *Invisible Loyaties: Reciprocity in Intergenerational Family Therapy.* 2nd edn. New York: Harper & Row, Brunner/Mazel.

Corbetta, M., Shulman, G.L. (2002, March). Control of Goal-Directed and Stimulus-Driven Attention in the Brain. *Nature Reviews Neuroscience*, 3, 3, 201–215.

De Saussure, F. (1916). *Cours De Linguistique Générale.* C. Bally, A. Sechehaye (Eds.). With the Assistance of A. Riedlinger. Lausanne, Paris: Payot.

Edelman, G., Tononi, G. (2000). *A Universe of Consciousness: How Matter Becomes Imagination.* New York: Basic Books.

Fox, M.D., Snyder, A.Z., Vincent, J.L., Corbetta, M., Van Essen, D.C., Raichle, M.E. (2005). The Human Brain is Intrinsically Organized into Dynamic, Anticorrelated Functional Networks. *Proceedings of the National Academy of Sciences*, 102, 27, 9673–9678.

Freeman, W.J., Vitiello, G. (2005). Nonlinear Brain Dynamics and Many-Body Field Dynamic. *Electromagnetic Biology and Medicine*, 24, 1–9.

Freeman, W.J., Vitiello, G. (2006). Nonlinear Brain Dynamics as Macroscopic Manifestation of Underlying Many-Body Field Dynamics. *Physics of Life Review*, 3, 93–118.

Freeman, W.J., Vitiello, G. (2008). Dissipation and Spontaneous Symmetry Breaking in Brain Dynamics. *Journal of Physics A: Mathematical and Theoretical*, 41, 304042, 1–17.

Freeman, W.J., Vitiello, G. (2016). Matter and Mind Are Entangled in Two Streams of Images That Guide Behavior and Inform the Subject Through Awareness. *Mind and Matter*, 14, 1, 7–24.

Glasser, M.F., Coalson, T.S., Robinson, E.C., Hacker, C.D., Harwell, J., Yacoub, E., Ugurbil, K., Andersson, J., Beckmann, C.F., Jenkinson, M., Smith, S.M., Van Essen, D.C. (2016). A Multi-Modal Parcellation of Human Cerebral Cortex. *Nature*, 536, 171–178.

Griffin, D.R. (1976). *The Question of Animal Awareness. Evolutionary Continuity of Mental Experience.* New York, NY: Rockfeller University Press.

Gusnard, D.A., Akbudak, E., Shulman, G.L., Raichle, M.E. (2001). Medial Prefrontal Cortex and Self-Referential Mental Activity: Relation to a Default Mode of Brain Function. *Proceedings of the National Academy of Sciences*, 98, 4259–4264.

Gusnard, D.A., Raichle, M.E. (2001, October). Searching For a Baseline: Functional Imaging and the Resting Human Brain. *Nature Reviews Neuroscience*, 2, 10, 685–694.

Hamann, K., Warneken, F., Greenberg, J.R., Tomasello, M. (2011). Collaboration Encourages Equal Sharing in Children but not in Chimpanzees. *Nature*, 476, 7360, 328–331.

Jung, C.G. (1927/1931). The Structure and Dynamics of the Psyche. In: *The Collected Works of C.G. Jung*. Vol. 8. London, New York: Routledge.

Jung, C.G. (1937). Psychological Factors Determining Human Behavior. In: *The Collected Works of C.G. Jung*. Vol. 8. London, New York: Routledge.

Jung, C.G. (1948). A Psychological Foundation of Belief in Spirits. In: *The Collected Works of C.G. Jung*. Vol. 8. London: Routledge.

Langer, S.K. (1967). *Mind: An Essay on Human Feeling.* Vol. 1. Baltimore, MD: Johns Hopkins Universities Press.

Pezzulo, G., Zorzi, M., Corbetta, M. (2021, September). The Secret Life of Predictive Brains: What's Spontaneous Activity For? *Trends in Cognitive Sciences*, 25, 9, 730–743.

Sander, L., Amadei, G., Bianchi, I. (2014). *Living Systems, Evolving Consciousness, and the Emerging Person. A Selection of Papers from the Life Work of Louis Sander.* London, New York: Routledge.

Selvini Palazzoli, M., Boscolo, L., Cecchin, G., Prata, G. (1994). *Paradox and Counter-paradox*. New York: Jason Aronson.

Sperber, D., Hirschfeld, L. (1999). *Culture, Cognition, and Evolution*, pp. cxi-cxxxii. Cambridge, MA: MIT Encyclopedia of the Cognitive Sciences (MIT Press).

Stern, D.N. (1985). *The Interpersonal World of the Infant: A View from Psychoanalysis and Developmental Psychology*. English edn. Karnac Books (Edizione Del Kindle).

Tagliagambe, S., Malinconico, A. (2018). *Tempo e Sincronicità. Tessere il Tempo*. Milano: Mimesis.

Tomasello, M. (2014). *A Natural History of Human Thinking*. Cambridge, MA: Harvard University Press.

Tomasello, M. (2019). *Becoming Human. A Theory of Human Ontogeny*. Cambridge, MA, London: Bellknap Press.

Trevarthen, C. (1979). Communication and Cooperation in Early Infancy. A Description of Primary Intersubjectivity. In: *Before Speech: The Beginning of Human Communication*, pp. 321–347. M. Bullowa (Ed.). London: Cambridge University Press.

Vitiello, G. (2023). Cervello, Mente E Cuore. *Atque*, 30–31, 75–96.

Winnicott, D.W. (1960, January 1). The Theory of the Parent-Infant Relationship. *The International Journal of Psycho-Analysis*, 41.

Chapter 11

Numinosum and Individuation[1]

Let's briefly summarize what I have discussed so far.

- Affects are the evolutionary oldest, most basic functions by which the organism – hence, we humans – integrate their phenomenal experience into subjectivity, ensuring an ongoing homeostatic condition at all levels: the level of bodily needs, feelings, conceptual problems, relational challenges, etc.
- Affects confer meaning and teleological orientation to psychic activity.
- Primary affects seem to be innate and quickly develop within co-evolutionary, *deeply social* interactions into secondary emotions, hence, expressing highly complex, shared, cultural, *emotional thoughts and values (meanings)*.
- These complex psychological formations triggered and organized by innate affects and their offspring – secondary and tertiary emotions – have from the beginning of ontogenetic life an imaginal form, which in humans is mostly, yet absolutely not, exclusively visual. Inner images, such as dream images, are, therefore, the (re)presentational forms of the affects. Through ontogenesis, the abstraction of such visual images produces thoughts.
- The secondary emotions that emerge from primary affects and cognitive competences may be normative or descriptive, yet they transcend concrete individual predicaments, *although they pervasively involve the whole subject, as they are always personal experiences*, which at this point are "abstracted" into *universalized* (at least *culturally* universalized) forms. As we have briefly seen, this happens already from the third year of age, with the birth of normative fairness.

Speaking of affects and, therefore, complexes, I could not ignore the issue of archetypes, whose components Jung claimed to be organized around a common set of meanings ultimately derived from evolutionary biology. Therefore, it was necessary to discuss the issues involving the archetypes and some of the criticisms to this part of Jung's theory. As I said, several of these criticisms that reject the archetypal hypothesis refer to cognitive research on representations and conceptual development, without the necessary integration with affects and emotions. After all, what is clinically important is not really the patient's intellectual finesse but his/

DOI: 10.4324/9781003586258-11

her becoming himself/herself, and it is the affects and the emotions that may organize or disrupt this process, which we call the individuation process.

As I already pointed out, opening this book, I do not wish to discuss and debate the different specific criticisms of Jung's theory that have been published in the last decades. Instead of adopting a "polemic" approach, I chose to take a constructive one and try to see the role of emotional life with its connection to Jung's archetypal hypothesis. In this last chapter, I want to go back to the psychotherapeutic situation, to which, after all, all my work is dedicated. Hence, I will refer to two brilliant articles by John Merchant (2016, 2019) as a "doppelgänger" to let me better express my point of view, not necessarily against his positions or those of other critics but to explore the legitimacy of Jung's theory under the light of Merchant's position.

I found Merchant's articles useful and clinically very sound. I believe his observations to be precious for our work, and I wish to thank him for them and to, somehow, excuse myself for using them "instrumentally". Yet I also think that Merchant's paradigm is debatable and would like to add a few remarks *from it*, remarks that might be appropriate for this discussion.

The central point of interest for my discussion is that, in a few words, Merchant maintains that there is no evidence for any production of meaningful species-specific imagery from genetic activity. This is as undisputable as the fact that the Earth is not flat. There is no discussion.

Merchant, quoting the work of Jean Knox, argues:

Noticeably, Knox's (2003) model would also agree with Goodwyn's definition of the archetype as "the collection of psychological constraints and biases, of whatever origin, that work in concert to create one or more resonant attractor states in the narrative field" (Goodwyn, 2013, p. 400).

(Merchant, 2019, p. 711)

I do agree with this definition, adding that the main organizer of this plurality of constraints and attractors (many of which are well-known and some of which I described) is precisely the affect, which integrates the different complexes and, at a different level, the Self itself.

Moving away from Jung's top-down approach, Merchant mostly refers to the cognitive literature, some of which I have also used in this book, and uses a bottom-up approach – the same that I used here. But in doing so, in his 2016 article, Merchant describes a beautiful case of a patient who had an archetypal experience and interprets it as follows:

we do not have to see my patient's vision as expressing something archetypal in the classical sense, that is, it is not the result of some innate archetype but rather of either imaginal reconstructions of remembered real events or metaphoric visionary constructions that reflect the intense and traumatic emotional effects upon him.

(Merchant, 2016, p. 72)

In a few words, the archetype would be a product of a trauma and would represent a derivative of a personal complex that the mind could not yet properly form. Hence, the archetype would derive from the personal complex and not vice-versa. A very interesting idea, indeed. Nevertheless, when Merchant ties archetypes, their imagery and their numinous quality to early relational traumas which disrupt the Ego capacity to integrate his experience in viable personal complexes, it seems to me that he sees any archetypal outcome just as a symptom.

Jung describes the experience of an archetype as *numinous*. In *Psychology and Religion*, he defines the latter with the following words:

> a dynamic agency or effect not caused by an arbitrary act of will. . . . The numinosum – whatever its cause may be – is an experience of the subject independent of his will. . . . The numinosum is either a quality belonging to a visible object or the influence of an invisible presence that causes a peculiar alteration of consciousness.
>
> (Jung, 1938, §6)

In Jung's thinking, the numinosum is both a quality inherent to an object or an experience that comes over a person, often inadvertently (Jung, 1938).

Rudolf Otto and Jung provide a wealth of explicit qualities people are likely to feel when in the presence of the holy. First, it must be noted that the numinosum is a paradox (Otto, 1958, p. 29) containing both positive and negative aspect, both of which we may experience simultaneously in any encounter with the Divine. Some of the positive qualities of the numinosum include sublimity, awe, excitement, bliss, rapture, exaltation, entrancement, fascination, attraction, allure (Ibid. pp. 17–37) and what Otto called an "impelling motive power" (Ibid. p. 67).

Other qualities testify to the somatic involvement of such a pervasive emotional state and, hence, its primary archaic affective quality: feeling overwhelmed, fear, trembling, weirdness, eeriness, urgency, stupor, bewilderment, horror, mental agitation, repulsion and haunting, daunting, monstrous feelings that "overbrim the heart" (*Ibid*. p. 80).

Otto speaks at length of *the mysterium tremendum et fascinans*, the fascinating mystery that makes us tremble (in awe). Because it "grips or stirs the mind", such an experience is not one we forget. Jung tells us that such an experience is always a "defeat for the ego", something to which the ego must surrender. In fact, a further characteristic of the numinous is an acute sense of unworthiness, a deeply humbling feeling.

In this sense, it is true that Ottos' *ganz andere* (the "wholly other") nature of the archetypal experience is inherently *traumatic* and represents the core of any symptomatology to the extent for which a symptom damages the Ego's critical integrative functions and acts upon it in a compulsive, compelling way.

These observations, which are at the root of Jung's original discussions on schizophrenia, go back to the opening considerations of this book and to the relationship between affects, effectivity and reality. In fact, from the perspective of the

numinosum – which seems to be the deepest and most direct psychological manifestation of the libido – the domain of primary embodied a-noetic affects expresses
itself as a religious experience. For Jung, the most general quality of *any* unconscious content is its religious nature: the farther away a content is from the Ego, the
more "religiously" it is felt.

Now being a defeat for the Ego, there is no discussion that the irruption of the
numinosum *may* be a sign of a symptomatic state, yet is this the whole truth? I see
in Merchant's position, as in many other Jungian cognitive contributions to complexes which refer to bottom-up theories like attachment, or theories inspired by
Freudian or some post-Freudian trends, the risk of reductionism and of a sudden,
yet not explicit, radical shift from some core aspects of analytical psychology.

Let me summarize my thoughts:

Merchant is right. It is wholly possible that his patient was traumatized as a
fetus, and a numinous, traumatic experience was, therefore, produced *from the
immature Ego*. Yet if this is interpreted as being the only possible way numinous
experiences happen, it seems that:

a) The numinous is always a symptom of a sort of maladaptation within a *situational* theory of the psyche, i.e., a vision for which we are built to be molded
   and shaped by outer stimuli. This option is contrary to the co-evolutionary principles I referred to earlier.
b) In such a situation, therefore, the numinously charged content must be cured and
   interpreted as a product of immature experiences in childhood, therefore, in a
   causal way.
c) The aim of individuation is *not* to experience such numinous state and the
   imagery that expresses it but to reduce it to those everyday issues that the immature mind could not yet comprehend.

If, and only if, these conditions are true, these are my questions:

1. Could the numinosum *not* be a psychopathological symptom but also an emotional feature of an emerging symbolic experience – *of the formation of a new
   gnostic metaphor*?
2. Why should we equate immaturity with infancy? Could development be a
   potentially *constant* challenge for the Ego throughout life if and when its structure cannot integrate potentially meaningful new and/or very intense emotional
   experiences/thoughts that may occur throughout life? Can't a breakdown also
   be a breakthrough?

From the perspective of evolutionary psychology, this long quote from Tooby,
Cosmides and Barkow clarifies this point quite well:

developmentally timed to have the necessary adaptations for that stage, regardless of whether, as a side effect, they happen to appear before or persist after they

are needed. . . . Hence, the Standard Model assumption-critical to its logic-that the mental organization present in adults but absent from newborns must be "acquired" from the social world has no conceptual foundation and is, in many cases, known to be empirically false. In the worldview of the SSSM, [Standard Social Science Model] biological construction goes on in the uterus, but at birth the child is "biologically complete" except for growth; at this point, it is surrendered into the sole custody of social forces, which do the remainder of the construction of the individual. This, of course, reflects folk biology, captured in the two dictionary definitions of innate as "present from birth" and as "intrinsic". Social constructivist arguments frequently take the form that because thus-and-such is absent at birth, or doesn't appear until after age seven, or until after puberty, it is obviously "learned" or "socially constructed". As a result, a common, but generally irrelevant feature of "nativist" versus "environmentalist" debates is over what is "present from birth". This confuses (among other things) the question of whether something is expressed at the time of birth with whether there exists in the individual evolved developmental mechanisms that may activate and organize the expression of an adaptation at some point in the life cycle. Developmental processes continue to bring additional adaptations on line (as well as remove them) at least until adulthood, and there is an increasing amount of evidence to suggest that age-driven adaptive changes in psychological logical architecture continue throughout adulthood.

(Barkow et al., 1992, pp. 81–82)

Not all features of evolved human design are or can be present at any one time in any one individual. Thus, the genetically universal may be developmentally expressed as different maturational rational designs in the infant, the child, the adolescent, and the adult; in females and males; or in individuals who encounter different circumstances.

(Barkow et al., 1992, p. 82)

Contrary to this position, to which I subscribe, it seems that the cognitive, situational approach, when looking at the images and at the emotional and cognitive competence of a person, assumes that only a mind that is not *yet* formed may produce numinous experiences due to the lack of conceptualization. This would imply that, once a cognitive competence has matured – therefore, after the developmental age – any irruption of the numinous experience would be a sign of a psychological breakdown (the case of schizophrenia is the easiest example).

Yet if we do not split affects from cognition and if we refer to emotional thoughts (like in Jung but also in Bion), then even a reflection of light on a tin plate – as in Jacob Boehme – may produce a numinous experience, which I do not wish to psychiatrize or reduce to the possibility that Boehme was not properly hugged by his mother, *even if this may be factually true.*

Why should we unilaterally pathologize the numinosum into a purely negative trauma and not also interpret it as an extreme need for second-degree systemic changes – what Jung rightly called *transformations*? Why should not *any* mind at *any* time be challenged as the mind of a child (or of a fetus, as in Merchant's clinical case) in order to emotionally *transcend* (and cognitively: abstract and generalize) his subjective feelings, therefore, transcending his own subjective identity towards a feeling of universality?

In my opinion, a view like Merchant's runs the risk of transforming the Jungian approach into a post-Freudian one, in which the unconscious is a former repressed child or a blind beast, who wishes only to mate and kill[2] and who could not adequately adapt to the situation.

So as we are dealing with affects, let's once again take into consideration Jung's position regarding the issue of what is development and psychopathology in relation to the numinosum and what Jung claimed were the universal images that always accompany it. Therefore, let me share three aspects of Jung's position from his ideas of the role of the numinosum, transference and dreams.

11.1   Numinosum

The features of the numinosum, as in Merchant's case, are associated with images that convey a sense of impersonality/universality and describe a compelling emotional experience. The question is this: Is the experience of the numinosum and of impersonal images *always* a causal problem (a pathology), or could they also represent a teleological solution? Jung's answer is *yes*.

In a letter to P.W. Martin (20 August 1945), the founder of the International Study Center of Applied Psychology, Jung wrote:

> It always seemed to me as if the real milestones were certain symbolic events characterized by a strong emotional tone. You are quite right; the main interest of my work is not concerned with the treatment of neuroses but rather with the approach to the numinous. But the fact is that the approach to the numinous is the real therapy and inasmuch as you attain to the numinous experiences you are released from the curse of pathology. Even the very disease takes on a numinous character.
>
> (Jung, 1953, vol. 1, p. 377)

I wholeheartedly agree with Jung. For me, for my personal and professional analytical life, without having ever been in contact with what we call "numinosum" (I guess that Bion would have referred to O), my life and that of my patients would be utterly meaningless. In fact, this is the core and the key to what Jung claimed to be his own original and specific contribution to psychology and psychotherapy – what he called "transformation". In his *General Problems of Psychotherapy* (Jung, 1954/1966), where he discusses the process of psychotherapy, Jung is clear in setting its goal and its intrinsic potential aim and destiny. In fact, the "phases" of "confession", "elucidation" and "adaptation" must lead towards a "transformation".

11.2   Transference

Jung's reflections on the therapeutic relationship and the therapeutic process are one of the most valuable contributions to any psychotherapeutic approach and today are at least implicitly adopted by nearly every form of psychotherapy. In the Freudian field, many of Jung's ideas on the therapeutic relationship are now part of the official "technique", having modified the original "parameters" set by Kurt Eissler (1953) through the progressively more influential contributions by Ferenczi (1995). Suffice it to remember Jung's idea that, in fact, any psychotherapeutic method may work (something on which most contemporary research on the efficacy of psychotherapies agrees) since *what cures is the relationship* and that this relationship always involves the honest involvement of the total personalities of both the patients and the psychotherapist. This last issue involves the issue of *transference*, "the alpha and omega" of the whole endeavor. In this field, Jung had been from the beginning the real protagonist. He was the first advocate for the need to be analyzed before becoming an analyst and for the central role of the analyst's own transference *vs.* that of the patient, which implicitly means that the analyst *must always also recognize himself as a patient in a reciprocal relationship.*

All this does not mean to be an apology of Jung's importance but is meant to emphasize that any structural changes within Jung's theory of transference might represent a radical, essential departure from the core of his ideas and that, in this case, such changes must be taken very seriously.

During his Tavistock Lectures (1935), Jung delivered a lecture on transference, in which he theorized the following four stages:

1) Elaboration of the projections of "personal" images ("subjectivation").
2) Discrimination between personal and impersonal contents.
3) Differentiation of the personal relationship with the analyst from the impersonal factors and images.
4) Objectivation of the impersonal images.

The aim of the whole process is the awareness of the subjective importance and meaning of personal and impersonal contents within the transference, including those from childhood.

The first three stages aim at the fourth one, in which the psychological images are objectified and a new form of consciousness may finally develop within the transference.

In essence, this describes the essential goal of psychotherapy. Should this change, the very essence of Jung's vision of psychotherapy will be radically modified. In such a case, this should be clearly stated, also not to incur misunderstandings or unpleasant mixing of incompatible thoughts.

Jung follows these principles quite consistently – so much so as to write the main text on transference from an archetypal perspective, in which the protagonists are *Rex* and *Regina* (the countersexual unconsciouses of the two Egos of patient and analyst). An important example of this aim may also be taken from a challenging clinical case that Jung discusses at length in *Psychology of the Unconscious* (1917/1926, Chapters VI–VII, pp. 80–113). Jung's main purpose for the discussion of this clinical case is to precisely to highlight the *differences and the peculiarity* of his method and "philosophy", which *does not limit itself to a causal approach based on the patient's history as a traumatized child*. In fact, such an approach deals with the contents of the *personal unconscious*, i.e., those contents that have been repressed in infancy. Therefore, all interpretations and, in general, the whole aim of psychotherapy at this stage is that of restructuring the Ego in relation to its shadow-contents through an *analytical-reductive* approach. This is what all psychotherapies do, from psychoanalysis to cognitive-behavioral psychotherapy, not analytical psychology. The reason being that the Jungian approach is not centered on the Ego but on the Self, and this difference changes the whole perspective.

The personal, conscious or unconscious Ego-related contents are obviously fundamental; no one is disputing this. Yet they do not represent the core of the issue.

> It matters little that, even today, the view prevails in many quarters that analysis consists mainly in "digging up" the earliest childhood complex in order to pluck out the evil by the root. This is merely the aftermath of the old trauma theory. Only in so far as they hamper the patient's adaptation to the present have these historical contents any real significance. The painstaking pursuit of all the ramifications of infantile fantasy is relatively unimportant in itself; the therapeutic effect comes from the doctor's efforts to enter into the psyche of his patient, thus establishing a psychologically adapted relationship. For the patient is suffering precisely from the absence of such a relationship. Freud himself has long recognized that the transference is the alpha and omega of psychoanalysis.
>
> (Jung, 1921a, §276)

Discussing his clinical case, it is at the moment in which his patient has a certain dream in which the image of the analyst is transformed in a numinous way that Jung understands that the patient's infantile elements are not relevant any longer.

To insist upon them would literally kill the whole process and make it sterile. Therefore, Jung, following what the patient is experiencing – and not a particular explanation *about* such experience – dismisses the analytical method and introduces his *synthetic approach*. This doesn't just exclude the causally oriented analytical perspective but encompasses it, putting it into a teleological perspective so that all the contents from the Ego's past may reveal their perspectival meaning towards the patient's present, in which wholly new creative contents not yet lived in infancy are finally about to emerge. *And these contents are impersonal* (not yet been personalized).

From these four stages in the transference, we see that for Jung, psychotherapy can happen through the analysis of (co)transference, which, in its ultimate stage, should go exactly in the opposite direction of causal, retrospective, pathomorphic and stereotypical interpretations,[3] i.e., towards the numinous quality of life as an empirical container of universal emotional – and at a certain level *symbolic* – values.

This is a truly crucial point, as it directly involves the core of Jung's ideas of the psyche, psychopathology and psychotherapy. Departing and substituting these core concepts radically changes the nature of analytical psychology. Should this occur, it must be openly declared, and a new name should be given to the new paradigm.

Nowadays, all psychotherapies are engrossed in the reductive and causal paradigm. For what concerns us more closely, it is imperative that the unilaterally Ego-centered theory[4] of the psyche that derives from Jean Knox's approach and those that concur in such a position are openly recognized, also to better contribute to a fruitful debate.

It is precisely because of such a reductive perspective that the aim of psychotherapy may be defined as Jean Knox has coherently done:

The development of affect regulation developing the capacity for mentalization and reflective function facilitating the development of self-agency can be correlated with three main therapeutic approaches:

- interpretation, allowing conscious awareness of repressed or dissociated mental contents.
- new relational experiences, in which the analyst is a new object for the patient.
- facilitating regression (*reculer pour mieux sauter*).

(Knox, 2009, p. 15)

Here, I wish to be clear: although I do not mean that such objectives and methods are not cogent, grounded and essential for Ego structuring, the identification of analytical psychology with these aims and methods *represents a tragedy*.

To assert, as a general principle, that a reductive analysis is unnecessary would of course be short-sighted and no more intelligent than to deny the value of all research into the causes of war. The doctor must probe as deeply as possible into the origins of the neurosis in order to lay the foundations of a subsequent synthesis. As a result of reductive analysis, the patient is deprived of his faulty adaptation and led back to his beginnings. The psyche naturally seeks to make good this loss by intensifying its hold upon some human object – generally the doctor, but occasionally some other person, like the patient's husband or a friend who acts as a counterpole to the doctor.

(Jung, 1921b, §282)

A great part of my own work deals with such issues and refers to such theories. What I mean with my criticism is that if they are taken as the only aims, they are dangerously unilateral and reductive, *as they only refer to the Ego formation, i.e., to that essential condition through which the Self embodies itself,* the place where it progressively indwells. Reducing the Ego and the personality to their infancy and throwing the Self away means destining the patient to a neutralized, harmless adaptation. Under this light, *not even* Freud's "normal unhappiness" would be left.

The analyst would have to try to "cure" that unhappiness, perhaps by a tender holding of the regressed patient.[5]

Perhaps none of the authors that concur with the paradigm that Jean Knox has authoritatively defended intends to do so, yet the implicit, inevitable result of such theories converges with the Foucauldian aims of psychiatry as a tool for normalization.

Knox's point of view, like that of several others who seem to endorse it, as well as the references to infantile traumas as factual occurrences to be dealt with as the real goal of psychotherapy, transform analytical psychology into a *radically* different theory and clinical approach. This approach ultimately deals exclusively with the formation of the Ego, its relationships and the *personal* unconscious – i.e., only on the contents repressed from the experiences of the Ego and not on the layer *from which* the Ego and everything else keeps emerging: the Self. In such a case, there is no need for any analytical psychology. Others have done a very good job already.

Most psychologies, like the Freudian and post-Freudians – except for Bion's and Winnicott's – along with attachment theory, behavioral cognitive theory and, basically, all theories that refer to past traumas, are fundamentally Ego-psychologies. Their aim is the Ego and, in one way or another, *adaptation*. The real exception to this Ego-centered perspective is analytical psychology, for which infancy is the first condition for the development of the personality, not its origin, for which the goal of psychotherapy is not just the (obviously indispensable and preliminary) formation of an Ego but also its transcendence through the integration of parts of the collective unconscious.

Within this perspective, the Ego is a means and not an end for a process in which becoming myself is the necessary path to becoming *another*. This explains the meaning of Jung's idea of the two moments of the analytical process – a "first" one devoted to the Ego and the "second" part in which the Ego is called to step back – or of the existence of both interpretation and amplification. In fact, in the first part of an analysis (but this should *not* be interpreted diachronically, as the second part is always embedded in the first one), the protagonists are the Ego itself, the Persona and the Shadow. During this preliminary phase, the analysis of the Ego-related contents would aim at the coalescence of an Ego to let the Ego transform itself and progressively integrate the non-Ego (the unrepressed unconscious).

In the second part of the analytical process, the Ego (provided it was ever formed) must retreat. This is an aspect of the psychotherapeutic process wholly overlooked by all psychotherapies, with their pseudo-medical idea of psychotherapy[6] as something that should heal somebody of his/her "defects".

With few exceptions, this radical, fundamental aim for an eventual retreat of the Ego is totally absent in today's psychotherapies except for analytical psychology. Centered exclusively on the Ego and its personal unconscious, they seem to look at the present only in reference to a causal past and not to the past and the present as movements towards a creative future.

When the analyst is looking for the lost/repressed contents, interpretation, as a convergent way to look for meaning, does have its role; it does not when the Ego must finally divergently grow out of its shell and try to integrate something wholly new, something intrinsically future, intrinsically *other*. At this moment, the personal unconscious and the issues that relate to the Ego become petty infantilized issues, and the discussions on them turns out to be desperately boring for both patient and analyst. It is *now* that amplification becomes the real tool to approach the symbolic aspect of the unknown/new that wants to finally happen – the future of childhood: adult life.

If confession, elucidation and education deal with the constitution and safeguard of the Ego (Jung, 1954/1966) – and all psychotherapies deal with this (and they may do a good job in studying, explaining and doing so) – only analytical psychology has *creativity* as the real attractor of the whole process. Creativity means the becoming something *other* than the Ego that had formed throughout infancy, youth and young-adult life.

What Knox quotes (interpretation, new relational experiences, regression) are fundamental *instrumental* developmental means *for* something – that something that Jung calls individuation, which *begins* in infancy, and hopefully does not *end* when infancy ends. In a few words, it means being able to age because, as Shakespeare wrote, "Ripeness is all" (*King Lear*, V sc. II).

The same consequences derive from the reduction of *any* numinous, religious experience – as it happens when this is expressed by "archetypal" images – if this is reduced to a pathogenic infantile trauma or, in any case, to a pathogenic trauma of the Ego which should be healed. In this sense, the risk arises of precipitating into the ultimately desperate view of life as a process of adaptation as theorized by Ego psychology.

> When I was a child, I spake as a child, I understood as a child, I thought as a child: but when I became a man, I put away childish things.
>
> (1 Corinthians 13:11, King James Version)

The hypnotic interest of the studies on development – which I personally very much appreciate – may cause the tragic loss of the fundamental core of Jung's legacy: the openness to the embodiment in the finitude of life of something infinite and *felt as* universal.

Finally, the exclusive mention of repressed/dissociated material to be *interpreted* tragically defines the totality of human life and of the human psyche as just a residue of a lost childhood (a seemingly post-behavioristic reaction to a mere cause) and confines the body itself – the body as an unattainable mystery – to its just-so material/biological nature. At this point, the factual, shallow observation of the patient's behavior (is this also perhaps the meaning of "evidence based"?) and the prescription of drugs celebrate their dangerous *coniunctio*.

11.3 Dreams

Jung's suggestion about the analysis of dreams also goes towards this direction.

> I should like to distinguish between the prospective function of dreams and their compensatory function. The latter means that the unconscious, considered as relative to consciousness, adds to the conscious situation all those elements from the previous day which remained subliminal because of repression or because they were simply too feeble to reach consciousness. This compensation, in the sense of being a self-regulation of the psychic organism, must be called purposive.
>
> The prospective function, on the other hand, is an anticipation in the unconscious of future conscious achievements, something like a preliminary exercise or sketch, or a plan roughed out in advance. Its symbolic content sometimes outlines the solution of a conflict, excellent examples of this being given in Maeder. The occurrence of prospective dreams cannot be denied. It would be wrong to call them prophetic, because at bottom they are no more prophetic than a medical diagnosis or a weather forecast. They are merely an anticipatory combination of probabilities which may coincide with the actual behaviour of things but need not necessarily agree in every detail. Only in the latter case can we speak of "prophecy". That the prospective function of dreams is sometimes greatly superior to the combinations we can consciously foresee is not surprising, since a dream results from the fusion of subliminal elements and is thus a combination of all the perceptions, thoughts, and feelings which consciousness has not registered because of their feeble accentuation. In addition, dreams can rely on subliminal memory traces that are no longer able to influence consciousness effectively. With regard to prognosis, therefore, dreams are often in a much more favourable position than consciousness.
>
> (Jung, 1916/1948, §492–493)

Hence, as we have already seen for transference, Jung's attitude and method regarding dreams differentiates between interpretations and amplifications and, therefore, between the prospective and compensatory function of dreams.

The interpretive method is aimed at reducing the present situation to its causal components and, therefore, to compensate and adapt the psyche to the circumstances of the present. Therefore, such a method looks into the past, into repetitions and restorations of pathogenic – possibly traumatic – experiences. Hence, the patient is interpreted as a former child whose total development ended when his "developmental process" ended – at the end of adolescence.

Differently from Freud, Jung did not think that the *via regia* to the unconscious was the dream; he thought it was the complex (Jung, 1948), not meaning the "personal complexes" but *all* the complexes – including the archetypical ones. This shift from the personal complex (for psychoanalysis, the only one – the Oedipus) to the archetypes implies the need to let go of the Freudian technical "golden rule", free association.

In fact, Jung argues:

When you start to associate freely, you will eventually arrive at your complexes. So, you can arrive at their complexes *in whatever way* because they are what is attractive and attracts everything. The following happens: in free association, the chain of associations leads to some complex. This happens quite naturally and, so to speak, without inhibition; you just "fall into" the complex. So, if you discover a complex by free association, this does not necessarily mean that this complex is also contained in your dream image. I concluded that this method is not applicable because, although the person's complexes are invariably arrived at, this does not say that exactly these complexes are contained in the dream. *It could even be the case that the unconscious had to free itself of precisely these complexes to be able to deal with them! Maybe just this is the achievement of the unconscious!*

(Jung, 2010, p. 25. Last italics mine)

For the way I interpret this passage, Jung is suggesting that the whole, *ultimate* effort of the psyche is *to get rid* of all egocentric identifications to promote the experience of what is felt as infinite and universal and that is felt so, in one's life, *always through the individual and finite vessel of the Ego.* This is the opposite of any psychotherapy whose aims are those described before by Jean Knox.

A further observation may come out from another quote from Jung's letters:

In the deepest sense we all dream not out of ourselves but out of what lies between us and the other.

(Jung, 1953, vol. 1, p. 172)[7]

This quite revealing statement seems to be fully convergent with the in-between nature of archetypes, whose possible existence I have defended in this book, since through the dream, the possibility of liberating the soul from its projections deriving from personal complexes may re-establish a true relationship with the others based on a *non-personalistic* basis. This would, therefore, attain the same aim of psychotherapy, as explained by Jung in his analysis of transference: the objectivation of the impersonal images.

I think that these examples from Jung are very telling, as they maintain that what may be a sign of a breakdown may also be a breaking-in, a breakout and especially a breakthrough: the very purpose of individuation.

Analytical psychology should welcome a rational, adequate bottom-up theory, yet we should be careful about mistaking explanations with experiences and falling into a reductionist causal approach, which would refer all life to its causal childhood, without noticing that this will radically change the nature of our psychology. I wish to stress that this would be fine, provided we are aware of it.

As I said in my introductory remarks, the welcoming of bottom-up theories involves the sphere of *scientia* – of *epistemic knowledge*. In my personal experience and for my personal taste, I am interested in amplifying my fantasies about the world and my experience of it by adding different contingent points of touch of the sphere of reality, which are represented, for instance, by neurobiology or developmental psychology. Yet it must be clear that these forms of knowledge have little to do with what is essential: the psychological experience of what is real through the numinous images by means of which psychological life happens – precisely what Jung did through his *Red Book*. Seen in this way, the practice of analytical psychology is a form of practical art, which requires the heart and mind of an artist, and more *esprit de finesse* than *esprit de géométrie*. This special, empirical art rests on the progressive process of symbolizing our underlying, embodied affective essence and corresponds to the possibility of realizing our subjective lives with what fully completes us: our social "objects" and our cultural milieu.

This further process of transformation of our embodied affective psychology into a meaningful social and cultural community is the theme of the second volume.

Notes

1 Part of this chapter has been published in Carta, S. (2024). Jungian and Interdisciplinary Analyses of Emotions, Edition by Elizabeth Brodersen, Isabelle Meier, Valeria Céspedes Musso, Copyright © 2025 by Routledge. Reproduced by permission of Taylor & Francis Group.

2 In the biological world, this is true only for animals held in captivity, i.e., held in impossible conditions for the animal's health (the animals whose behaviors most zoologists studied before the birth of ethology in the 20th century). The idea of the blind, unconscious, unrestrained beast unfortunately applies only to humans. The problems do not derive from the unconscious but from the disrupting phylogenetic effects of consciousness. Indeed, the *felix culpa* of eating the apple had a price.

3 See here not only Jung but especially Peterfreund, E., *The Process of Psychoanalytic Therapy: Models and Strategies*, 1983.

4 These theories may include a self – like Kohut does – but this self is still interpreted in a radically different way from Jung's, as it corresponds to the sum of the parts that the Ego needs to adapt to reality, which are not yet integrated because of some past trauma. The fact that Kohut refers to the self when he speaks of narcissism and the role he gives to self-objects is quite telling about the different paradigm. Once again, Kohut's observations are invaluable, but they must be encompassed within a larger perspective.

5 This is what is already happening as a manifestation of the spirit of the time: the colossal inflation of the nosography of the DSM is, besides other disquieting reasons related to the profit-pursuing drug industry, an example that *everything must be cured*, i.e., repressed no matter what. The Ego *must* be soothed because any non "normality" must be a sign of a "trauma" of some sort. Yet this crusade against suffering, behind its titanic and apparently benevolent attitude, has a dark shadow. For instance, "curing" and, therefore, normalizing the ADHD child *not to touch* the conditions that contribute to his symptoms: the brokenness of the family, the distorted way of living in our cities, the absurd emptiness and isolation of our "evolved" societies, the collapse of sociality, the mad materialism that has transformed everything into a fetish and a commodity, etc.

Only a healthy person may produce a symptom. A symptom is not just a sign of a trauma (of something dysfunctional) but it is also the testimony that "something" intrinsically healthy, the Self, is trying to say something essential.

6 Although I am aware that I am stating something like a blasphemy, sometimes I have the feeling that the standard idea that analytical thoughts, ideas, experiences, etc., must always contain a clinical case or a clinical vignette comes from the latent vision of an analyst with a white coat – a medical pathologist with his clinical case.

I am not criticizing the importance of clinical cases. What I am saying is that the expectation, especially in specialized journals and conferences, that something is "clinical" only if it refers to a clinical case is a product of a reduction of the true nature of the life we want to care for as analysts.

This impression is often increased when the clinical cases or the vignettes seem to be presented *to confirm and justify* what the analyst has just expressed and not the other way around.

What I miss are clinical cases written by patients.

7 I am indebted to Sonu Shamdasani for reminding me of this quote from Jung.

References

Barkow, J., Cosmides, L., Tooby, J. (Eds.). (1992). *The Adapted Mind: Evolutionary Psychology and the Generation of Culture*. Oxford, New York, Toronto: Oxford University Press.

Carta, S. (2024). Perceptions, (E)Motions, Cognition. Paradigmatic Anomalies, Images and the Development of the Personality. In: *Jungian and Interdisciplinary Interface(s) between Emotions: Emplacement of Engagement. Vol. 1: I Feel, therefore I Am*. E. Brodersen et al. (Eds.). London: Routledge.

Eissler, K. (1953). The Effect of the Structure of the Ego on Psychoanalytic Technique. *Journal of the American Psychanalytic Association*, 1, 104–143.

Ferenczi, S. (1995). *The Clinical Diary of Sándor Ferenczi*. J. Dupont (Ed.). Cambridge, MA, London: Harvard University Press.

Goodwyn, E. (2013). Recurrent Motifs as Resonant Attractor States in the Narrative Field: A Testable Model of Archetype. *Journal of Analytical Psychology*, 58, 3, 387–408.

Jung, C.G. (1917/1926/1943). The Psychology of the Unconscious. In: *The Collected Works of C.G. Jung*. Vol. 7. London: Routledge.

Jung, C.G. (1921a). Psychological Types. In: *The Collected Works of C.G. Jung*. Vol. 6. London: Routledge.

Jung, C.G. (1921b). The Therapeutic Value of Abreaction. In: *The Collected Works of C.G. Jung*. Vol. 16. London: Routledge.

Jung, C.G. (1916/1948). General Aspects of Dream Psychology. In: *The Collected Works of C.G. Jung*. Vol. 8. London: Routledge.

Jung, C.G. (1935/1972). The Tavistock Lectures. In: *The Collected Works of C.G. Jung*. Vol. 15. London: Routledge.

Jung, C.G. (1938/1969). Psychology and Religion: West and East. In: *The Collected Works of C.G. Jung*. Vol. 11. London: Routledge.

Jung, C.G. (1948). A Review of the Complex Theory. In: *The Collected Works of C.G. Jung*. Vol. 8. London: Routledge.

Jung, C.G. (1953). *Letters. Selected and Edited by Gerhard Adler in Collaboration with Aniela Jaffé*. 2 Vols. Princeton: Princeton University Press.

Jung, C.G. (1954/1966). General Problems of Psychotherapy. In: *The Collected Works of C.G. Jung*. Vol. 16. London: Routledge.

Jung, C.G. (2010). *Children's Dreams: Notes from the Seminar Given in 1936–1940*. L. Jung, M. Meyer-Grass (Eds.). E. Falzeder, T. Woolfson (Transl.). Princeton: Princeton University Press.

Knox, J. (2003). *Archetype, Attachment, Analysis: Jungian Psychology and the Emergent Mind*. London, New York: Routledge.

Knox, J. (2009). The Analytic Relationship: Integrating Jungian, Attachment Theory and Developmental Perspectives. *British Journal of Psychotherapy*, 25, 1, 5–23.

Merchant, J. (2016). The Image Schema and Innate Archetypes: Theoretical and Clinical Implications. *Journal of Analytical Psychology*, 61, 1, 63–78.

Merchant, J. (2019). The Controversy Around the Concept of Archetypes and the Place for an Emergent/Developmental Model. *Journal of Analytical Psychology*, 64, 5, 701–719.

Otto, R. (1958). *The Idea of The Holy*. New York: Oxford University Press.

Peterfreund, E. (1983). *The Process of Psychoanalytic Therapy: Models and Strategies*. London: Routledge.

Appendix

An Overview: Mapping the Connection of Affects and Cognition

In the following diagrams, I first tried to sketch the different paths of cognitive, semiotic and epistemic development (Figure A.1) then that of the development of affects (Figure A.2). Figure A.3 summarizes the developmental pathways that these two lines take and the way they cross each other.

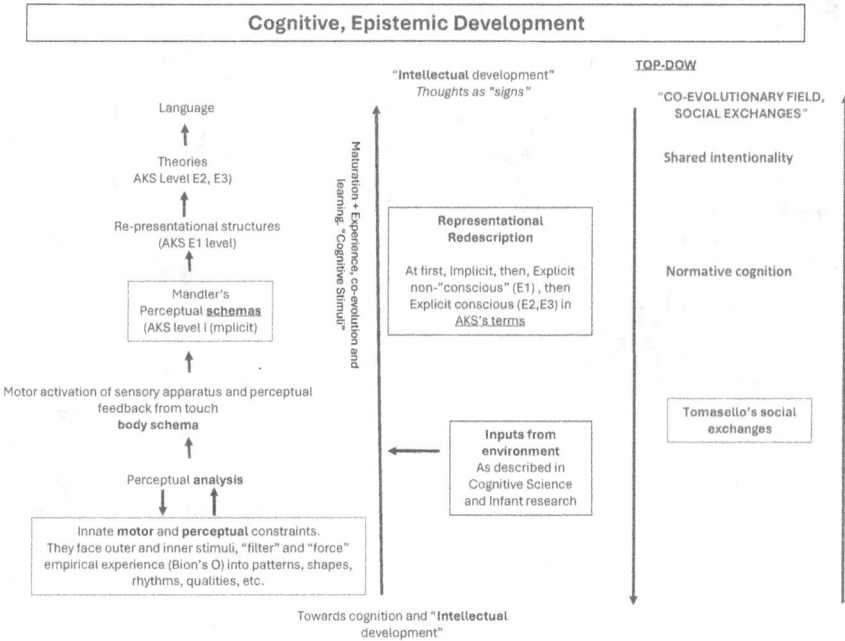

Figure A.1 Cognitive/epistemic development, indicating cognitive processes and contents described through a neo-Piagetian model (Karmiloff-Smith), cognitive processes involved in a neo-Vygotskyan perspective (Tomasello), and sensory-motor elements.

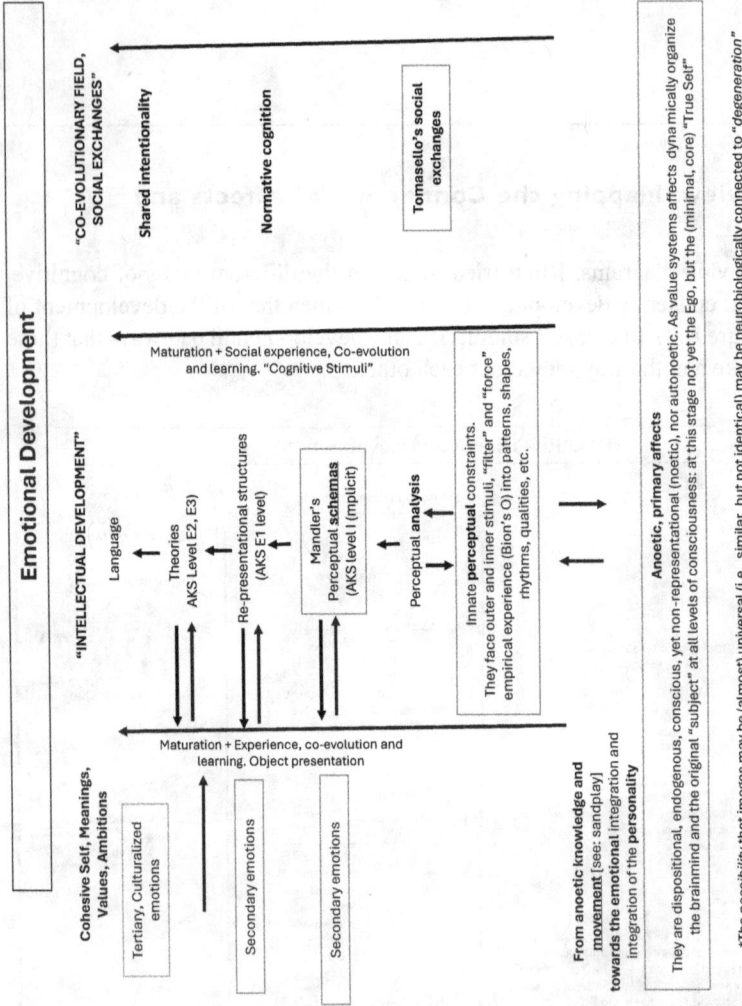

Figure A.2 Emotional development. The orange indicates emotional contents and development. The red indicates cognitive processes and contents described through a neo-Piagetian model (Karmiloff-Smith), blue cognitive processes involved in neo-Vygotskyan perspective (Tomasello), while the green sensory-motor elements.

Perception + Affectivity + Cognition = Personality Development

Cohesive Self, Meanings, Values, Ambitions

"Intellectual development"

TOP-DOWN

Representational Redescription

At first, Implicit, then, Explicit non-"conscious" (E1), then Explicit conscious (E2, E3) in AKS's terms

Inputs from environment

As described in Cognitive Science and Infant research

Unfiltered stimuli (Beta elements)?

Towards cognition and "Intellectual development"

Maturation + Social experience, Co-evolution and learning. "Cognitive Stimuli"

Language

Theories AKS Level E2, E3)

Re-presentational structures (AKS E1 level)

Mandler's Perceptual **schemas** (AKS level I(mplicit)

Perceptual **analysis**

Innate **perceptual** constraints. They face outer and inner stimuli, "filter" and "force" empirical experience (Bion's O) into patterns, shapes, rhythms, qualities, etc.

Anoetic affects

They are dispositional, endogenous, conscious, yet non-representational (noetic), nor autonoetic. As value systems affects dynamically organize the brainmind and the original "subject" at all levels of consciousness: at this stage not yet the Ego, but the (minimal) "True Self"

Maturation + Experience, co-evolution and learning. Object presentation

BOTTOM-UP

From anoetic knowledge and movement [see: sandplay] **towards the emotional integration and integration of the personality**

NOT Stimulus, but Winnicottian Object presentation

Imagines

Imagines are representation of emotional action patterns. Collected through mind wondering (DMN) [see: active imagination.] The cognitive schemas give imaginative representation to the affects. Schemas become **"Complexes".** They may carry transcultural resemblances* as blueprints derived from their affective and perceptually constrained origins.

*The *possibility* that images may be (almost) universal (i.e., similar, but not identical) may be neurobiologically connected to "*degeneration*"

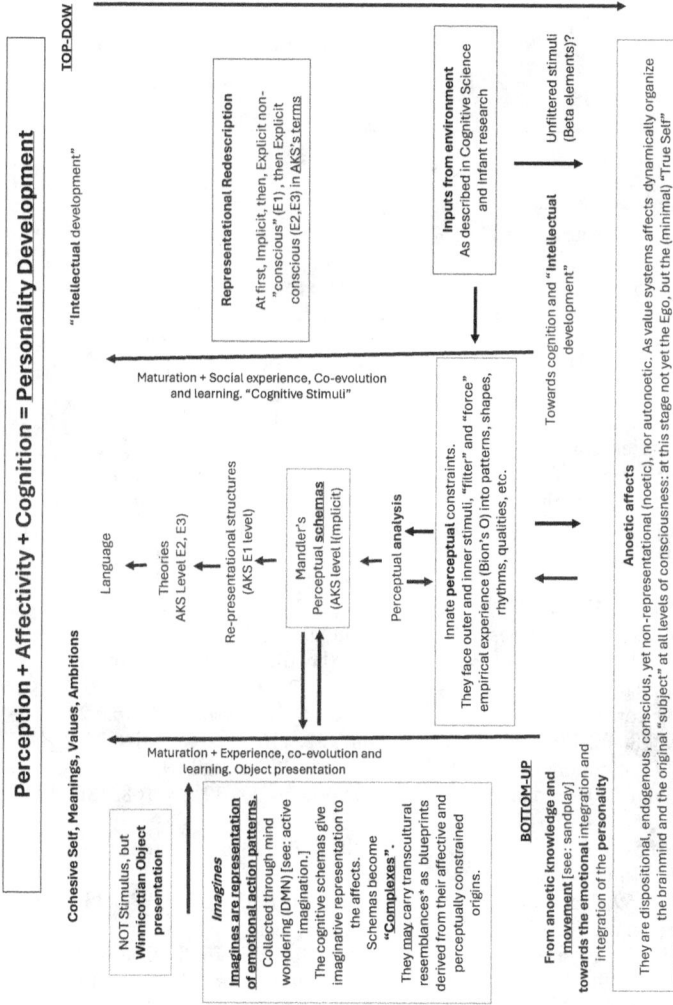

Figure A.3 The development of the personality. This diagram describes the elements and processes involved in the development of the whole personality. The orange indicates emotional contents and development. The red indicates cognitive processes and contents described through a neo-Piagetian model (Karmiloff-Smith), blue cognitive processes involved in neo-Vygotskyan perspective (Tomasello), while the green sensory-motor elements.

Index

Page locators in **bold** indicate a table
Page locators in *italics* indicate a figure

For Product Safety Concerns and Information please contact our EU
representative GPSR@taylorandfrancis.com
Taylor & Francis Verlag GmbH, Kaufingerstraße 24, 80331 München, Germany

www.ingramcontent.com/pod-product-compliance
Lightning Source LLC
Chambersburg PA
CBHW050350270326
41926CB00016B/3685